Cretney & Lush on
Enduring Powers of Attorney

D1556617

Cretney & Lush on Enduring Powers of Attorney

Fifth Edition

Denzil Lush BA, MA, LLM
Solicitor, Master of the Court of Protection

JORDANS
2001

Published by
Jordan Publishing Limited
21 St Thomas Street
Bristol BS1 6JS

© Jordan Publishing Limited 2001

British Library Cataloguing-in-Publication Data

A catalogue record for this book is available from the British Library.

ISBN 0 85308 735 0

Typeset in-house
Printed by Henry Ling Limited, The Dorset Press, Dorchester DT1 1HD, UK

ACKNOWLEDGEMENT

The official typography of Forms EP1 to EP7 in Appendix 4 (from Statutory Instrument 2001/825) are reproduced with the permission of the Controller of Her Majesty's Stationery Office.

PREFACE

When the fourth edition of this book was published in September 1996, we thought it would be the final one and that we would soon start planning a new work on continuing powers of attorney. Eighteen months earlier, in March 1995, the Law Commission had recommended that the Enduring Powers of Attorney Act 1985 be repealed and replaced by a Mental Incapacity Act, enabling donors to create continuing powers whereby their attorneys can make medical and personal decisions in addition to financial decisions. This recommendation has not yet been implemented, although the Lord Chancellor has said that he will introduce the necessary legislation as soon as parliamentary time allows.

During the last 5 years there have been several major developments in this field that warrant the publication of a new – fifth – edition now. In chronological order they have been:

- the Trustee Delegation Act 1999;
- the decisions in *Re C*, *Re E* and *Re W*; and
- the Court of Protection (Enduring Powers of Attorney) Rules 2001, which came into force on 1 April 2001 and were necessitated by the demise of the Public Trust Office and the resurrection of its mental health sector as the Public Guardianship Office.

The most significant change over the last 5 years, however, has been neither legislative nor judicial, but a growing awareness among professionals and the public alike, both at home and abroad, that enduring powers of attorney facilitate financial abuse. The extent to which abuse occurs will never be known. No one could categorically claim that, for example, 16,453 attorneys are exploiting their donors at any one time. Its prevalence depends on how one defines abuse, which can cover anything between ethically questionable conduct, at one extreme, and a criminal fraud involving substantial assets at the other. For this reason, we have included in this edition a chapter on financial abuse, which attempts to describe how it occurs, why it occurs, and suggests one or two ways in which it can be prevented.

For this fifth edition, the book has been retitled *Cretney & Lush on Enduring Powers of Attorney* reflecting Stephen Cretney's involvement as author of the first three editions and co-author of the fourth. As a Law Commissioner, he was involved in the recommendations which led to the Enduring Powers of Attorney Act 1985, but his academic interests have now moved into other areas and he has not been involved in the preparation of this edition.

The law is stated as at 1 July 2001.

DENZIL LUSH

August 2001

CONTENTS

TABLE OF CASES

References are to paragraph numbers. References in *italics* are to Appendix page numbers.

TABLE OF STATUTES

TABLE OF STATUTORY INSTRUMENTS

References are to paragraph numbers. References in *italics* are to Appendix page numbers.

TABLE OF INTERNATIONAL MATERIALS

References are to paragraph numbers.

TABLE OF LAW SOCIETY GUIDANCE

References are to paragraph numbers. References in *italics* are to Appendix page numbers.

TABLE OF ABBREVIATIONS

1971 Act	Powers of Attorney Act 1971
1983 Act	Mental Health Act 1983
1985 Act	Enduring Powers of Attorney Act 1985
1989 Act	Law of Property (Miscellaneous Provisions) Act 1989
1990 Regulations	Enduring Power of Attorney (Prescribed Form) Regulations 1990
1999 Act	Trustee Delegation Act 1999
2001 Rules	Court of Protection (Enduring Powers of Attorney) Rules 2001
CPA	continuing power of attorney
EPA	enduring power of attorney
Law Com Paper No 30	*Powers of Attorney* (1970)
Law Com Paper No 122	*The Incapacitated Principal*
Law Com Paper No 220	*The Law of Trusts: Delegation by Individual Trustees* (1994)
Law Com Paper No 231	*Mental Incapacity* (1995)

Chapter 1

ENDURING POWERS OF ATTORNEY IN CONTEXT

1.1 INTRODUCTION

1.1.1 What is a power of attorney?

A power of attorney is a formal arrangement created by a deed in which one person ('the donor') gives another person ('the attorney') authority to act in his name and on his behalf. A survey conducted by the Consumers' Association found that the most common reasons for ordinary people using a power of attorney were health problems and foreign travel. In most cases, the power was granted by a parent to a grown-up child. Powers of attorney are also widely used in commercial and business transactions.

1.1.2 The legal framework

The law relating to powers of attorney forms part of the general law of agency. The common law of agency, therefore, still applies insofar as it has not been affected by subsequent legislation. Reference should be made to the standard works on agency, for example *Bowstead and Reynolds on Agency* 16th edn (Sweet & Maxwell, 1996).

In practice, the law governing powers of attorney is now largely contained in statute, although the law has never been formally codified. The most important statute is the Powers of Attorney Act 1971 (the 1971 Act), which gave effect to the recommendations contained in the Law Commission's report *Powers of Attorney* (1970) Law Com Paper No 30. The Act is reproduced in Appendix 1 to this book and its main features are as follows.

1.1.3 Execution as a deed

At common law, there was no rule that agency must be created by a deed, except where the agent himself was to be empowered to execute a deed. Powers of attorney could be granted in writing, although in practice they were almost universally granted by a document under seal. Section 1 of the 1971 Act now requires that an instrument creating a power of attorney be executed as a deed. This means complying with the rules now embodied in the Law of Property (Miscellaneous Provisions) Act 1989.

1.1.4 The effect of the Law of Property (Miscellaneous Provisions) Act 1989

Section 1(3) of the Law of Property (Miscellaneous Provisions) Act 1989 (the 1989 Act) provides that an instrument is validly executed as a deed by an individual if, and only if:

- it is *signed*, which includes making one's mark, by him in the presence of a witness who attests the signature; *or*
- it is signed by someone else *at his direction*, in his presence and in the presence of two witnesses who each attest the signature; *and*
- the instrument is *delivered* as a deed by him or by a person authorised to do so on his behalf.

The Enduring Powers of Attorney (Prescribed Form) Regulations 1990 (SI 1990/1376) were specifically made to apply these provisions to enduring powers of attorney (see para **2.6**).

1.1.5 Proof of power of attorney

The Law of Property Act 1925 had made provision for the filing of powers of attorney and for the provision of office copies of a filed power. The 1971 Act abolished the filing of powers in the Central Office of the Supreme Court, although documents already filed may still be proved by means of an office copy.

Section 3(1) of the 1971 Act states that a photocopy of a power of attorney, provided that it is duly certified in the manner prescribed in the Act, shall be sufficient evidence of the contents of the power. The certificate must appear on the copy, and must be signed by the donor, a solicitor or a stockbroker. A notary public can also certify a copy of the power (Courts and Legal Services Act 1990, s 125(2), Sch 17, para 4). The certificate must be at the end of the document and must state that the copy is a true and complete copy of the original. If the original consists of two or more pages, there must be a certificate at the end of each page of the copy to the effect that it is a true and complete copy of the corresponding page of the original. Where a copy has been certified in this manner, the contents of the instrument may also be proved by means of a copy of that copy, provided that the copy itself complies with s 3(1).

1.1.6 Protection of attorneys and third parties

The 1971 Act did nothing to affect the rule whereby a power of attorney is revoked by the subsequent mental incapacity of the donor (*Drew v Nunn* (1878) 4 QBD 661). It did, however, contain a number of provisions protecting attorneys and third parties against the consequences of the power having terminated by such revocation or otherwise. These are considered in Chapter 8 of this book.

1.1.7 Power to delegate trusts

Section 25 of the Trustee Act 1925 contained a restricted power for a trustee to delegate his trusteeship during his absence abroad. The 1971 Act replaced those provisions, and these, in turn, have been replaced by the provisions contained in the Trustee Delegation Act 1999. The effect of the 1999 Act is described in detail in Chapter 11.

1.1.8 Automatic revocation on mental incapacity

In practice, powers of attorney are often executed by elderly people who want to authorise somebody else to act for them when their own ability to deal with business affairs has become impaired. However, the supervening mental incapacity of the donor of a power of attorney revokes the attorney's authority at precisely the time when it is most needed. This rule has caused a great deal of inconvenience.

1.1.9 Reference to the Law Commission

In the consultation leading up to the enactment of the 1971 Act, there was some discussion of the possibility that a power might be granted under which the attorney would be entitled to carry on handling the donor's affairs notwithstanding the donor's incapacity.

The Law Commission said that its information confirmed the view that it was often difficult to gauge whether the donor of the power was originally capable of granting the power, and even more difficult to assess whether and when decreasing mental capacity, because of old age or illness, had caused the donor to become legally incapable. The Commission noted that, in a great many cases, attorneys continued to act, notwithstanding the fact that the donor had become incapacitated. It remarked that, in doing so, they were performing a valuable service since, if the jurisdiction of the Court of Protection were invoked in all these cases, the court's resources would not be able to cope with the resulting increase in work. Nevertheless, the Commission pointed out that, in so acting, attorneys were running a considerable risk, because technically they did not have any legal authority or effective protection if their acts were subsequently challenged.

The Law Commission concluded in 1970 that this was not a matter which could be dealt with properly 'in isolation from a complete review of the present procedure for dealing with the property of persons of unsound mind' (*Powers of Attorney* (1970) Law Com Paper No 30, para 27). In fact, such a review has only recently been completed, and the Commission's proposals can be found in its report, *Mental Incapacity* (1995) Law Com Paper No 231.

In 1973, the Lord Chancellor asked the Law Commission to 'consider the law and practice governing powers of attorney and other forms of agency in relation to the mental incapacity of the principal, and to make recommendations'. The Commission's report, *The Incapacitated Principal* (1983) Law Com Paper No 122, contained a draft Bill which forms the basis of the Enduring Powers of Attorney Act 1985.

In *Re R (Enduring Power of Attorney)* [1990] 2 All ER 893 at 895b, Vinelott J stated:

> 'The 1985 Act made a very remarkable change in the law. It creates a regime for the administration of the affairs of somebody who becomes incapable of managing their affairs, which is supplemental to that provided by the Mental Health Act 1983. In effect, the Act permits a person, while capable of managing his affairs, to select somebody who will be responsible for managing his or her affairs if there is a supervening incapacity, so avoiding the expense and (possibly, in the minds of some) the embarrassment of invoking the full jurisdiction of the Court of Protection.'

1.2 SOURCES OF LAW

The Enduring Powers of Attorney Act 1985 (the 1985 Act) was brought into force by the Enduring Powers of Attorney Act 1985 (Commencement) Order 1986 (SI 1986/125). It came into force on 10 March 1986 and extends only to England and Wales.

The Court of Protection (Enduring Powers of Attorney) Rules 2001 (SI 2001/825) govern the procedure of the Court of Protection in connection with applications under the 1985 Act. These Rules, which came into force on 1 April 2001, replaced earlier Rules in 1986 (SI 1986/127) and 1994 (SI 1994/3047).

The Enduring Powers of Attorney (Prescribed Form) Regulations 1990 (SI 1990/1376), which came into force on 31 July 1990, replaced two earlier sets of Regulations (SI 1986/126 and SI 1987/1612). The Regulations prescribe the mandatory form of enduring power, which is considered in detail in para **2.5**.

1.3 LIMITATIONS ON THE SCOPE OF THE 1985 ACT

Two important limitations on the scope of the 1985 Act should be noted at the outset.

— First, it is not a codifying Act. It builds on the provisions of the common law and the Powers of Attorney Act 1971 and cannot be understood in isolation. It simply enables powers of attorney to be created which will survive any subsequent mental incapacity of the donor.
— Secondly, it has no effect on other parts of the law of agency. In particular, a mandate given by a customer to his bank will still be terminated by the customer's supervening incapacity.

1.4 THE POLICY OF THE 1985 ACT

In *The Incapacitated Principal* (1983) Law Com Paper No 122, the Law Commission stated that two particular difficulties were caused by the rule that supervening mental incapacity revokes the attorney's authority. One was the identification of incapacity, and the other was a reluctance to apply to the Court of Protection for the appointment of a receiver.

1.4.1 Identification of incapacity

In practice, it is often difficult to know whether and when the donor has lost capacity. The Law Commission noted that:

'A particular difficulty in this area is the identification of incapacity. A donor's failure to manage his affairs properly may be as easily attributable to lack of inclination as to positive lack of mental incapacity. He may have "good" as well as "bad" days. Applying any definition of "incapacity" inevitably involves taking a subjective rather than an objective view. The donor's doctor may consider that he is incapable while his wife may attribute his behaviour to eccentricity' (Law Com Paper No 122, para 3.3).

1.4.2 Reluctance to invoke the Mental Health Act 1983 jurisdiction

When the donor of the power had become incapacitated, the proper action was to arrange for the appointment of a receiver by the Court of Protection under the provisions of Part VII of the Mental Health Act 1983. But this was not always done:

> 'The underlying complaint is not that the Court of Protection is unapproachable or unnecessarily slow or inflexible. It is none of these things. Inevitably, however, it has procedures, and procedures always involve time and expense. For example, before making a receivership order the court always requires production of *medical evidence* because it has to be satisfied that the proposed patient is indeed a "patient". The originating application must usually be accompanied by a substantial *affidavit* to enable the court to judge the suitability of the proposed receiver and (looking to the future) to assist the court to give directions on questions relating to the administration of the patient's estate. Furthermore, the receiver may as a condition of his appointment be required to provide security. He will also usually be required to render annual *accounts* to the court and he may have to attend the court to have these passed. Finally, in order to finance the court's activities, *fees* are payable by the patient's estate. At the outset each originating application bears a commencement fee. Additionally, there are fairly substantial fees charged annually on the patient's clear annual income as well as "transaction fees" for some individual dealings with the patient's estate' (Law Com Paper No 122, para 2.27).

1.4.3 Abolish the automatic revocation rule?

The Law Commission considered, but rejected, proposals which would simply have abolished the rule that the donor's mental incapacity terminates the attorney's power. However, it found overwhelming support for a new type of power which would, subject to conditions and safeguards, continue in force despite the donor's subsequent incapacity. However, its consultation was by no means unanimous as to the detailed provisions which should be made for such a power. In particular, there was no general consensus about the safeguards needed to protect the donor against the danger of exploitation. There were two conflicting needs which had to be balanced:

> 'First, the need to provide a simple, effective and inexpensive method of allowing powers to continue despite the donor's incapacity. Secondly, the need to protect the donor's interests against exploitation. Both needs are perfectly valid. Unfortunately they are not easily reconciled' (Law Com Paper No 122, para 3.9).

1.4.4 Commonwealth enduring power of attorney (EPA) schemes

In seeking to balance these conflicting needs, the Law Commission investigated a number of EPA schemes in other parts of the Commonwealth and in the United States. It concluded that these schemes were generally popular. They were seen as fulfilling a previously unmet need, particularly by providing an inexpensive and useful alternative to receivership proceedings. However, 'there was no such thing as an internationally accepted form of EPA scheme' (Law Com Paper No 122, para 3.16).

1.4.5 Safeguards

Most of the foreign schemes examined by the Law Commission contained some basic provisions designed to protect the donor's interests. For example, a requirement that the enduring power contain a statement by the donor showing his intention that the power should survive his mental incapacity; a requirement that the donor's signature be witnessed by someone other than the attorney; and machinery whereby the power could be terminated or controlled by the intervention of a court or some other official body. Some schemes contained more extensive protective measures.

1.4.6 Basic protection would be inadequate

In the light of this examination, the Law Commission concluded that it could not recommend the adoption of a scheme which had only the basic level of protection outlined above. It considered that such a scheme would fail to provide sufficient protection for the donor. In particular, it was concerned by the fact that many enduring powers would be granted by elderly donors whose mental state was already beginning to deteriorate. Such people were likely to be highly suggestible and do whatever the prospective attorney said was best, perhaps without even appreciating the effect of granting an enduring power.

1.4.7 Protective scheme preferred

The scheme embodied in the 1985 Act, therefore, contains a number of provisions specifically designed to protect the donor. Indeed, it has been said that the exercise of the power 'is hedged about on all sides with statutory protection for the donor' (*Re K; Re F (Enduring Powers of Attorney)* [1988] 2 FLR 15 at 20, per Hoffmann J).

In particular, an enduring power must be in a *prescribed form* which contains explanatory information stating the general effect of creating and accepting the power for both the donor and the attorney. It must also contain prescribed statements by the parties. For example, the donor must state, 'I intend that this power shall continue even if I become mentally incapable'. The attorney must state, 'I also understand my limited power to use the donor's property to benefit persons other than the donor'.

However, the key provision of the 1985 Act is that, when he has reason to believe that the donor is or is becoming mentally incapable, the attorney must apply to the Court of Protection for the *registration* of the power. As a preliminary to registration, the attorney must also *serve notice on the donor and the donor's relatives*. The relatives are thus given an opportunity to consider the attorneyship and, if necessary, to object to the attorney's operation of the power.

1.5 THE IMPACT OF THE 1985 ACT

It would be impossible to assess the number of enduring powers that have been executed since the Act came into force in March 1986, but the number of applications for registration has grown steadily, as the following table shows.

1986	605
1987	1,476
1988	2,215
1989	2,842
1990	3,649
1991	4,309
1992	5,189
1993	5,767
1994	6,637
1995	7,562
1996	8,921
1997	9,548
1998	10,726
1999	11,337
2000	12,340

By contrast, new applications to the Court of Protection for the appointment of a receiver under the Mental Health Act 1983 have remained fairly constant, at about the 6,000 level, since 1986, whereas until then there had been an average growth rate of 6.6% per year.

Applications under the Mental Health Act 1983 relate to four main client groups:

– older people, mainly with Alzheimer's disease or multi-infarct dementia;
– people with mainstream mental illnesses, such as schizophrenia;
– people with learning difficulties; and

– people who have suffered a head injury as a result of a car accident, an accident at work, an assault, or who have suffered brain damage as a result of clinical negligence, and have been awarded damages.

For various reasons, the uptake of enduring powers is almost exclusively confined to older people, and it is doubtful whether EPAs are really suitable for the other client groups. People with learning difficulties often lack the capacity to create an EPA in the first place. Where people suffer from mainstream 'revolving door' mental illnesses, the problems of registering the power, cancelling registration on recovery, re-registering, etc, may be a disincentive to the creation of an EPA. In addition, it is not uncommon for people who are mentally ill to fall out with their attorney and seek to revoke the power.

People who have suffered brain damage in an accident or assault often lack the capacity to create a power after the accident, and most of the leading personal injury and clinical negligence lawyers consider that, as a matter of policy, EPAs are unsuitable for the management and administration of a substantial damages award because of the lack of accountability and security. Indeed, damages awards often contain a specific order that an application be made to the Court of Protection for the appointment of a receiver.

Seventy-four per cent of donors of EPAs are female, and the average age of the donor on an application to register a power is 85. Sixty per cent of donors appoint only one attorney; 34% appoint joint and several attorneys; and 6% appoint joint attorneys.

The period between the creation of an EPA and the application to register it is currently less than 1 month in 7% of applications; 1–3 months in 11%; 3–6 months in 9%; 6–12 months in 15%; and over 12 months in 58%. These figures differ dramatically from the research findings back in 1991, when only 10% of applications related to powers more than a year old (see S Cretney, G Davis, R Kerridge and A Borkowski *Enduring Powers of Attorney: A Report to the Lord Chancellor* (Lord Chancellor's Department, June 1991), p 26).

1.6 PROPOSED REFORMS

1.6.1 The Law Commission's report on mental incapacity

In March 1995 the Law Commission published its report *Mental Incapacity* (1995) Law Com Paper No 231, which, among other things, proposed that the 1985 Act be repealed and that, instead, it should be possible for a donor to create a continuing power of attorney (CPA). CPAs are conceptually quite different from EPAs, although both serve the common purpose of providing the machinery whereby decisions can be made on behalf of a person who lacks capacity.

1.6.2 Differences between EPAs and CPAs

The main differences between EPAs and the proposed CPAs are as follows.

Range of decisions that can be made by an attorney

Under an EPA the attorney can generally do anything that the donor could do with his own property and financial affairs, but cannot make decisions about the donor's personal welfare or health care. Under a CPA the attorney will be able to make any decision that the donor is unable to make himself at that time about his property, finances, personal welfare and health care. Personal welfare decisions include, for example: where the donor should live; with whom the donor should live; whom the donor should see and not see; and decisions about the donor's diet and dress.

The ability of the donor to participate in the decision-making process

Until an EPA is registered the donor and the attorney have concurrent authority, and both can make decisions about the donor's property and finances. Once an EPA is registered, the donor no longer has the authority to make decisions about his property and financial affairs. With a CPA, the donor will be able to carry on making decisions himself, provided he has the capacity to make such a decision at the time it needs to be made. The attorney acting under a CPA will only be able to make decisions that the donor is incapable of making, or which he reasonably believes the donor is incapable of making, at that time.

When the power comes into operation

Unless the donor specifically states that it will not come into operation until he has become mentally incapable of managing his affairs, an EPA comes into effect immediately. An attorney acting under a CPA will not be able to act under the power until it has been registered with the registration authority.

Registration of the power

Before applying to the court for the registration of an EPA, the attorney must give written notice of his intention to register the power to the donor and the donor's nearest relatives. The donor or the relatives can object on various grounds if they oppose the intended registration. The procedure on registration of a CPA will be as follows. Before applying to the registration authority, the attorney must give the donor notice of his intention to register the power. The donor will be able to object if he disagrees with the intended registration. The donor's relatives will not be notified before registration of the power. Instead, the registration authority will give notice of registration to not more than two people whom the donor has specifically nominated as being entitled to be notified.

1.6.3 Making decisions

In December 1997 the Lord Chancellor's Department issued a consultation paper, *Who Decides?*, Cm 3808, followed by a policy statement, *Making Decisions*, Cm 4465, on 27 October 1999, which set out the Government's response to the proposals in the Law Commission's report, *Mental Incapacity*.

The Government has decided that:

- as with EPAs, there will be a mandatory prescribed form of CPA;
- the form must be accompanied by evidence that the donor was mentally capable at the time it was created. That evidence could be provided by either a separate medical certificate or a signed statement by a doctor in the CPA form itself;
- donors will be able to appoint substitute attorneys in case their first choice of attorney loses mental capacity or dies. The Court of Protection will not, however, have the power to appoint a substitute attorney, as had originally been proposed by the Law Commission;
- it will not be possible to convert an existing financial EPA into a CPA, as was originally proposed by the Law Commission. The legislation will contain appropriate transitional arrangements in respect of EPAs to ensure a smooth transition;
- there will be a compulsory registration system and a registration authority. All CPAs must be registered before the attorney can use them.

The Government has pledged to introduce the necessary legislation 'when Parliamentary time allows' (*Making Decisions*, para 7).

1.6.4 Quinquennial Review of the Public Trust Office

The Quinquennial Review of the Public Trust Office was carried out between May and October 1999 by Miss Ann Chant CB (see para **5.2**), whose report was published in November 1999. The report states that:

'An EPA bestows virtually unfettered control of someone's financial assets once it is brought into force. While its objective (to put someone's financial affairs in the hands of an individual they have pre-selected, rather than surrendering them to the Court of Protection) fits entirely with the objective of keeping the state out of family affairs unless there is no alternative, if an EPA goes wrong the results can be catastrophic for the person concerned. Although comparatively rare, there are plenty of instances where the system has been deliberately or accidentally abused and getting the position rectified through the court is a long and difficult process' (para 47).

The report proposed that there should be various enhancements to the present system to instigate essential regulation and oversight. 'It is the lack of them which prevents current EPA arrangements being confidently recommended to the public by Ministers as a practical alternative for some people to the Court of Protection' (para 48).

The proposed enhancements to the current legislation, which are set out in Annex 4 to the report, include:

- first registration on creation of the power;
- second registration on incapacity;
- provision in the prescribed form inviting the donor to nominate an independent professional person who will supervise the attorney;
- a legal requirement for attorneys to keep annual accounts;
- that the attorney would be expected to produce the annual accounts to the supervisor;
- that if the attorney failed to account satisfactorily, the supervisor would be obliged to inform the registration authority.

Chapter 2

GRANTING AN ENDURING POWER OF ATTORNEY

2.1 INTRODUCTION

2.1.1 Essentials of an enduring power of attorney (EPA)

In order that a power of attorney can qualify as an EPA:

- the donor must be an individual who has the capacity to grant the power;
- the donee must not be disqualified from acting as attorney under an enduring power;
- the instrument must be in the prescribed form, and must incorporate the prescribed explanatory information;
- the power must not fall into one of the categories of power of attorney which cannot be enduring powers.

2.1.2 Is a defective EPA valid as an ordinary power?

An instrument which does not satisfy the requirements of an enduring power may, nevertheless, take effect as an ordinary power. That this is what Parliament intended can be seen from s 11(4) of the Enduring Powers of Attorney Act 1985 (the 1985 Act) which, in respect of joint and several powers, provides that:

> 'a failure, as respects any one attorney, to comply with the requirements for the creation of enduring powers, shall prevent the instrument from creating such a power in his case without however affecting its efficacy for that purpose as respects the other or others or the efficacy in his case for the purpose of creating a power which is not an enduring power.'

This question was considered by Arden J in *Re E (Enduring Power of Attorney)* [2000] 1 FLR 882. In that case it was held that an EPA which was technically invalid because of an inconsistency in the appointment of joint attorneys, took effect as an ordinary power even if it could not take effect as an enduring power.

2.2 THE DONOR

2.2.1 The donor must be an individual

Only an *individual* can grant an enduring power (s 1(1)). Partnerships, companies, and others who are not individuals cannot do so.

2.2.2 The donor must have mental capacity at the time of granting the power

It is a fundamental principle that the donor must, at the time when he grants the power, have the mental capacity to grant it. The 1985 Act does not specify the capacity required to create an enduring power but, in *Re K; Re F (Enduring Powers of Attorney)* [1988] 2 FLR 15, it was held that the relevant question is whether the donor had, at the time, the mental capacity, with the assistance of such explanation as he may have been given, to understand the nature and effect of the power. The validity of the power does not depend upon whether the donor would, hypothetically, have been able to perform all the acts which it authorises (at 19, per Hoffmann J).

In that case, a power was held to have been validly granted by a woman who, at the date of execution, enjoyed a period during which she was able to understand that a named individual was to be her attorney under an EPA, and who understood what an enduring power was, even though she was at the time incapable, by reason of mental disorder, of managing her property and affairs.

Hoffmann J stated (at 20):

> 'Plainly one cannot expect that [a] donor should have been able to pass an examination on the provisions of the Act. At the other extreme, I do not think that it would be sufficient if he realised only that it gave [the donee] power to look after his property.'

Hoffmann J went on to accept the following summary, put forward by counsel for the Official Solicitor acting as *amicus curiae*, as a statement of the matters which should ordinarily be explained to the donor and which the evidence should show that he had understood:

> 'First (if such be the terms of the power), that the attorney will be able to assume complete authority over the donor's affairs. Secondly (if such be the terms of the power), that the attorney will in general be able to do anything with the donor's property which he himself could have done. Thirdly, that the authority will continue if the donor should be or become mentally incapable. Fourthly, that if he should be or become mentally incapable, the power will be irrevocable without confirmation by the court' (at 20).

As a result, someone with limited capacity may, nevertheless, execute a valid power even though he may be incapable, by reason of mental disorder, of managing and administering his property and affairs.

The decision in *Re K; Re F* has been criticised for being inconsistent with the common law rules affecting the creation of powers of attorney (Roderick Munday 'The Capacity to Execute an Enduring Power of Attorney in New Zealand and England: A Case of Parliamentary Oversight?' (1989) 13 *New Zealand Universities Law Review* 253).

It has also been criticised for imposing too simple a test of capacity to create an EPA (see the discussion in S Cretney, G Davis, R Kerridge and A Borkowski *Enduring Powers of Attorney: A Report to the Lord Chancellor* (Lord Chancellor's Department, June 1991), para 2.7). Whether the test is simple or hard, however, depends largely on the explanation given and the questions asked by the person assessing the donor's capacity. For example, if the four pieces of basic relevant information described by the judge in *Re K; Re F* were recited to the donor and he was asked 'Do you understand this?' in such a way as to encourage an affirmative reply, he would probably pass the test with flying colours and, arguably, it would be too simple. If, on the other hand, after an explanation about the nature and effect of the transaction had been given in broad terms and simple language, the assessor were specifically to ask 'What will your attorney be able to do?' and 'What will happen if you become mentally incapable?', the test would be substantially harder.

Such matters were considered by the Court of Appeal in *In re W (Enduring Power of Attorney)* [2001] 2 WLR 957 at 962. Sir Christopher Staughton said:

> 'For my part, I would not be inclined to rely on evidence of one interview. No doubt it is right to ask questions when it is contemplated that a donor shall execute an enduring power; but that is not by any means the final way of determining whether there is the necessary capacity.'

2.2.3 Evidence of mental capacity

If the donor did not have capacity at the time of grant, an objection may subsequently be made to the registration of the power on the ground that it was not valid (s 6(5)(a)). If such an objection is established, registration of the power must be refused, and the instrument must be delivered up for cancellation (s 6(6) and (8)). Moreover, the attorney may be liable to third parties for misrepresenting his authority; and dealings with third parties may be affected, since the power will never have existed (see para **8.3.3**).

It is clearly important to minimise the risk of a power being invalidated on this ground, and it would be wise to ensure that, where the donor has borderline capacity, evidence of his capacity to grant the power is obtained and preserved.

There is no statutory requirement that a person who witnesses the donor's signature should be specially qualified, for example, a solicitor or a doctor. Indeed, the Law Commission specifically rejected proposals that there should be such a requirement (*The Incapacitated Principal* (1983) Law Com Paper No 122, para 4.19). However, in cases involving testamentary capacity, there is a golden if tactless rule that 'when a solicitor is drawing up a will for an aged testator or one who has been seriously ill, it should be witnessed or approved by a medical practitioner, who ought to record his examination of the testator and his findings' (*Kenward v Adams* (1975) *The Times*, November 29, per Templeman J). This warning was repeated by the same judge in *Re Simpson, Deceased: Schaniel v Simpson* (1977) 121 SJ 224 and has been reiterated recently in *Buckenham v Dickinson* [1997] CLY 661 and *In the Estate of Lily Louisa Morris (Deceased)* (Rimer J, Lawtel 15/5/2000).

It is recommended, therefore, that if there is any doubt about the donor's capacity to create an enduring power, a formal assessment of his capacity should be carried out by a registered medical practitioner, who should record his examination and findings and, where appropriate, witness the donor's execution of the power. In any event, it would be sensible to ensure that the attesting witness is someone who is familiar with the donor's mental state, and who will subsequently be in a position to give credible evidence.

The British Medical Association's Private Practice and Professional Fees Committee recommends fees in respect of EPAs. These fees are revised annually with effect from 1 April each year. From 1 April 2001, the recommended fee for completing an examination to determine whether a person is capable of executing an EPA is £84, and the recommended fee for witnessing an EPA is £42.50.

2.2.4 Other incapacity

In theory, there seems to be no reason why a minor or undischarged bankrupt should not grant an enduring power insofar as he can grant an ordinary power but, in practice, it is unlikely that such appointments will be made (Law Com Paper No 122, para 4.5, and footnote 109; and see *Bowstead and Reynolds on Agency* 16th edn (Sweet & Maxwell, 1996)).

2.2.5 Where the donor is already a patient

Although the Mental Health Act 1983 (the 1983 Act) predated and did not anticipate the provisions of the Enduring Powers of Attorney Act 1985, ss 95(1)(d) and 96(1)(a) of the 1983 Act confer sufficient powers on the Court of Protection to authorise a patient to execute an EPA.

Until recently, however, it was not the court's practice to allow patients to create an EPA. A Master's Direction to that effect was issued on 20 May 1992. (A Master's Direction is a purely internal direction to the staff of the Court of Protection, whereas a Practice Direction applies both internally and externally.) The reasons were as follows.

In *Re Walker* [1905] 1 Ch 160 the Lords Justices in Lunacy held that a patient cannot, even during a lucid interval, execute a valid deed dealing with or disposing of his property. Such a deed is entirely null and void. The rationale is that, if a patient were free to execute a deed dealing with or disposing of his property, there would be a conflict of control between the patient and the receiver to whom the court has delegated control of the patient's property and affairs. In *Re Barnes* [1983] VR 605, Beach J, of the Supreme Court of Victoria, Australia, specifically held that an EPA created by a patient was void for this reason.

However, there need not be any conflict of control if the court itself approves and oversees the transfer of control from a receiver to an attorney and, in principle, the Court of Protection will approve the execution of an EPA by a patient, provided it is satisfied that:

(1) having regard to all the circumstances, the execution of an enduring power of attorney is in the patient's best interests;
(2) the patient has the capacity – and the evidence shows that he has the capacity – to understand the nature and effect of the transaction, namely, that he is transferring the management of his financial affairs from a receiver to an attorney; what the differences are between the two schemes; and why he considers it necessary or expedient to transfer from a receivership to an attorneyship;
(3) it is the patient's own autonomous wish to execute an EPA, and not simply a device by the receiver to be relieved of various obligations, such as his duty to account, or to obtain unsupervised control of the patient's finances.

If the court approves the application to transfer control from a receiver to an attorney, it will issue an order along the following lines:

'The patient is AUTHORISED to execute an enduring power of attorney appointing (*name*) of (*address*) to be his attorney with general authority to act on his behalf in relation to all his property and affairs subject to the restriction and condition that the attorney will have no authority to act as attorney until the instrument has been registered by the Court of Protection.'

As soon as the enduring power has been registered, the court will issue an order discharging the receiver. This procedure is appropriate only where the patient is still incapable, by reason of mental disorder, of managing and administering his property and affairs. If he has recovered capacity, the appropriate application is for an order determining proceedings.

2.3 THE ATTORNEY

A power of attorney cannot be an enduring power unless the attorney is a *trust corporation* or an *individual* who has attained the age of 18 (1985 Act, s 2(7)). A donor cannot constitute a partnership or a company, other than a trust corporation, as an attorney under an enduring power.

2.3.1 Trust corporations

Trust corporation means the Public Trustee or a corporation appointed by the court to be a trustee or entitled by rules under s 4(3) of the Public Trustee Act 1906 to act as a custodian trustee (1985 Act, s 13(1)). Despite this definition, the Public Trustee does not act as an attorney. Since 1 April 2001 the offices of Public Trustee and Official Solicitor have been combined.

The relevant rules under s 4(3) of the Public Trustee Act 1906 are the Public Trustee Rules 1912 (SR&O 1912 No 348), r 30, as substituted by SI 1975/1189 and amended by SIs 1976/836, 1981/358, 1984/109, 1985/132, and 1994/2519. The following corporations are currently entitled to act as custodian trustees:

'(a) the Treasury Solicitor;
(b) any corporation which:
    (i)   is constituted under the law of the United Kingdom or of any part thereof, or under the law of any other Member State of the European Economic Community or of any part thereof;
    (ii)   is empowered by its constitution to undertake trust business (which for the purpose of this rule means the business of acting as trustee under wills and settlements and as executor and administrator) in England and Wales;
    (iii) has one or more of its places of business in the United Kingdom; and
    (iv) is a company incorporated by special Act or Royal Charter, or
         a company registered (whether with or without limited liability) in the United Kingdom under the Companies Act 1948 or under the Companies Act (Northern Ireland) 1960 or in another Member State of the European

Economic Community and having a capital (in stock or shares) for the time being issued of not less than £250,000 (or its equivalent in the currency of the State where the company is registered), of which not less than £100,000 (or its equivalent) has been paid up in cash, or

a company registered without limited liability in the United Kingdom under the Companies Act 1948 or the Companies Act (Northern Ireland) 1960 or in another Member State of the European Economic Community and of which one of the members is a company within any of the classes defined in this sub-paragraph;

(c) Any corporation which is incorporated by special Act or Royal Charter or under the Charitable Trustees Incorporation Act 1872 which is empowered by its constitution to act as a trustee for any charitable purposes, but only in relation to trusts in which its constitution empowers it to act;

(d) Any corporation which is constituted under the law of the United Kingdom or of any part thereof and having its place of business there, and which is either:

    (i) established for the purpose of undertaking trust business for the benefit of Her Majesty's Navy, Army, Air Force or Civil Service or of any unit, department, member or association of members thereof, and having among its directors or members any persons appointed or nominated by the Defence Council or any Department of State or any one or more of those Departments, or

    (ii) authorised by the Lord Chancellor to act in relation to any charitable ecclesiastical or public trusts as a trust corporation, but only in connection with any such trust as is so authorised;

(e) (i) any Regional Health Authority, Area Health Authority or special health authority, but only in relation to any trust which the authority is authorised to accept or hold by virtue of section 21 of the National Health Service Reorganisation Act 1973;

    (ii) any preserved Board as defined by section 15(6) of that Act, but only in relation to any trust which the Board is authorised to accept or hold by virtue of an order made under that section;

(f) the British Gas Corporation, but only in relation to a pension scheme or pension fund established or maintained by the Corporation by virtue of section 36 of the Gas Act 1972;

(g) the London Transport Executive, but only in relation to a pension scheme or pension fund:

    (i) which is established or administered by the Executive by virtue of section 6 of the Transport (London) Act 1969, or

    (ii) in relation to which rights, liabilities and functions have been transferred to the Executive by an order under section 74 of the Transport Act 1962 as applied by section 18 of the Transport (London) Act 1969;

(h) Any of the following, namely:

    (i) the Greater London Council,

    (ii) the corporation of any London borough (acting by the council),

    (iii) a county council, district council, parish council or community council,

    (iv) the Council of the Isles of Scilly,

but only in relation to charitable or public trusts (and not trust for an ecclesiastical charity or a charity for the relief of poverty) for the benefit of the inhabitants of the area of the local authority concerned and its neighbourhood, or any part of that area.'

In some cases, particularly where an application is made to register an enduring power appointing an unfamiliar trust corporation to act as attorney, the court will require sight of the corporation's memorandum and articles and proof that it satisfies the requirement as to paid-up share capital. The court also usually requires an up-to-date list of the authorised signing officers and specimens of their signatures.

2.3.2 Individuals

(1) Minors cannot be EPA attorneys

At the time when he executes the power, the attorney must have attained the age of 18 (1985 Act, s 2(7)(a)). The fact that the attorney was under 18 when the power was granted will not prevent it taking effect as an enduring power, provided that the attorney, having attained the age of 18, executes the power before the donor loses capacity. The Enduring Powers of Attorney (Prescribed Form) Regulations 1990 (SI 1990/1376), reg 3(1) provides that execution by the donor and attorney need not be contemporaneous.

(2) Bankrupts cannot be EPA attorneys

The attorney, when he executes the power, must not be bankrupt (s 2(7)(a)). If he is subsequently made bankrupt, his authority is terminated, whatever the circumstances of the bankruptcy (s 2(10)).

2.3.3 Office-holders

In its report, *Mental Incapacity* (1995) Law Com Paper No 231, the Law Commission commented that there might be occasions where a public official should be available to act as attorney of last resort (eg 'the manager for the time being of the X branch of the Y Bank' or 'the Director of Social Services of Z Region'). Although there are a handful of cases in which an office holder – mainly a Director of Social Services – has been appointed as attorney under an enduring power, the Law Commission suggested that:

> 'There will often be good reasons for avoiding the appointment of an office holder. The result of local government or NHS re-organisation, or of business changes in a solicitors' firm or a financial institution, might mean that there is no person fulfilling the description of the attorney when the (power) is needed' (Law Com Paper No 231, para 7.21).

2.3.4 Substitute and successor attorneys

A power of attorney which gives the attorney, as distinct from the donor, a right to appoint a substitute or successor cannot be an enduring power (s 2(9)). However, the donor may appoint a substitute or successor attorney, although the draftsman could encounter difficulties with the rules relating to joint or joint and several attorneys (s 11). In practice, if the donor envisages that the power could continue for many years, he may be well advised to consider appointing joint and several attorneys to diminish the risk of there being no attorney available to act when the need arises. The special rules on joint, and joint and several, attorneys are considered in detail in Chapter 7, and a way of providing for a succession of attorneys is considered at para **7.2.3**.

2.4 THE FORM OF THE POWER

The form and content of an EPA are, and were intended to be, matters of the greatest importance (Law Com Paper No 122, para 4.10). To ensure that both the donor and attorney appreciate the nature and effect of the instrument, the 1985 Act provides that a power cannot be an enduring power unless it is in the prescribed form (s 2(1)(a)).

The Prescribed Form Regulations, which are made by the Lord Chancellor under powers conferred in s 2(2) of the Act, give detailed effect to the statutory requirement that a power of attorney must, if it is to qualify as an enduring power, be in the prescribed form and contain prescribed explanatory information. The Regulations also contain provisions about execution by the donor and attorney.

2.5 THE PRESCRIBED FORM

2.5.1 Use of prescribed form is mandatory

The prescribed form set out in the Schedule to the Enduring Powers of Attorney (Prescribed Form) Regulations 1990 (SI 1990/1376) (reproduced in Appendix 5 to this book), must be used if the power of attorney is to be an enduring power within the meaning of the 1985 Act. In particular, the power must include all the explanatory information headed *About using this form* in Part A, and the relevant marginal notes to Parts B and C (reg 2(1)). Regulation 2(3) permits the form of execution to be adapted to provide for cases where a party signs by means of a mark, and for cases where the attorney is a trust corporation.

Regulation 2(2) requires the exclusion, either by omission or deletion, from the prescribed form of one and only one of any pair of alternatives. For example, the references to *all my property and affairs* or *the following property and affairs*. Regulation 2(2) also permits the exclusion of certain matters, for example, marginal notes corresponding to any words which have been excluded. These provisions may make it easier for draftsmen to 'present each client with a version tailored to his needs, containing everything he wants, nothing he does not want, and no messy deletions' (RT Oerton (1990) 137 SJ 971 at 973).

Paragraph 9 of the explanatory information in the current form prescribed in 1990 refers to the Court of Protection (Enduring Powers of Attorney) Rules 1986. These were revoked when the Court of Protection (Enduring Powers of Attorney) Rules 1994 (SI 1994/3047) came into force in December 1994, but no new form of EPA was prescribed. Nor was a new form of EPA prescribed by the present Court of Protection (Enduring Powers of Attorney) Rules 2001 (SI 2001/825), which came into force on 1 April 2001. The court has no objection to the reference in the explanatory information being corrected to cite the 1994 or 2001 Rules, as the case may be.

2.5.2 Permitted variations

Although reg 2(4) of the Enduring Powers of Attorney (Prescribed Form) Regulations 1990 (SI 1990/1376) (the 1990 Regulations) provides that, in general, an instrument which seeks to exclude any provisions contained in the Regulations is not a valid EPA, some freedom of choice is permitted. In particular, an enduring power may also include 'such additions (including paragraph numbers) or restrictions as the donor may decide' (reg 2(1)). The following are examples.

2.5.3 Additions

(1) Authorising the attorney's remuneration
It is preferable that the instrument should contain an express power for a professional attorney or a trust corporation to make charges for acting if it is intended that such an attorney be appointed (*Frith v Frith* [1906] AC 254). The Law Commission suggested that it was desirable for an enduring power to state whether or not the attorney was to be remunerated and, if so, on what basis (Law Com Paper No 122, para 4.83(iv)). However, even in the absence of an express charging clause, it would seem that the attorney will be entitled to be indemnified from the donor's estate for costs and expenses he incurs in the execution of his responsibilities (*Curtis v Barclay* (1826) 5 B & C 141).

Section 3(4) of the 1985 Act provides that an attorney under an enduring power may only benefit himself to meet his *needs* (see para **4.4**). It might be argued that a right for a professional or other attorney to charge for his services constitutes a more extensive power to benefit himself, and this view can be supported by reference to authorities on the effect of professional charging clauses in wills (see, eg, *Re Pooley* (1888) 40 ChD 1). However, it can also be argued that other provisions of the 1985 Act (notably s 8(2)(b)(iii), discussed in para **5.6**) clearly envisage that an enduring power may validly provide for the attorney's remuneration. This view seems to be supported by para 6 of the prescribed explanatory information, which says: 'If your attorney(s) are professional people, for example solicitors or accountants, they may be able to charge for their professional services as well. You may wish to provide expressly for remuneration of your attorney(s) (although if they are trustees they may not be allowed to accept it)'.

The Law Society recommends that where a solicitor acts as an attorney, the instrument should contain a professional charging clause (see para **10.2**).

(2) Authorising the attorneys to delegate the management of investments

As in the case of ordinary powers, an attorney acting under an enduring power has an implied power to delegate any of his functions which are not such that the donor would have expected him to have attended to them personally. Any wider power to delegate must be expressly provided for in the instrument (Law Com Paper No 122, para 4.22). See, generally, the discussion on this point at para **9.4**.

(3) Authorising disclosure of the donor's will to the attorney

The donor could authorise a solicitor to disclose to his attorney the contents of his will, provided that the power is registered, and provided that the solicitor considers disclosure to be necessary or expedient for the proper exercise of the attorney's functions. The attorney may need to know about the donor's will in order to avoid acting in a manner contrary to his wishes. The Law Society, in *The Guide to the Professional Conduct of Solicitors* 8th edn (1999), states, at Principle 16.01, that 'a solicitor is under a duty to keep confidential to his or her firm the affairs of clients and to ensure that the staff do the same'. The Law Society's advice on disclosing the donor's will to an attorney is considered at para **10.5**.

(4) Requiring the attorney to notify additional people of his intention to apply for registration

It is not possible to derogate from the statutory list of relatives who are entitled to receive notification of the attorney's intention to apply for registration of an enduring power, but it is possible to add to the list. The donor may want to include among those entitled to receive notice, for example, a partner; friend; step-relation; brother- or sister-in-law; solicitor; GP; priest; social worker; home-help; next-door neighbour; or the proprietor of the residential care home or nursing home in which he is residing.

(5) Requiring the attorney to keep accounts

An attorney has a common law duty to keep accounts and to be ready to produce them constantly. However, the explanatory information in Part A of the prescribed form omits to mention this duty. If the donor wishes to describe the accounts and records the attorney should keep, it might be sensible to require the attorney also to prepare an inventory of the donor's assets when he first assumes his functions as attorney.

(6) Requiring the attorney to account periodically to a third party

A possible safeguard against misuse of the power by an attorney is for the donor to require the attorney periodically to provide an account of his dealings under the power to a third party. The third party might be a solicitor or accountant, or even a member of the family. It is advisable to specify the date on which the account is to be produced: for example, on 5 April each year, or on the first and every subsequent anniversary of the registration of the power.

2.5.4 Restrictions

The prescribed explanatory information warns the donor that an attorney who has general power in relation to all the donor's property and affairs will be able to deal with the donor's money and property and may be able to sell his house. In addition, if the donor does not want the attorney to have such wide powers the donor 'can include any restrictions you like' (para 3 of the prescribed explanatory information). Among restrictions commonly found are the following.

(1) Not to make gifts

A donor could restrict or exclude the power of the attorney to benefit himself and persons other than the donor, and to make gifts of the donor's property (1985 Act, s 3(4) and (5)). For an example, see *Re R (Enduring Power of Attorney)* [1991] 1 FLR 128, where the donor also provided that the attorney was not to have power in respect of an investment portfolio managed by a named person.

(2) Not to dispose of specified property

The donor may like to include a restriction that the attorney should not be entitled to dispose of a specified property, such as the family home – an asset expressly referred to in para 2 of the prescribed explanatory information.

(3) Consent of third party required

The donor might provide that certain dispositions are not to take place without the concurrence of a third person. For instance, he might impose a restriction that his family home is not to be disposed of without the consent of his wife.

(4) Powers only effective on registration

The donor could stipulate that the attorney is not to have any authority unless and until he has reason to believe that the donor is or is becoming mentally incapable (1985 Act, s 4(1)). It may be preferable to express such a provision in the above terms, rather than state that the attorney is to have no authority unless and until the power has been registered because, pending registration of the power (which takes a minimum of 5 weeks), it may be necessary for the attorney to exercise his limited powers of maintenance and prevent loss to the donor's estate (s 1(2)). The attorney's function to apply to the court for the registration of the instrument is a duty, rather than a power, and his duty to register arises before he has authority to act in such a case (s 4(1)–(3)). For the distinction between *duties* and *powers*, see Chapter 9.

2.5.5 Short form of EPA

The omission of unused alternatives and corresponding marginal notes, permitted by reg 2(2) of the 1990 Regulations, makes it possible to draw up a short and simple form of general, unrestricted power.

Regulation 2(1) requires all the explanatory information to be included in every case, but the donor is told in para 11 of Part A of the prescribed form that 'some of these explanatory notes may not apply to the form you are using if it has already been adapted to suit your particular requirements'.

2.5.6 Transitional provisions

Regulation 5 of the 1990 Regulations revokes the rules governing the form of enduring power prescribed by the Enduring Powers of Attorney (Prescribed Form) Regulations 1987 (SI 1987/1612), but provides that a power executed before 31 July 1991 in the form prescribed in 1987 shall be capable of being a valid enduring power, whether or not seals are affixed to it.

This follows the pattern of previous regulations prescribing new forms, and the result can be summarised as follows:

— a power executed between 10 March 1986 and 31 October 1987 must be in the form prescribed by the 1986 Regulations;
— a power executed between 1 November 1987 and 30 June 1988 (both dates inclusive) could be in the form prescribed by either the 1986 or 1987 Regulations;
— a power executed between 1 July 1988 and 30 July 1990 must be in the form prescribed by the 1987 Regulations;
— a power executed between 31 July 1990 and 30 July 1991 could be in the form prescribed by either the 1987 or 1990 Regulations;

- a power executed on or after 31 July 1991 must be in the form prescribed by the 1990 Regulations.

Regulation 5 of the 1990 Regulations makes it clear that the relevant date of execution for this purpose is the date of execution by the donor.

2.5.7 Prescribed form in Welsh

The Welsh Language Act 1993 requires the Minister responsible for an Act of Parliament to prescribe forms in Welsh. Two statutory instruments came into force simultaneously with the Trustee Delegation Act 1999 on 1 March 2000.

The Powers of Attorney (Welsh Language Forms) Order 2000 (SI 2000/215) provides translations of the trustee power of attorney in s 5(6) of the Trustee Delegation Act 1999 and the general power of attorney in Sch 1 to the Powers of Attorney Act 1971.

The Enduring Powers of Attorney (Welsh Language Prescribed Form) Regulations 2000 (SI 2000/289) prescribe a Welsh form of *Atwrneiaeth Barhaus* which may be used instead of the English form set out in the 1990 Regulations. The prescribed form is set out in Appendix 6 to this book.

Welsh translations of forms EP1 to EP7 are acceptable by virtue of the Court of Protection (Enduring Powers of Attorney) Rules 2001 (SI 2001/825), r 3(2)(c).

2.6 EXECUTION OF THE POWER

Section 2(1)(b) of the 1985 Act provides that the instrument which creates the power must be executed in the prescribed manner by the donor and the attorney. If there are joint attorneys, all must execute the power (s 11(2)).

2.6.1 The requirements of execution and attestation

The Law of Property (Miscellaneous Provisions) Act 1989, which came into force on 31 July 1990, changed the law relating to deeds and their execution, and necessitated the making of the 1990 Regulations.

Regulation 3 provides that:

- an enduring power must be executed by both the donor and the attorney;

- execution by the donor and attorney need not necessarily take place at the same time (indeed, there is no reason why execution by an attorney should not be postponed, provided that it takes place before the donor becomes mentally incapable);
- execution by the donor and attorney(s) must take place in the presence of a witness, but not necessarily the same witness, who must sign the form and give his full name and address;
- the donor and an attorney must not witness each other's signature;
- one attorney must not witness the signature of another attorney.

In *Re R* (unreported) 23 February 1988, Knox J, the donor, Mrs R, executed an EPA on 26 July 1986, 4 days after it had been executed by the attorney. The Master of the Court of Protection refused to register the power, holding that the donor must execute the instrument before the attorney because one cannot accept an obligation until it has been conferred. Allowing an appeal by the attorney, Knox J held that 'one has to find affirmatively in the Act or in the Regulations something which compels the conclusion that the order of execution has to be donor first, attorney second. I have come to the conclusion that there is no material from which that conclusion by way of implication can be reached'. The decision in *Re R* is now largely academic, because the 1990 Regulations expressly state in Part C, 'Don't sign this form before the donor has signed Part B'; nevertheless, the principle still applies to any instruments executed under the first Prescribed Form Regulations.

2.6.2 Execution – special cases

The 1990 Regulations make provision for special cases. Regulation 2(3) allows the prescribed form to be adapted to provide for a case where the donor or an attorney signs by means of a mark. Regulation 3 allows an enduring power to be executed at the direction of the donor or attorney.

If the instrument is signed by someone else at the direction of the donor or attorney:

- it should include, in Part B or Part C as appropriate, a statement that the instrument has been executed at the direction of the donor or attorney;
- the person signing should not be the donor, the attorney or any of the witnesses to the signature of either the donor or an attorney; and
- it must be signed in the presence of two witnesses, each of whom must sign the form and give their full names and addresses (reg 3(3) and (4)).

Although the Regulations do not specifically state that, when someone signs the power at the direction of the donor, the signatory must do so *in the presence of* the donor, it is essential that the donor is present, otherwise the deed will not have been validly executed in accordance with the provisions of the Law of Property (Miscellaneous Provisions) Act 1989, s 1(3)(a)(ii).

If the donor is blind, it has been suggested that the attestation clause should be amended to show the circumstances in which the donor has executed the instrument, and that if the power is registered, the court will need an explanation from the attorney or his solicitors as to how the donor was notified of the intention to apply for registration (PD Lewis (1987) LSG 1219). A blind person cannot witness the donor's or attorney's signature. *Witness* means, with regard to things audible, someone who has the faculty of hearing, and, with regard to things visible, someone who has the faculty of sight. Because the execution of a deed is a visible transaction, it cannot be signed *in the presence of* a blind person (*Re Gibson (Deceased)* [1949] P 434).

2.6.3 Trust corporations

Regulation 2(3) of the 1990 Regulations provides that the form of execution by an attorney of an enduring power may be adapted to provide for execution by a trust corporation (see the Companies Act 1985, s 36A, inserted by the Companies Act 1989, s 130).

2.6.4 Attestation by spouse

The marginal notes on the prescribed form warn the donor, though surprisingly not the atttorney, that 'It is not advisable for your husband or wife to be your witness'. The reason for the inclusion of this warning is to be found in s 14(1) of the Civil Evidence Act 1968 which provides, in effect, that a spouse would not necessarily be a compellable witness in proceedings attacking the power.

2.6.5 Alterations

The 1990 Regulations contain no requirement that alterations to the document be initialled, and there is a general presumption that alterations to a deed have been made before execution.

2.7 CONSEQUENCES OF FAILURE TO COMPLY WITH THE FORMALITIES

If the formal requirements set out above are not complied with, the instrument cannot take effect as an enduring power. It may, of course, be effective as an ordinary power (see para **2.1.2**), but such a power will be revoked by the donor's supervening mental incapacity. The 1985 Act contains two minor modifications to the general principle that failure to observe the prescribed formalities will prevent the power taking effect as an enduring power.

2.7.1 Presumption that the prescribed information was incorporated

If the instrument is in the prescribed form, and purports to have been executed in the prescribed manner, it shall, in the absence of any evidence to the contrary, be taken to be a document which incorporated, at the time of execution by the donor, the prescribed explanatory information (s 2(5)). This provision is limited in scope. It does not provide a general presumption in favour of due compliance with the prescribed formalities but merely a presumption that one particular requirement – namely, that prescribed explanatory information be endorsed on the EPA – was satisfied at the relevant time.

2.7.2 Material and immaterial differences

Where an instrument differs in an immaterial respect in form or mode of expression from the prescribed form, the instrument shall be treated as sufficient in point of form and expression (s 2(6)). The scope of this provision is slightly obscure, but guidance on its application was given in two articles by PD Lewis ((1986) LSG 3455 and (1987) LSG 1219).

For example, the Court of Protection has ruled that:

– the omission of the prescribed statement by the donor – 'I intend that this power shall continue even if I become mentally incapable' – constitutes a material difference, with the result that the instrument in question would be incapable of taking effect as an enduring power;
– leaving in both alternatives, *jointly* and *jointly and severally*, is a material difference and will invalidate the instrument as an enduring power;
– crossing out both alternatives, *all my property and affairs* and *the following property and affairs*, is also a material difference. The earlier words, *with general authority to act on my behalf*, are not sufficient on their own;
– omitting the date on which the donor or attorney signed the instrument is immaterial, provided that it can be established by extraneous affidavit evidence;
– the omission of the witness's address is considered to be an immaterial difference. Extraneous evidence is acceptable.

2.7.3 Severance of illegal clauses

The Court of Protection may agree to the registration of an instrument subject to the severance of an offending clause, applying the common law doctrine that 'where you cannot sever the illegal from the legal part of a covenant, the contract is altogether void, but, where you can sever them, whether the illegality be created by statute or by the common law, you may reject the bad part and retain the good' (*Pickering v Ilfracombe Railway* (1868) LR 3 CP 235 at 250). Examples of clauses which the court has severed from instruments include: a provision that any two of three attorneys appointed jointly may act together; clauses in which the donor purports to authorise the attorney to make gifts without restriction; and clauses which purport to authorise the attorney to make medical treatment decisions on the donor's behalf.

2.8 CERTAIN TYPES OF POWER CANNOT BE ENDURING POWERS

The 1985 Act contains two provisions which prevent certain powers qualifying as enduring powers even though they would otherwise do so.

2.8.1 Attorney given power to appoint a substitute or successor

Section 2(9) states that a power of attorney which gives the attorney a right to appoint a substitute or successor cannot be an enduring power. This provision is considered in detail at paras **2.3.4** and **7.2.1**.

2.8.2 Trustee powers

Section 2(8) of the 1985 Act provided that a power of attorney under s 25 of the Trustee Act 1925 (whereby a trustee may grant a power of attorney delegating his trusts, powers and discretions for a period not exceeding 12 months) could not be an EPA. Section 2(8) has now been repealed by s 12 of the Trustee Delegation Act 1999, and s 6 of the 1999 Act enables a donor to delegate his functions as trustee. However, the requirements of s 25 of the Trustee Act 1925 (as amended by s 5 of the 1999 Act), such as duration, notice and wording, will apply to any such delegation.

Chapter 3

ACTION REQUIRED AT ONSET OF MENTAL INCAPACITY

3.1 THE SIGNIFICANCE OF THE ONSET OF MENTAL INCAPACITY

Provided the donor remains fully mentally capable, an enduring power of attorney (EPA) is operated in the same way as an ordinary power of attorney, and the duties of the attorney are largely the same as those of an attorney under an ordinary power. In particular, in the absence of any express or implied contractual obligation, the attorney owes no duty to the donor to operate the power (see para **9.2**).

The only significant difference between an ordinary and an enduring power at this stage lies in the fact that, if the power is an enduring power, the extent to which the attorney may benefit himself and third parties and make gifts is governed by express statutory provisions to be found in s 3(4) and (5) of the Enduring Powers of Attorney Act 1985 (the 1985 Act). These provisions are fully explained in paras **4.4** and **4.5**.

An ordinary power will be revoked by the donor's incapacity, but it is expressly provided that an enduring power shall not be revoked by the donor's subsequent mental incapacity (s 1(1)(a)).

It does not follow from this that the donor's supervening mental incapacity is irrelevant in the case of an enduring power. The onset of such incapacity has two important consequences. First, if the donor becomes incapable, the powers of the attorney are restricted until the power has been registered by the Court of Protection (s 1(2)). Secondly, s 4 of the 1985 Act imposes special duties on the attorney if he 'has reason to believe that the donor is *or is becoming* mentally incapable' (s 4(1)) (emphasis added). Since these special duties may, in point of time, arise before it becomes necessary to consider the effect of the donor's incapacity on the extent of the attorney's powers, they are examined first.

3.2 ATTORNEY'S DUTIES WHEN THE DONOR IS BECOMING MENTALLY INCAPABLE

If the attorney under an enduring power has reason to believe that the donor is or is becoming mentally incapable, he has two specific duties:

- a duty to give notice to the donor and prescribed relatives; and
- a duty to apply to the Court of Protection for registration.

These duties arise in the context of the donor's mental incapacity, and s 13(1) of the 1985 Act provides a definition of mental incapacity for this purpose.

3.2.1 Mental incapacity

Section 13(1) states that:

> ' "Mentally incapable" or "mental incapacity" ... means, in relation to any person, that he is incapable by reason of mental disorder of managing and administering his property and affairs and "mentally capable" and "mental capacity" shall be construed accordingly.'

3.2.2 Mental disorder

It will be noted that the donor's inability to deal with his property and affairs must arise by reason of mental disorder. This term has the same meaning as in s 1(2) of the Mental Health Act 1983, which states that:

> ' "mental disorder" means mental illness, arrested or incomplete development of mind, psychopathic disorder and any other disorder or disability of mind.'

Surprisingly, 'mental illness' is not defined in either the Mental Health Act 1983 or the Enduring Powers of Attorney Act 1985. In *W v L* [1974] QB 711 at 719, Lawton LJ said that the words mental illness are 'ordinary words of the English language. They have no particular medical significance. They have no particular legal significance ... (and) should be construed in the way that ordinary sensible people would construe them'. In 1976, in an appendix to its review of the Mental Health Act 1959, the Department of Health and Social Security issued the following guidelines on the symptoms commonly associated with mental illness.

> 'Mental illness means an illness having one or more of the following characteristics:
>
> - more than temporary impairment of intellectual functions shown by a failure of memory, orientation, comprehension, and learning capacity;

- more than temporary alteration of mood of such a degree as to give rise to the patient having a delusional appraisal of his situation, his past or his future, or that of others, or to the lack of any appraisal;
- delusional beliefs: persecutory, jealous or grandiose;
- abnormal perceptions associated with delusional misinterpretation of events;
- thinking so disordered as to prevent the patient making a reasonable appraisal of his situation or having reasonable communication with others.'

The first set of characteristics is similar to the standard definition of *dementia*: 'an acquired global impairment of intellect, memory and personality but without impairment of consciousness ... as such, it is almost always of long duration, usually progressive, and often irreversible, but these features are not included as part of the definition' (WA Lishman *Organic Psychiatry: The Psychological Consequences of Cerebral Disorder* 2nd edn (1987)).

3.2.3 Incapable of managing his property and affairs

In *F v West Berkshire Health Authority* [1989] 2 FLR 376 at 423H, Lord Brandon stated that "*Property and affairs*" means "business matters, legal transactions and other dealings of a similar kind"'. It does not include matters relating to personal welfare (such as where the donor should live, or with whom he should have contact) or medical treatment. Neither the Court of Protection nor an attorney acting under an enduring power has any jurisdiction or authority to make personal or medical decisions on behalf of the donor, although inevitably *power over the purse* will confer some degree of *power over the person*.

Assessing the donor's capacity to manage and administer his property and affairs is very subjective. His ability to cope depends largely on the value and nature of his property and affairs and the extent to which he may need to be protected from his own rashness or from exploitation by others – often members of the family.

The standard textbook on Court of Protection practice, Heywood and Massey, *Court of Protection Practice*, 12th edn (Sweet & Maxwell, 1991), p 17 cites an unreported decision of Wilberforce J, *Re CAF* (1962), as the authority for stating that 'the degree of incapacity of managing and administering a [person's] property and affairs must be related to all the circumstances, including the state in which [he] lives and the complexity and importance of the property and affairs which he has to manage and administer'.

Although the decision in *Re CAF* was never reported, and there is not even a surviving transcript of the judgment, there has been a lively debate in the Australian courts as to whether an individual's capacity to manage his affairs is subjective (following *Re CAF*) or objective. In one case the judge tried to introduce a more objective test and decided that a person must be 'incapable of dealing, in a reasonably competent fashion, with the ordinary routine affairs of man, and by reason of that incompetence there is a real risk that either he or she may be disadvantaged in the conduct of such affairs or that such moneys or property which he or she may possess may be dissipated or lost' (*PY v RJS* [1982] 2 NSWLR 700). However, in another case a different judge followed *Re CAF* and upheld the subjective test because the Act itself speaks of 'managing *his* affairs', rather than 'the ordinary routine affairs of man' (*Re MacGregor* [1985] VR 861).

For a more detailed discussion of this type of capacity, see The Law Society/BMA *Assessment of Mental Capacity: Guidance for Doctors and Lawyers* (1995), pp 25–30.

3.2.4 Becoming mentally incapable

There may be little difficulty in the attorney being able to decide that he has reason to believe that the donor *is* mentally incapable, but his duties under the 1985 Act arise at an earlier stage if he has reason to believe that the donor *is becoming mentally incapable*.

The 1985 Act gives no help on the construction of this imprecise formula. In particular, it should be noted that the Act gives no indication of the proximity required to actual incapacity for the duties to arise.

In the circumstances, it is suggested that the 'ordinary sensible person's test', referred to in para **3.2.2**, would apply. The view that this would be a correct interpretation derives some support from the following passage in the Law Commission's Report *The Incapacitated Principal* (1983) Law Com Paper No 122, para 4.35:

> '[The duty to register] would operate only when the attorney had "reason to believe". The reason for this is the difficulty in deciding when a person has lost capacity: such decisions can be very much a matter of opinion. It would perhaps have been possible to require that the attorney should obtain an expert medical opinion; but medical evidence (which is required in receivership proceedings) is liable to cause embarrassment both to the donor and attorney and might detract from the acceptability of the proposed EPA scheme as a whole. In any event, our recommendation is intended to cover not only the incapable donor but also the donor who is *merely becoming* incapable. We feel that our choice of words would help prevent the risk that the conscientious attorney might delay his application until (perhaps years later) he was absolutely certain that the donor was incapable. Our proposal would also in many cases enable the attorney to register his EPA before his authority became inoperable by the donor's actual incapacity.'

See para **3.7.4** which considers the meaning of *not yet becoming mentally incapable*.

3.2.5 Early registration is desirable

In practice, the prudent attorney will apply to register as soon as he has any grounds to suspect that incapacity could reasonably be alleged. Apart from anything else, once the registration process is underway, his powers are severely restricted (s 1(1)(b) and see para **4.6**). There may, however, be cases in which he will be deterred from timely registration because of embarrassment caused by the requirement that he must first notify the donor of his intention to apply for registration, and by the fact that the donor may object to registration on the ground that the application is premature (s 6(5)(c), and see para **3.7.4**).

3.3 THE NOTIFICATION REQUIREMENT

Before making an application for registration, the attorney must give notice to the donor and certain specified relatives of the donor of his intention to do so (Sch 1, para 1). It should be noted that Form EP1 (set out in Appendix 4 to this book) cannot properly be served until the enduring power has been executed. This is because the form refers to an enduring power already in existence.

3.3.1 Power to dispense with notification

Before applying for registration of the power, the attorney may apply to the Court of Protection to be dispensed from the requirement to give notice to the donor or to any of the specified relatives of the donor (Sch 1, paras 3(2) and 4(2)). Such an application will be granted if the court is satisfied:

– that it would be undesirable or impracticable for the attorney to give him notice; or
– that no useful purpose is likely to be served by giving him notice (Sch 1, paras 3(2) and 4(2)).

Applications for dispensation may, perhaps, be made in two classes of case. First, the attorney may feel that although the donor is or is becoming mentally incapable, he still retains sufficient understanding to be distressed by the service of a notice on him. Secondly, there may be cases in which the facts suggest that relatives who are entitled to be notified are unlikely to take a concerned interest in the matter. For example, the donor's wife may have been long separated from him.

It should be noted that there are circumstances (eg, the fact that a person's whereabouts cannot be discovered) in which it is not necessary to notify a relative who would otherwise be entitled (see para **3.3.5**). In such cases, there is no need for any application to the court for dispensation.

An application for dispensation should be made in the general form, Form EP3, prescribed in Sch 1 to the Court of Protection (Enduring Powers of Attorney) Rules 2001 (SI 2001/825) (the 2001 Rules). These Rules are set out in full in Appendix 4 to this book.

It has been said that an application to dispense with service on the donor on the grounds that he is incapable of understanding the registration procedure is unlikely to succeed. Moreover, applications on other grounds are 'unlikely to succeed unless there is clear medical evidence that service would be detrimental to the donor's health' (see PD Lewis (1986) LSG 3566 at 3567). In the absence of a successful application for dispensation, notice must be given as stipulated in the 1985 Act.

3.3.2 Notice to the donor

Unless the court has dispensed him from the requirement, the attorney must give the donor notice of his intention to apply for registration in Form EP1. The notice must be given to the donor personally (2001 Rules, r 15(1)). Service by post is not sufficient. The wording of the rule would seem to require service by the attorney personally, but it has been said that no point has been taken where the notice, although served personally on the donor, was served by an agent acting on the directions of the attorney (see PD Lewis (1986) LSG 3566 at 3567).

The Law Commission gave the following explanation for requiring service on the donor:

> 'Whilst we appreciate that there might be cases where the sight of a formal letter of notification might cause the donor worry or distress it seems to us on balance more undesirable that the donor should be unaware of the proposed registration or learn of the proposed registration at second hand, perhaps from a notified relative. The donor's notice would merely inform him of the attorney's intention to apply for registration and of the fact that the donor, once the power was registered, would not be able to revoke the power effectively without the revocation being confirmed by the court' (Law Com Paper No 122, para 4.42).

The Commission suggested that it would be a sensible practice for the attorney to discuss the matter with the donor before giving him the formal notice.

Although, as suggested in para **3.3.1**, there may be cases where the attorney will prefer to apply to the court to dispense with the need to notify the donor on the ground that such notification would be undesirable or impracticable, or that it would be unlikely to serve any useful purpose, it would appear that the prospects of such an application being successful are not high.

Prior to 1 April 2001, when the Court of Protection Rules 2001 (SI 2001/824) came into force, there were similar provisions whereby the court could dispense with notification on an alleged patient of an application for the appointment of a receiver under the Mental Health Act 1983. It was considered that these provisions were incompatible with the Human Rights Act 1998, and r 24 of the Court of Protection Rules 2001 requires notification to be given in all cases.

3.3.3 Notice to relatives

The notification to relatives required by Sch 1, para 1 to the 1985 Act is the initial stage in the registration procedure, which was said by the Law Commission to constitute 'the keystone of the protective part' of the scheme established by the Act. The Commission explained the importance it attached to the registration requirement in these words:

> 'Under our scheme the initial responsibility for the selection of the attorney rests with the donor. Since, however, for a variety of reasons the attorney may not be suitable to act on the donor's behalf without supervision, our scheme would ensure that the donor's relatives would have an opportunity to consider whether it would be safe to allow the attorney to continue acting once the donor's capacity was in doubt' (Law Com Paper No 122, para 4.36).

3.3.4 Power to dispense classes of attorney from notification requirement

It will become apparent that the provisions requiring notification to relatives are of some complexity, and that compliance with the stipulated procedures may sometimes involve considerable cost.

The Law Commission recognised that it would be possible to justify exemptions from the requirement that relatives be notified on the basis that the donor's interests were adequately safeguarded, for example, where the attorney was subject to professional standards and discipline (Law Com Paper No 122, para 4.43). Section 12(1) of the 1985 Act, therefore, contains a power for the Lord Chancellor by order to exempt attorneys of such descriptions as he thinks fit from the requirement to give notice to relatives prior to registration. Such attorneys would, however, still have to comply with the provisions governing notification to the donor. No such order has been made.

3.3.5 Who are the specified relatives?

Schedule 1, para 2(1) to the 1985 Act specifies a list of relatives of the donor who are entitled to receive notice of an intended application for registration. However, Sch 1, para 2(2) provides that a person who falls within the definition is, nevertheless, not entitled to receive notice if, *either* his name or address is not known to the attorney and cannot be reasonably ascertained by him, *or* the attorney has reason to believe that the relative has not attained 18 years of age or is mentally incapable. A decision by the attorney to this effect may have the practical consequence that notice will have to be given to other relatives (see para **3.3.6**, and compare the position where the court dispenses with the requirement to give notice to a particular relative, discussed in para **3.3.8**).

The Law Commission stated that the specified classes of relatives had been drawn up to reflect:

> '(in descending order) those relatives who would be most likely to know the donor best (and, perhaps, the attorney also) and have an interest in his well-being. As these relatives would also probably be the persons most nearly concerned in the donor's estate after his death, non-objection by them would be the best available guarantee that the attorneyship would not be fraught with difficulties caused by friction within the family' (Law Com Paper No 122, para 4.39).

The classes of relatives are as follows:

- the donor's husband or wife. A separated spouse would qualify under this head, but a divorced spouse would not. However, divorce is only effective for this purpose on the making of a decree absolute (*Re Seaford* [1968] P 53);
- the donor's children. A stepchild of the donor is not included in this or any other class. An illegitimate child is for these purposes to be treated as if he were the legitimate child of his mother and father (Sch 1, para 8(1)). However, there will, no doubt, be cases in which the existence or whereabouts of such a child are not known, and the child will, presumably, then not be entitled to be notified because of the rule set out above;
- the donor's parents. For the reasons stated above this expression includes the natural father of an illegitimate child. Once again, there will be many cases in which such a father will not have to be notified because his whereabouts are unknown;
- the donor's brothers and sisters, whether of the whole blood or half blood;
- the widow or widower of a child of the donor. It is not clear whether such a person ceases to be entitled to notice on remarriage, and it has been suggested that 'for safety's sake they should be notified, and anyone in the next class as well' (PD Lewis (1986) LSG 3566 at 3567);
- the donor's grandchildren;

- the children of the donor's brothers and sisters of the whole blood;
- the children of the donor's brothers and sisters of the half blood;
- the donor's uncles and aunts of the whole blood; and
- the children of the donor's uncles and aunts of the whole blood.

3.3.6 How many relatives have to be notified?

In principle, only *three* of the donor's relatives are entitled to receive notice, and those three come from the class appearing first in the list above. Thus, if the donor is married, his spouse (even if separated from the donor) will always be entitled to receive notice unless either her whereabouts are not known to the attorney and cannot reasonably be ascertained, or the court has dispensed with notification under the procedure described in para **3.3.1**. If the donor has children, those children (if they are 18 or over, and subject to the same exceptions) are then entitled to be notified; and so on down the list.

Although, in principle, no more than three persons are entitled to be notified (Sch 1, para 2(3)), it is provided that if there is any relative in a particular class who is entitled to be notified in order to make up the requirement of three, then every member of that class must be notified – even if that means notifying five, six or more relatives (Sch 1, para 2(4)). The principle is that the attorney is not to be allowed to choose which relatives in a particular class should be notified. It should be noted that the legislation is couched in terms of giving certain relatives an entitlement to be notified of the application. It can never be wrong to notify a relative who is not so entitled. Accordingly, if there is any doubt as to entitlement it would be safer to notify.

If the donor has fewer than three relatives falling into the specified categories, only those relatives need be notified. If he has no relatives within the specified categories, no notification need be given to any relative or friend – even if, for example, the donor has been sharing a common household with another person for many years. However, where there are no relatives entitled to be notified the court will not register the power until it has made or caused to be made such inquiries as it thinks appropriate (s 6(4)(b)).

3.3.7 Examples of notification requirement

Some examples may make the operation of the notification rules clearer.

- The donor has a wife and four surviving children, all of whom are aged 18 or over. Notice must be given to all five.
- The donor has one child, one parent and eight grandchildren. All 10 relatives must be notified, except for any grandchild under the age of 18.

- The donor has a spouse and two adult children. These three relatives are entitled to notice. It is not necessary to notify anyone else.
- The donor has a wife from whom he has been separated for 20 years, and a 'common law' wife of 10 years' standing. He lives with her and the three children of her marriage. Only his lawful wife need be notified.
- The donor has a spouse, two children (one aged 16 and one aged 18) and a mentally incapable uncle who has three adult children. The spouse, the 18-year-old child and the three cousins are entitled to be notified. The 16-year-old child is not so entitled, nor is the uncle.
- The donor has a spouse, two children under the age of 18, one parent and three adult brothers. The children are not entitled to receive notice. Hence the spouse, the surviving parent, and the donor's brothers are all entitled to receive notice.

3.3.8 Effect of the court dispensing with notification

It seems that a successful application under the procedure explained in para **3.3.1** to dispense with service on a relative does not have the consequential effect of adding to the class of relatives who must be notified in order that three or more will actually be notified. This is because the 1985 Act provides that 'no more than three persons are entitled to receive notice' (Sch 1, para 2(3)). In the situation under discussion, the court has merely dispensed with the requirement to serve a person who is so entitled. It has not altered the fact that such a person falls within the statutory description of being a person 'entitled to receive notice'.

3.3.9 Attorney a specified relative

It will often happen that the attorney will himself be a member of one of the specified classes of relatives. Such an attorney is not required to notify himself (Sch 1, para 3(1)), but he continues to count as a person entitled to receive notice for the purpose of the rule that no more than three persons are entitled to receive notice. For example, if a donor, who has a wife and two adult daughters, appoints his wife as his attorney, it is necessary for the attorney to notify the daughters, but nobody else.

3.3.10 Notice must be in the prescribed form

The notices to be given under the provisions explained above must be in the prescribed Form EP1, as set out in the 2001 Rules, Sch 1, and reproduced in Appendix 4 to this book (see the 1985 Act, Sch 1, para 5(a)). The prescribed form of notice explains that the attorney proposes to apply to the Court of Protection for registration of the power, and that the recipient may object to the proposed registration by notifying the court within 4 weeks from the date on which such notice is given. It summarises the grounds on which objection may be made, and reminds the donor that, while the enduring power of attorney remains registered, the donor will not be able to revoke it until the Court of Protection confirms the revocation. The form of notice should be signed by all the attorneys who are applying to register the EPA.

3.3.11 Service on the donor

The notification to the donor must be given to him personally (2001 Rules, r 15(1)). See para **3.3.2**.

3.3.12 Service on relatives

Rule 15(2) of the 2001 Rules provides that notification to relatives may be effected by sending the prescribed notice (Form EP1) to the relative concerned:

- by first-class post;
- through a document exchange;
- by fax; or
- by other electronic means.

3.3.13 Service on a solicitor

It is provided that if a solicitor acting for the person to be given a document endorses on that document or on a copy of it a statement that he accepts the document on behalf of that person, the document should be deemed to have been duly sent to that person and to have been received on the date on which the endorsement was made (r 16). However, this procedure is not available in respect of the notice to be served on the donor. A notice 'sent' to him has not been 'given to him personally', as required by r 15(1).

3.3.14 Substituted service

Where it appears to the court that it is impracticable for any document to be sent to a person by first-class post, document exchange, fax or e-mail in accordance with r 15(2), the court may give such directions for the purpose of bringing the document to the notice of the person to whom it is addressed as it thinks fit (r 17). Even in the unlikely event of it being appropriate, substituted service cannot be used in respect of the donor because the notice is not required to be 'sent' to him, but must be given to him personally (see para **3.3.11**).

3.3.15 Notice to co-attorney

Schedule 1, para 7 to the 1985 Act stipulates that an attorney under a joint and several power must give notice of his intention to apply for registration to any other attorney under the power who is not joining in the application. No such notice need be given if the co-attorney's address is not known to the applying attorney and cannot reasonably be ascertained by him, or if the applying attorney has reason to believe that the co-attorney has not attained 18 years of age, or is mentally incapable (Sch 1, para 7(2)). The court also has power, as in the case of notification of relatives and the donor, to dispense with the giving of notice to a co-attorney (Sch 1, para 7(1)). The form of notice sent to the co-attorney is identical to that given to the relatives and donor (Form EP1).

3.3.16 Notices to be served within 14 days of each other

The notices to the donor, relatives and any co-attorney of the attorney's intention to register the power (Form EP1) must be served within 14 days of each other (2001 Rules, r 6(1)).

3.4 APPLICATION FOR REGISTRATION

3.4.1 Application must be made as soon as practicable

Section 4(2) of the 1985 Act provides that the attorney shall apply for registration as soon as practicable if he has reason to believe that the donor is, or is becoming, mentally incapable. However, the notification requirement must be dealt with as set out in the preceding paragraphs before the application can be made.

If the attorney is not sure whether the power is, in fact, valid as an enduring power, for example because he is uncertain whether the donor had the necessary mental capacity to grant it (see para **2.2.2**), he may, and perhaps should, apply to the court to have the validity of the power determined rather than apply for registration (see PD Lewis (1987) LSG 1219 at 1221). This facility is expressly provided for in s 4(5), and the attorney must comply with any direction given to him by the court on such a determination.

3.4.2 Ten days after last notice

Rule 7 of the 2001 Rules provides that an application must be lodged with the court office not later than 10 days after whichever is the later of the date on which:

- notice has been given to the donor and every relative entitled to receive notice and every co-attorney; or
- leave has been given to dispense with notice.

For these purposes, a notice given by post is to be regarded as given on the date on which it was posted (1985 Act, Sch 1, para 8(2)). However, days on which the court office is closed are excluded in computing this period of time (2001 Rules, r 5(1)).

The time-limit for lodging Form EP2 was extended from 3 days to 10 when the Court of Protection (Enduring Powers of Attorney) Rules 1994 (SI 1994/ 3047) came into force in December 1994. The former 3-day limit was extremely short, and quite a number of applications were made to the court, under what is now r 14(3), to have the time extended. Referring to applications to extend what was then a 3-day limit, PD Lewis, the former Assistant Public Trustee, said that 'each case is decided on its own merits, so it is very important to consider carefully the form of wording of the application, to bring out the strength of the application' ((1987) LSG 1219 at 1221). Even though the time-limit has now been extended to 10 days, there may still be cause for an application to be made to the court for an extension under r 14(3). For example, the donor's condition may have deteriorated since the last Form EP1 was served, and the attorney, in the belief that the donor's death was imminent, may have deferred submitting the application to register. The donor then makes an unexpected recovery, and the attorney finds that the 10-day time-limit has expired. An application to have the time-limit extended should be made on Form EP3.

3.4.3 Form of application

The application for registration must be in the prescribed form (Form EP2) which is set out in Appendix 4 to this book (1985 Act, s 4(4); 2001 Rules, r 7 and Sch 1). The application states that the attorney has reason to believe that the donor is, or is becoming, mentally incapable, gives details of the persons to whom notice has been given, and contains a certificate that the provisions of the Act have been complied with. It should, perhaps, be noted that these statements are less comprehensive than those envisaged by the Law Commission (Law Com Paper No 122, para 4.44).

The application must be accompanied by the original power and a cheque for £75 made payable to the 'Public Guardianship Office' in respect of the prescribed fee (2001 Rules, r 26 and Sch 2).

Technically, the so-called 'registration fee' of £75 is payable 'on lodging an application for registration of an enduring power of attorney'. If, for any reason, the application is unsuccessful or the registration does not proceed (perhaps because the donor has died), the fee is not recoverable. See also para **5.14**.

3.4.4 Reasons why EPAs are defective

If the instrument itself – rather than the application – is defective, the applicant or his solicitors will receive a letter from the Public Guardianship Office informing him that the application to register the power has been rejected. The main reasons for failure are:

– the power omits the donor's date of birth (this can be put right by sending a copy of the donor's birth certificate);
– the explanatory information (Part A) has been omitted;
– the marginal notes have been omitted at ...;
– the power fails to appoint the attorneys either 'jointly' or 'jointly and severally';
– the power fails to show the extent of the attorney's(s') authority;
– the power fails to show the extent of the property over which the attorney(s) has (have) authority;
– the power was not dated when it was executed by the donor/attorney(s).

3.4.5 Reasons why applications to register are defective

If the application is defective the applicant will receive a letter from the Public Guardianship Office stating:

'Thank you for your application to register the above donor's enduring power of attorney. We cannot yet register it for the following reason(s), as shown with a tick:

The date(s) the notices (forms EP1) were given to the relatives or the donor is/are missing. Please insert. If the date(s) are after the date the attorney(s) signed the application form (EP2), would the attorney(s) please re-sign and re-date form EP2 and return it to this office.

The attorney(s) signed the application for registration (form EP2) before giving the notices of intention to register (form EP1). Would the attorney(s) please re-sign and re-date form EP2 and return it to this office.

The attorney(s) have not signed the application for registration (form EP2). Would the attorney(s) please sign it and return it to this office.

Please confirm that there are no other relatives entitled to notice of the application.

Please confirm that the notices (form EP1) served on the relatives and donor showed the correct date the enduring power of attorney was made, ie ... If not, a fresh application must be made and the notices re-served.

No additional Part C was used for the second attorney. Please provide evidence from the witness that he/she witnessed both attorneys' signatures.

The application to register has not been made by both or all the attorneys. If you intend registration to be limited to … please confirm that the notice(s) of intention to register (form EP1) served on the donor and relatives showed that attorney's or those attorneys' names only.

or

If you intend registration to be limited to the above-named attorney(s), please confirm that the notice(s) of intention to register (form EP1) served on the donor and relatives showed both or all the attorneys' names.

The application for registration was lodged out of time. Rule 7 of the Court of Protection (Enduring Powers of Attorney) Rules 2001 prescribes that the application should be sent to this office within 10 days of the last notice of intention to register (form EP1). Will you please (explain the delay) (seek a formal extension of time using form EP3 enclosed) or (serve fresh notices of intention to register and submit a fresh application for registration).

The notices of intention to register (form EP1) were not given to the Donor and relatives within 14 days of each other as prescribed by Rule 6 of the Court of Protection (Enduring Powers of Attorney) Rules 2001. Will you please (explain the delay) (re-serve the donor) (re-serve the relatives) and re-sign and re-date the application.'

3.5 FUNCTIONS OF THE COURT ON AN APPLICATION FOR REGISTRATION

The Law Commission regarded it as an important feature of the EPA scheme that registration by the court should normally be a simple administrative operation. In the great majority of cases, applications for registration were to involve the court in doing no more than checking that the relevant documents were in order and that no objections had been made. The Commission thought it essential to the success of the EPA scheme, both in terms of court resources and of public acceptability, that the court should be bound to grant the application and register the power 'in the absence of a valid objection or any other reason for not doing so'. In particular, the court was to have no duty to make independent inquiries unless there were suspicious circumstances, and the court would not normally be expected to check that those relatives whose names and addresses appeared in the registration application had actually been notified (Law Com Paper No 122, para 4.46).

3.5.1 Court's duty to register if the application is formally correct

The 1985 Act, accordingly, provides that the court *shall* register the instrument to which a formally correct application relates, save in two groups of exceptional cases (s 6(1)). However, it is important to emphasise that the duty to register arises only in the case of an application which is made in accordance with the provisions relating to formality and notification discussed above. Thus, the court would refuse to register an application if the donor's signature to the power were not attested, if the power had not been executed by an attorney, or if it were apparent on the face of the application that the notification requirements had not been satisfied.

3.5.2 Court may waive failure to notify

There is one exception to the principle that the application must be formally correct. If it is apparent from the application that notice has not been given to a relative who is entitled to receive notice under the 1985 Act, the court will, nevertheless, treat the application as properly constituted, if it is satisfied that as regards each such relative:

– it was undesirable or impracticable for the attorney to give him notice; or
– no useful purpose is likely to be served by giving him notice (s 6(3)).

These conditions are, in substance, identical to the grounds upon which the court could have dispensed with the notification requirement if an application in that behalf had been made before making the registration application (1985 Act, Sch 1, para 3(2)).

3.5.3 Competing applications for receivership and registration of power

Sometimes, applications to register an enduring power appointing one person as attorney and requesting the appointment of someone else as a receiver under the Mental Health Act 1983 arrive simultaneously, or in quick succession. The practice of the court in such circumstances is:

> 'to follow the EPA route as far as possible, only considering the appointment of a receiver when it proves impossible to register the EPA. The reasoning behind this is that, on the face of it, the donor chose to execute an EPA in preference to having his affairs handled by a receiver. If his wishes can be respected, they should be' (PD Lewis (1987) LSG 1219 at 1222).

As a matter of procedure, it is possible that once a conflict between two applications becomes apparent, the court will require a hearing in order to identify the issues and attempt to dispose of them, or may try to move the matter forward by encouraging the parties to correspond with each other and the court.

The principal exception to 'following the EPA route' is in cases where an individual has sustained head injuries, perhaps as a result of a road traffic accident, and there is likely to be a substantial award of damages. Quite often in such cases an enduring power, executed after the accident, is produced, and there are doubts as to whether the donor had the requisite capacity to create the power. Furthermore, it may be preferable for those responsible for managing a large award to have the supervision and back-up provided by the court through the appointment of a receiver (see para **1.5**).

3.5.4 Completion of Form EP2

Detailed guidance on the completion of the prescribed form of application for registration, Form EP2, has been given by PD Lewis (1986) LSG 3566 at 3568. This includes:

− the age of the attorney may be shown as 'over eighteen', although the exact age is more informative;
− if there are no relatives falling within the classes entitled to be notified, it avoids an inquiry from the court if the block is completed expressly stating that there are no relatives, rather than being left blank or crossed through;
− if there is only one attorney, the references in the sixth block to notification of a co-attorney should be crossed out;
− the final block should be checked to see that it has been signed and dated and that the address to which notices should be sent has been inserted;
− any discrepancy between the spelling of the donor's or attorney's name in the enduring power and in Form EP2 should be explained in a covering letter, as should any discrepancy between the donor's address on the form and the address at which he was served.

3.6 CIRCUMSTANCES IN WHICH FURTHER INQUIRIES ARE MADE

The general principle is that the court *must* register *provided* that the application is formally correct. However, there are three exceptional cases in which the court will not immediately register the power but will, instead, cause further inquiries to be made. In the light of those inquiries, it may then refuse to register the power.

These three situations, set out in s 6(4) of the 1985 Act, are where:

- a valid notice of objection has been made (see para **3.7**); or
- it appears from the application form that no one has been notified (see para **3.8**); or
- the court has reason to believe that inquiries might reveal evidence on which an objection to registration could be founded (see para **3.9**).

3.7 VALID NOTICE OF OBJECTION

3.7.1 Time-limits

If a valid notice of objection to the registration is received by the court before the expiry of 5 weeks beginning with the latest date on which the attorney gave notice to any person entitled to receive notice under Sch 1 to the 1985 Act, the court shall neither register the instrument nor refuse the application until it has made or caused to be made 'such inquiries (if any) as it thinks appropriate in the circumstances of the case' (s 6(4)(a)).

If an objection to registration is received by the court on or after the date of registration, it will be treated as an application to cancel the registration (2001 Rules, r 9(2)), see para **5.7**.

Rule 5 of the 2001 Rules contains various provisions relating to the computation of time.

3.7.2 Valid grounds for objection

Section 6(5) of the 1985 Act provides that a notice of objection is valid if the objection is made on one or more of the following five grounds, namely:

- that the power purported to have been created by the instrument was not valid as an EPA;
- that the power created by the instrument no longer subsists;
- that the application is premature because the donor is not yet becoming mentally incapable;
- that fraud or undue pressure was used to induce the donor to create the power;
- that, having regard to all the circumstances and in particular the attorney's relationship to or connection with the donor, the attorney is unsuitable to be the donor's attorney.

3.7.3 At this stage, it is immaterial whether the grounds are established

It should be emphasised that the question at this stage is whether the notice – rather than the objection itself – is valid, and such a notice will be valid if an objection is made on one or more of the specified grounds. If a valid notice is received by the court within the specified 5-week period, the court must neither register the instrument nor refuse the application until it has made or caused to be made such inquiries (if any) as it thinks appropriate in the circumstances (s 6(4)(a)). At this stage, it is immaterial whether or not those grounds are ultimately made out, although, if the objection were self-evidently frivolous or ill-founded, the court might well decide that no further inquiries were appropriate, and proceed to register the power.

3.7.4 Grounds for valid notice

The grounds on which a valid notice can be based must now be examined in detail.

(1) Power not valid

It would seem that an objection made on this ground might be based on two main (and rather different) grounds. First, the objector might claim that at the date when the power was purportedly created the *donor already lacked capacity* to grant it. It is a fundamental principle that a power cannot be valid unless the donor had mental capacity at the date of grant (see para **2.2.2**). If an objector can show that the donor then lacked sufficient mental capacity to understand the nature and effect of the power, it is not and never has been valid. The appropriate action in such a case may be for an application to be made to the court for the appointment of a receiver under Part VII of the Mental Health Act 1983.

The question of invalidity due to lack of capacity was considered in detail in *In re W (Enduring Power of Attorney)* [2000] 3 WLR 45.

The second ground on which an objection to the validity of the power might be made would be that the instrument purportedly creating the power was *formally defective*. The objection might be that the power omitted the obligatory statements stipulated in the prescribed form, that it was not executed by the parties, or that it was not properly witnessed. Again, the objection could be that for some other reason the power fell outside the definition of an EPA contained in s 2 of the 1985 Act and the regulations made thereunder, for example, because the attorney was an undischarged bankrupt or a minor, or that the attorney was not an individual or trust corporation.

(2) Power no longer subsists

This would cover cases where the donor had validly revoked the power, or the attorney had validly disclaimed it. Revocation and disclaimer are considered in Chapter 6.

(3) Donor not yet becoming mentally incapable

This head of objection is easy to state, but difficult to explain. Reference should be made to para **3.2.4** for comments on the elusive nature of the concept of 'becoming mentally incapable'.

The definition of mental incapacity in s 13(1) contains two prerequisites. A person must:

− have a mental disorder; and
− be incapable, or be becoming incapable, by reason of that mental disorder, of managing and administering his property and affairs.

These two prerequisites do not always coincide. A person with a mental disorder might be more than capable of looking after his affairs, and may even be financially astute. On the other hand, a person who has no kind of mental disorder could be totally incapable of managing and administering his property and affairs, perhaps because he is physically ill or disabled, not interested, poorly educated, or just lazy. The gerund *becoming* applies to the incapacity, rather than the mental disorder, and the incapacity must be preceded by some form of mental disorder as defined in s 1(2) of the Mental Health Act 1983. In other words, to succeed in objecting to registration of the power on this ground, it must be shown that either: (a) the donor is not suffering from mental disorder; or (b) even though he has a mental disorder, he is not yet becoming incapable, by reason of that disorder, of managing and administering his property and affairs.

The 1985 Act has changed common law rules on the burden of proof (*Re W (Enduring Power of Attorney)* [2001] 1 FLR 832, para 48). Accordingly, the onus is on the donor to prove that he is not yet becoming mentally incapable.

(4) Fraud or undue pressure was used to induce the donor to create the power

If objection is made on this ground, it is difficult to see how the objection could be dealt with other than at a hearing when the evidence could be fully considered. However, the mere making of the objection would, no doubt, almost invariably cause the court to defer a decision on registration pending further inquiries.

The existence of this ground of objection serves to emphasise the importance of keeping adequate records about the circumstances leading up to the grant of the power. It should be remembered that it will be possible to establish this ground of objection even if the attorney is a perfectly respectable person, and even if the 'pressure' in question had not been exercised by him but, for example, by well-intentioned relatives of the donor.

The burden of proof is on the objector to prove to the satisfaction of the court that:

– the donor was 'induced' to create the power;
– 'pressure' was used to induce him to create it; and
– such pressure was 'undue'.

The word 'induce' should be construed in its ordinary meaning, ie 'to persuade or to prevail upon to bring about' (*Commission of Racial Equality v Imperial Society of Teachers of Dancing* [1983] ICR 473). So, where, for example, the impetus or initiative to create an EPA comes from the donor personally, it can hardly be said that he had been induced to create the power.

To use 'pressure' means to behave in a manner whereby the will of the donor is overborne by the will of another person, so that in creating the power the donor is not acting of his own free will. Pressure can assume various forms: it can be physical, psychological, emotional, financial, and even pharmacological. Physical pressure constitutes any act or rough treatment directed towards the donor, whether or not actual physical injury results. Psychological or emotional pressure includes any behaviour that may diminish the donor's sense of identity, dignity and self-worth, including humiliation, intimidation, verbal abuse, threats, and isolation. Financial pressure includes the deliberate denial of the donor's access to his money or property. Excessive medication or the intentional withholding of medication would constitute pharmacological pressure.

The meaning of 'undue' has been considered judicially in the context of hardship and delay. For example, in *Liberian Shipping Corporation v A King & Sons Ltd* [1967] 1 All ER 934 at 938, CA, Lord Denning MR said, '"undue" simply means excessive. It means greater hardship than the circumstances warrant'.

(5) Attorney is unsuitable to be the donor's attorney
This ground, as the Law Commission pointed out (Law Com Paper No 122, para 4.49(e)), amounts, in effect, to a criticism of the donor's choice of attorney. It is, in practice, the ground which is most commonly alleged. As with the 'fraud or undue pressure' ground considered above, it will be an easy

matter to lodge a valid objection to registration on this ground, and that will of itself serve to delay registration pending the making of inquiries, and usually, no doubt, the holding of a hearing.

The ground leaves a considerable element of discretion with the court in deciding what criteria are to be regarded as rendering an attorney 'unsuitable'. The statutory reference to the attorney's relationship to or connection with the donor suggests that the court might well find this ground made out if the attorney were connected with the residential care home or nursing home in which the donor was residing and there were some grounds for thinking that financial advantage might, in consequence, be taken of the donor (see *Re Davey (deceased)* [1980] 3 All ER 342). However, the Law Commission stated that it would not wish the ground to be sustained 'merely because the attorney was not the sort of person that a particular relative would have chosen'. The Commission said:

> 'It is our wish that the donor's choice of attorney should carry considerable weight. Thus, for example, a mother might be content to appoint her son as her EPA attorney despite being aware of a conviction for theft. We would not want her choice of attorney to be upset simply because a particular relative would not want the son to be his attorney. The question should be whether the particular attorney is suitable to act as an attorney for the particular donor. In short, the court should examine carefully all the circumstances – particularly the relationship between donor and attorney' (Law Com Paper No 122, para 4.49(e)).

Unsuitability in the context of general hostility within the donor's family was considered in *In re W (Enduring Power of Attorney)* [2000] 3 WLR 45 and *In re E (Enduring Power of Attorney)* [2000] 3 WLR 1974.

3.7.5 Form of objection

The 2001 Rules do not specify the use of any particular form for making the objection to registration. Such an objection may be made by letter or otherwise in writing (r 8(1)). Rule 9(1) does, however, prescribe the content of an objection. The objection should state:

– the name and address of the objector;
– the name and address of the donor, if he is not the objector;
– any relationship of the objector to the donor;
– the name and address of the attorney; and
– the grounds for objecting to registration of the enduring power.

Even if these rules are not observed in every particular, it would seem that the court might still regard the notice of objection as being valid, since the 1985 Act defines that concept solely in terms of the grounds on which the objection is made, and does not require the objection to be in any particular form. The requirements of the 2001 Rules as to form would, therefore, seem to be merely directory.

Even if the objection fails to qualify as a valid objection (eg because it does not specify one of the grounds of objection set out in the 1985 Act), the court might, nevertheless, defer registration on the ground set out in s 6(4)(c) of the Act, namely, that it has reason to believe that appropriate inquiries might bring to light evidence on which it could be satisfied that one of the grounds for resisting registration had been established (see para **3.9**).

3.7.6 Procedure for determining objections

Where objections to registration have been lodged, the court may fix a preliminary hearing for the giving of directions, for example, relating to the filing of particulars of the objection, the filing of affidavit evidence, discovery and inspection of documents, and allocation of hearing date and costs (2001 Rules, r 10). It may be possible to avoid directions hearings if the issues can be identified in correspondence (PD Lewis (1987) LSG 1219 at 1220).

3.8 NO RELATIVE TO WHOM NOTICE HAS BEEN GIVEN

The Law Commission's protective scheme relies heavily on the specified relatives being likely to know the donor and to have an interest in his well-being. If a donor has no relatives within the specified classes, no notice can be given, and this element of protection will, accordingly, be absent. However, those who have no relatives may be most likely to need some protection against unscrupulous attorneys. It was for this reason that the Law Commission proposed that where no relative had been notified, the court should not register or refuse to register without 'first considering the possibility of making inquiries' (Law Com Paper No 122, para 4.48), and this proposal is implemented by s 6(4)(b) of the 1985 Act.

Such applications might be thought likely to receive special scrutiny by the court, but no indication has been given of what form this scrutiny is likely to take. There is, for example, no requirement that such an application be accompanied by specified information about the relationship (if any) between the donor and the attorney, but, presumably, it is information of this kind which would be relevant in enabling the court to discharge its task. There might, for example, be less cause for further inquiry if the attorney were the donor's solicitor or accountant, or his common law spouse, than if he were the proprietor of the residential care home or nursing home in which he is residing. Generally, it seems likely that the court may well find it difficult to make judgments as to whether or not further inquiries would be appropriate. The court may call for a report from one of the Lord Chancellor's Visitors (Mental Health Act 1983, s 103(2); 1985 Act, s 10(1)(a)).

3.9 APPROPRIATE INQUIRIES MIGHT PRODUCE EVIDENCE OF A GROUND FOR OBJECTION

This ground for deferring registration might cover cases where the court knew from other proceedings that there were suspicious circumstances relating to a particular attorney, or where it had received information (perhaps by an anonymous letter) which indicated grounds for concern. It must again be emphasised that what is in issue at this stage is simply whether the case is one of the exceptions where registration is not a simple and automatic administrative act.

3.10 EFFECT OF A GROUND OF OBJECTION BEING ESTABLISHED

If the court decides not to register the application until it has made inquiries or caused inquiries to be made, it must then, in the light of those inquiries, determine whether any of the five grounds of objection specified in s 6(5) (set out in para **3.7.2**) has, in fact, been established to its satisfaction.

If the court is satisfied that any of these grounds of objection has been established, it must refuse the application. However, if it is not so satisfied, the court is obliged to register the instrument to which the application relates. If the court is in doubt, it would appear that it should register the power but, in such a case, it might well decide to give directions to enable it to exercise appropriate supervision (see s 8(2); and para **5.6**).

3.10.1 Ancillary powers

If the court refuses to register a power, it may, in an appropriate case, exercise its powers under Part VII of the Mental Health Act 1983, specifically by appointing a receiver for the donor under s 99.

Where the court refuses an application for registration on the ground *either* that fraud or undue pressure was used to induce the donor to create the power, *or* that the attorney is unsuitable to be the donor's attorney, it *must* revoke the power created by the instrument (1985 Act, s 6(7)).

If the court refuses an application for registration on any ground other than that the application is premature, the instrument must be delivered up to be cancelled unless the court otherwise directs (s 6(8)).

3.11 REFUSAL TO REGISTER IF A RECEIVER HAS BEEN APPOINTED

If it appears to the court that an order under the Mental Health Act 1983 appointing a receiver for the donor is in force but the enduring power has not also been revoked, the court must not, unless it directs otherwise, exercise its functions in relation to the registration of the power but will refuse the application for registration (s 6(2)). The reason for this provision (which appears to have no counterpart in the draft Bill annexed to the Law Commission's Report, Law Com Paper No 122) is, no doubt, that a receiver has adequate powers to deal with the donor's affairs (see, generally, Mental Health Act 1983, s 99(2)).

3.12 OTHER CONSEQUENCES OF ACTUAL OR IMPENDING MENTAL INCAPACITY OF THE DONOR

There may be cases in which the attorney has doubts about the validity of the power and wishes to have these resolved before making an application for registration. Section 4(5) of the 1985 Act allows him to refer to the court for its determination any question as to the validity of the power. The attorney must comply with any directions given to him by the court on that determination.

Chapter 4

AUTHORITY AND POWERS OF AN ATTORNEY UNDER AN ENDURING POWER

4.1 INTRODUCTION

Section 3(1) of the Enduring Powers of Attorney Act 1985 (the 1985 Act) provides that:

'An enduring power of attorney may confer general authority (as defined in subsection (2) below) on the attorney to act on the donor's behalf in relation to all or a specified part of the property and affairs of the donor or may confer on him authority to do specified things on the donor's behalf and the authority may, in either case, be conferred subject to conditions and restrictions.'

In effect, there are four options – or potentially eight, if one counts the alternatives 'with' or 'without' any restrictions or conditions.

The options are to confer:

- *general authority* in relation to all the donor's property and affairs;
- *general authority* in relation to a specified part of the donor's property and affairs;
- *specific authority* in relation to all the donor's property and affairs; and
- *specific authority* in relation to a specified part of the donor's property and affairs.

The expression *property and affairs* extends only to business matters, legal transactions and other dealings of a similar kind, and an attorney acting under an enduring power has no authority to make any decision relating to the donor's health care or personal welfare, such as where to live and with whom to have contact (see *Re F (Sterilisation: Mental Patient)* [1989] 2 FLR 376, particularly at p 423, per Lord Brandon).

4.2 GENERAL AUTHORITY

4.2.1 The effect of conferring general authority

If the donor wishes to confer general power authority on his attorney, he must use the words contained in the prescribed form, namely: 'I appoint *(name and address)* to be my attorney for the purpose of the Enduring Powers of Attorney Act 1985 with general authority to act on my behalf'.

The words *general authority* are crucial. It is only the use of this expression which will, by reason of the provision in the 1985 Act to that effect, confer the relevant powers on the attorney. General authority is defined in s 3(2) as follows:

> 'Where an instrument is expressed to confer general authority on the attorney it operates to confer, subject to the restriction imposed by subsection (5) below and to any conditions or restrictions contained in the instrument, authority to do on behalf of the donor anything which the donor can lawfully do by an attorney.'

The enduring power is a creature of statute and is effective only if the instrument is *expressed to confer* such general authority. The requirement that a particular form of words be used should be contrasted with the position under the Powers of Attorney Act 1971, s 10(1) of which provides that 'a general power of attorney in the form set out in Schedule 1 to this Act, or in a form to the like effect but expressed to be made under this Act, shall operate to confer on *(the donee(s))* authority to do on behalf of the donor anything which he can lawfully do by an attorney'.

It must also be remembered that the 1985 Act stipulates the use of a prescribed form. Failure to use that form will prevent the instrument from being an enduring power within the meaning of the Act (s 2(1)). The Enduring Powers of Attorney (Prescribed Form) Regulations 1990 use the formula set out in the section above and that should be clearly adopted in practice. However, a minor variation in wording (eg general authority to act as my attorney) would possibly, by reason of the rule that an instrument may differ in an immaterial respect in form and mode of expression from the prescribed form, not prevent the instrument from taking effect as an enduring power (s 2(6)) (see para **2.7.2**). On the other hand, failure to use the words *general authority* would, for the reasons given above, leave the extent of the attorney's powers in doubt.

4.2.2 What can a donor lawfully do by an attorney?

The extent of the authority conferred by an enduring power giving the attorney general authority is a matter, first, for the general law. This is because the 1985 Act provides that an instrument expressed to confer general authority to do on behalf of the donor *anything which the donor can lawfully do by an attorney* (s 3(2)).

The meaning of this expression was considered in *Clauss v Pir* [1988] 1 Ch 267, where it was held that the attorney could not lawfully swear an affidavit on the donor's behalf. The donor can lawfully do most things by an attorney, but there are three important exceptions:

– where statute requires the evidence of the donor's signature; or
– where the donor's competency to do the act arises by virtue of holding some office, public or otherwise; or
– where the donor's own authority or duty to do the act is of a personal nature, requiring skill or discretion for its exercise.

Therefore, by virtue of the first exception, an attorney could not execute a will on behalf of the donor because s 9 of the Wills Act 1837 provides that the will must be 'signed ... by the testator or by some other person in his presence and by his direction' (but see para **5.6.2**). Because of the second exception, the attorney of a bishop could not lawfully ordain a priest, and because of the third exception an attorney acting for a student could not lawfully sit an examination on the donor's behalf.

Statutory authority granted to a particular person cannot normally be delegated and, generally speaking, it is not possible for an attorney who is himself a delegate further to delegate his authority (see para **9.4**). As has already been noted, a power of attorney which gives the attorney a right to appoint a substitute or successor cannot be an enduring power (s 2(9)).

4.2.3 Acting for the donor as an administrator or executor

The attorney under an enduring power is not entitled to take over the powers of a donor who has been acting as an executor or administrator. The Non-Contentious Probate Rules 1987 (SI 1987/2024), r 35(2) provides that 'where a registrar is satisfied that a person entitled to a grant is by reason of mental incapacity incapable of managing his affairs, administration for his use and benefit, limited until further representation be granted' may be granted to the lawful attorney of the incapable person acting under a registered enduring power of attorney (EPA). Only a person specifically authorised by the Court of Protection to apply for a grant has a higher priority to seek a grant. The practice of the Family Division in applications for grants in favour of attorneys in cases of incapacity is set out in *Practice Direction – Enduring Powers of Attorney: Grants of Administration* [1986] 1 FLR 627, reproduced in Appendix 9 to this book.

4.2.4 General authority over part of the donor's property and affairs

Most EPAs relate to all the donor's property. According to a survey conducted by Bristol University in 1990, in no less than 98.4% of applications to register an enduring power, the EPA conferred on the attorney the general authority to act in relation to all the donor's property and affairs (S Cretney, G Davis, R Kerridge and A Borkowski *Enduring Powers of Attorney: A Report to the Lord Chancellor* (Lord Chancellor's Department, June 1991) p 27.

It is, however, possible to give the attorney the general authority only in relation to specified property, for example, 'my property situated in England' or 'my Blackacre estate' or 'my bank account at the Royal Bank of Scotland, Oxford Branch'. The prescribed form, accordingly, makes provision for the donor to give general authority in relation not only to *all my property and affairs* but also to *the following property and affairs*. In such a case, the attorney may do anything an attorney can lawfully do in respect of that property, but he has no powers over any other property.

4.2.5 Specific authority

It is possible to limit the scope of the attorney's authority to the carrying-out of specified transactions, for example, the transfer of a specific property. In such a case, the prescribed form will state that the attorney has authority 'to do the following on my behalf': for example, 'execute a transfer in relation to the following property and affairs, Blackacre'. If the power is limited to doing specified things on the donor's behalf, it will be a matter of construction of the words used as to what authority is conferred on the donee.

4.2.6 Subject to any conditions or restrictions

An enduring power, whether general or specific, may be granted subject to restrictions and conditions, which should be set out where indicated in the prescribed form. Paragraph **2.5.4** gives examples of some restrictions which are occasionally imposed in practice.

An enduring power is potentially extremely wide ranging, and in some cases the right to impose conditions and restrictions may be important. However, the Law Commission, in its report *The Incapacitated Principal* (1983) Law Com Paper No 122, para 4.31, sounded a note of caution about the excessive use of restricted powers. While accepting the general principle that people should be able to make such arrangements as they please for the management of their affairs, it emphasised that it would be important for the donor to ensure that the authority bestowed under his enduring power effectively covered the whole of his property and affairs. As the Commission said:

'If he leaves a "gap" so that part of his property and affairs is not covered by an EPA, it may be necessary for the court to intervene and appoint a receiver. And whilst we would not wish to prevent the donor giving his attorney such limited authority as he thought fit, the fact remains that the less authority that is given to the attorney, the greater is the risk that he would be unable to act for the donor at a later date. If by that time the donor were incapable so that he could not create a new power, the court might have to take over.'

4.2.7 Scope of authority: the 1985 Act's provisions

The 1985 Act contains a number of important provisions dealing with the scope of the attorney's authority, which will apply, regardless of whether the power is *general* or *limited*, unless the instrument itself contains any relevant special conditions or restrictions. These are:

– the power to exercise the trustee functions of the donor;
– the power to provide for the needs of persons other than the donor; and
– a circumscribed power to make gifts of the donor's money and property.

4.3 POWER TO EXERCISE TRUSTEE FUNCTIONS

The extent to which an attorney acting under an enduring power may exercise the functions of the donor as a trustee is now governed by the Trustee Delegation Act 1999, and is considered in detail in Chapter 11.

4.4 POWER TO PROVIDE FOR PEOPLE'S NEEDS

4.4.1 Section 3(4)

Section 3(4) of the 1985 Act provides that:

'Subject to any conditions or restrictions contained in the instrument, an attorney under an enduring power, whether general or limited, may (without obtaining any consent) act under the power so as to benefit himself or other persons than the donor to the following extent but no further, that is to say—

(a) he may so act in relation to himself or in relation to any other person if the donor might be expected to provide for his or that person's needs respectively; and
(b) he may do whatever the donor might be expected to do to meet those needs.'

Thus, in the absence of any express provision in the instrument creating the power, the attorney may provide for the *needs* of any person, including himself. Three questions need to be asked.

— First, is the provision in question required to meet a need of the person benefited?
— Secondly, might the donor be expected to provide for that person's needs?
— Thirdly, what might the donor be expected to do to meet those needs?

4.4.2 Needs

The authority is only to provide for *needs*. It is submitted that *needs* are not limited to maintenance in any narrow sense. The courts would probably adopt a reasonably generous view of what is comprised in this expression, extending it no doubt to the provision of suitable housing, clothing, holidays etc. In this context, decisions on the Inheritance (Provision for Family and Dependants) Act 1975 and the Matrimonial Causes Act 1973 may be relevant.

4.4.3 Might the donor be expected to provide for that person's needs?

Even if the provision in question is to satisfy someone's *needs*, the attorney may act only if the donor might be expected to provide for them. Suppose, for example, that the question is whether provision should be made towards the further education or training of the donor's adult child. First, it would have to be established that such provision constituted a *need*. Secondly, it would have to be asked whether this particular donor might be expected to provide for the needs of that child. Thirdly, it would have to be asked what this particular donor might have been expected to do to meet that need. For example, it might be clear that the donor had himself envisaged meeting the costs involved; conversely, it might be clear that he had decided against doing so.

Section 13(2) of the 1985 Act provides that any question as to what the donor might be expected to do shall be determined by assuming that he had full mental capacity at the time but otherwise by reference to the circumstances existing at that time. It would seem, therefore, that the donor's personality and preferences should be taken into account. For example, he may believe that adult children should be self-sufficient. However, matters stemming from the incapacity should be disregarded, for example, a delusion that the child in question has been neglectful or cruel. Again, an attorney could properly take account of the fact that the donor's means had much diminished, but should not take account of any delusional belief on the donor's part that he was extremely poor.

4.4.4 What might the donor be expected to do to meet those needs?

Some donors might be more generous than others in meeting needs. One might take the view that a spouse should have the best that money can buy while convalescing after an illness and, thus, provide on an appropriately extensive scale; another might take a more parsimonious view. The question for the attorney in all cases is: assuming that he had full mental capacity, what would *this particular donor* have done in the light of the facts as they are?

If the donor still has mental capacity, the best way of answering this question would be to ask him. However, this statutory power will also be available, provided that the power has been registered, after the onset of incapacity.

4.4.5 *Re Cameron (deceased)*

The provisions of s 3(4) of the 1985 Act were considered by Lindsay J in *Re Cameron (deceased)* [1999] 2 All ER 924, the facts of which were as follows. Mrs Marjorie Cameron had four sons, Donald, Iain, Alastair and Hamish, all of whom were educated at fee-paying schools. In 1974 she executed a will leaving her residuary estate to her sons in equal shares. In March 1989 she executed an EPA appointing three of her sons (though not Donald) jointly to be her attorneys with general authority to act on her behalf in relation to all her property and affairs. The power was registered in July 1989. In 1991 the attorneys, exercising their powers under s 3(4), paid £62,596 to trustees to provide for the private education of their brother Donald's son, Jamie. The payment was made on the basis that, as a portion, it would, by virtue of the rule against double portions, *adeem pro tanto* Donald's share of Mrs Cameron's residuary estate. At that time Donald was unemployed and living on state benefits. Mrs Cameron died in November 1992. Donald maintained that there had been no ademption of his share of the estate, contending, inter alia, that private education was not a 'need' within the meaning of s 3(4) of the Act.

Lindsay J held that, for the purposes of s 3(4), the education of a child was a 'need', and the provision of private education for a grandson came within that section. Furthermore, in the circumstances, Mrs Cameron might have been expected to provide for her grandson's needs, and the provision that the attorneys had made on her behalf was of a kind which she might have been expected to make, both to confer some benefit on Donald and to meet the need to provide an education for his son. Accordingly, the payment of £62,596 was a valid exercise of the power of attorney. With regard to the rule against double portions, the judge held that a gift by a grandparent for the benefit of a grandchild could be treated as being for the benefit of the grandchild's parent.

Accordingly, the payment adeemed Donald's share of his mother's residuary estate to the extent of that payment.

4.4.6 Effect of the donor's incapacity

The attorney's powers under s 3(4) of the 1985 Act are not affected by the onset of the donor's incapacity (s 1(2)) (see para **4.6.1**).

4.5 POWER TO MAKE GIFTS

4.5.1 Section 3(5)

Section 3(5) of the 1985 Act states:

> 'Without prejudice to subsection (4) above but subject to any conditions or restrictions contained in the instrument, an attorney under an enduring power, whether general or limited, may (without obtaining any consent) dispose of the property of the donor by way of gift to the following extent but no further, that is to say—
>
> (a) he may make gifts of a seasonal nature or at a time, or on an anniversary, of a birth or marriage, to persons (including himself) who are related to or connected with the donor; and
>
> (b) he may make gifts to any charity to whom the donor made or might be expected to make gifts,
>
> provided that the value of each such gift is not unreasonable having regard to all the circumstances and in particular the size of the donor's estate.'

4.5.2 Power to make gifts is in addition to the power to provide for needs

The power to make gifts operates 'without prejudice to' the power conferred by s 3(4) to provide for *needs*. The power to make gifts is, therefore, additional to the power to provide for needs and could be invoked if for some reason that power is inapplicable, for example, where no 'need' can be established. The power to make gifts is extremely limited.

4.5.3 Four conditions must be satisfied

Four conditions have to be established before the power to make gifts can be used:

– there must be *no restrictions* or conditions in the EPA itself which prohibit the attorney from making the gift;
– the *timing* of the gift must fall within the prescribed parameters;

- the *recipient* must either be a charity, or an individual who is related to or connected with the donor;
- the *value* of the gift must be not unreasonable.

4.5.4 There must be no restrictions in the instrument

There must be no restrictions or conditions in the instrument which would prohibit the attorney from making a gift of the donor's property. Where the EPA specifically states that no gifts are to be made to the donor's friends or relatives, the powers of the Court of Protection under s 8(2) of the 1985 Act do not extend to directing the attorney to make provision for a third party by way of gift or in recognition of a moral obligation owed by the donor (*Re R (Enduring Power of Attorney)*) [1991] 1 FLR 128).

4.5.5 Timing of the gift

A gift to charity can be made at any time of the year, but in the case of an individual, the gift must be either 'of a seasonal nature', or made 'at a time of a birth or marriage', or 'on an anniversary of a birth or marriage'. Seasonal gifts include, for example, Christmas or Easter presents, but it is doubtful whether *seasonal* extends to include the end of one tax year and the beginning of another. The 1985 Act does not specify on whose birthday or wedding anniversary the gift may be made, and for ethnic, cultural or other reasons the donor may have traditionally given presents on his own birthday, rather than the recipient's. Presents given on a christening, confirmation, barmitzvah, graduation, engagement or retirement are, effectively, excluded from the scope of s 3(5).

4.5.6 Recipient of the gift

An individual recipient, as distinct from a charity, must be someone *related to* or *connected with* the donor. Neither of these expressions is defined. Although Sch 1, para 2(1) to the 1985 Act defines the persons who are 'referred to in this Act as "relatives"', it is thought that the word *relatives* applies only to the persons who may be entitled to receive notice of the attorney's intention to register the enduring power, and that the expression *related to* is wider and may include, for example, a parent-in-law, son- or daughter-in-law, step-parent and stepchild, none of whom fall within the definition of relatives in Sch 1. In any event, these people are presumably *connected with* the donor.

The attorney may make gifts to any charity if the donor made or might be expected to make such gifts. The question whether or not the donor made such gifts is one of fact which should be comparatively easy to answer. The question whether he might be expected to do so is to be answered on the basis that he has full mental capacity (s 13(2)). The reported decisions on statutory wills give some useful guidance on the factors to be taken into account in ascertaining what an incapacitated person might be expected to do, assuming he had full mental capacity at the time (see *Re D (J)* [1982] Ch 237; *Re C (Spinster and Mental Patient)* [1992] 1 FLR 51; but compare *Re S (Gifts by Mental Patient)* [1997] 1 FLR 96). The wording of s 3(5) prima facie excludes any purposes which are not charitable: for example, political parties, animal rights groups, or the Voluntary Euthanasia Society.

4.5.7 Value of the gift

Even if the above conditions are satisfied, the gift must be of such an amount that it can only properly be described as *not unreasonable*. This involves a consideration of all the circumstances, but particular reference is made to the size of the donor's estate. A millionaire might reasonably make larger gifts than a person who lives solely on a State retirement pension. Although the attorney is the arbiter of what is *not unreasonable* in this context, if the matter is brought before the Court of Protection in an application for relief under s 8(2) of the 1985 Act, the court will decide whether what is proposed is reasonable. The court does not, and would be unwilling to, impose a quantum similar to that which applies to the 'small gifts' procedure in receivership cases.

In *In re W (Enduring Power of Attorney)* [2000] 3 WLR 45, at 51d, Jules Sher QC commented that 'the power of an attorney to make gifts of the donor's property is extremely limited, and certainly, without the authorization of the court after the power is registered, does not extend to the making of gifts as part of inheritance tax planning'.

4.5.8 No need to obtain consent

The attorney may exercise the power to make gifts of the donor's property without consulting the donor or, indeed, anyone else. If the donor still has mental capacity, he could either revoke the power or forbid the attorney to make a projected gift. The position would, of course, be different once the donor had lost capacity (see para **4.7.4**).

4.5.9 Wider authority to make gifts cannot be conferred in the EPA

Any provision in an enduring power which purports to give the attorney greater authority to make gifts is ineffective (Law Com Paper No 122, p 29, fn 134). It has been suggested, however, that it may be possible for the donor, while he is still mentally capable, to execute an ordinary power of attorney authorising the attorney to benefit others without limitation (ibid, fn 135).

4.5.10 Effect of registration on the power to make gifts

The attorney's power to dispose of the donor's property pending the registration of an enduring power is considered in para **4.6.3**, and the position once the power is registered is discussed in para **4.7.4**.

4.6 ATTORNEY'S AUTHORITY AND POWER AT THE ONSET OF DONOR'S INCAPACITY

When the donor of the power of attorney becomes mentally incapable, the power would at common law have been revoked. Section 1(1)(a) of the 1985 Act prevents such automatic revocation taking place, but it also provides that, once incapacity has supervened, the attorney may not do anything under its authority, subject to two exceptions which apply only if the attorney has made an application for registration. The inability of an attorney validly to exercise the power once mental incapacity has supervened constitutes an incentive for the donor to register (see *Re K; Re F (Enduring Powers of Attorney)* [1988] 2 FLR 15 per Hoffmann J).

4.6.1 Restricted powers pending registration

If an application for registration has been made, the attorney may (until the application has been initially determined) take action under the power for two purposes only, namely:

– to maintain the donor or prevent loss to his estate; or
– to maintain himself or other persons insofar as s 3(4) permits him to do so (s 1(2)).

The scope of the attorney's authority under these powers is narrow. He may not take action – such as, for example, subscribing for shares under a rights issue – unless his failure to do so would cause actual loss to the donor's estate.

The restricted powers described above do not arise unless and until an application for registration has been made, and that can be done only after notification for registration has been given to the donor and specified relatives (see para **3.3.3**). If a donor were suddenly totally incapacitated (eg comatose) the attorney would not be able to take any action under the instrument at all until an application had been made to register it.

The 1985 Act makes some limited provision for such an emergency situation. Section 5 provides that if the court has reason to believe that the donor of an enduring power may be, or may be becoming, mentally incapable, it may exercise any power which it could exercise under s 8(2) of the Act on registration of the power provided that it is *necessary* to do so. The powers of the court under this head would extend to giving directions with respect to the management or disposal by the attorney of the property and affairs of the donor (s 8(2)(b)(i)), and giving any authorisation which the attorney would have to obtain from a mentally capable donor (s 8(2)(d); see para **5.3.2**).

4.6.2 Authority only restricted when mental incapacity established

In many cases, there will be no gaps between the onset of mental incapacity and the registration of the power. This is because the attorney's authority under the power is only restricted in the way described above in circumstances in which the power would have been *revoked* at common law (s 1(1) and s 13(1)). That will not occur until the donor has, in fact, become incapable, and in many cases the power will by then already have been registered. As we have seen in para **3.2.4**, the attorney will have come under a duty to apply for registration at what will often be the earlier stage at which he had reason to believe the donor to be *becoming mentally incapable*.

4.6.3 No power to make gifts pending registration

As has been mentioned above, when an attorney has applied for registration of the power, then, until the application has been initially determined, the only action he can take is: (a) to maintain the donor or prevent loss to his estate; or (b) to maintain himself or other persons insofar as s 3(4) permits him to do so (s 1(2)). Thus, the attorney cannot make gifts in accordance with s 3(5) of the 1985 Act until the power has been registered. If, however, it is *necessary* to make gifts pending the completion of the registration procedure, an application could be made to the court under s 5 (see para **5.3.2**).

4.6.4 Attorney may not disclaim without notifying the court

Section 4(6) provides that, if the attorney has reason to believe that the donor is or is becoming mentally incapable, he may not disclaim unless and until he gives notice to the court (see para **6.3.1**).

4.7 ATTORNEY'S AUTHORITY AND POWERS WHEN THE POWER IS REGISTERED

4.7.1 Attorney may act under power

Once a power has been registered, the attorney will, in principle, have the same powers as he had before the onset of the donor's mental incapacity. He may then act under the authority conferred by the power (1985 Act, s 1(1)(b)).

4.7.2 Attorney cannot rely on the donor's further authorisation

Section 7(1)(c) provides that once the power has been registered:

> 'the donor may not extend or restrict the scope of the authority conferred by the instrument and no instruction or consent given by him after registration shall, in the case of a consent, confer any right and, in the case of an instruction, impose or confer any obligation or right on or create any liability of the attorney or other persons having notice of the instruction or consent.'

Hence, whether or not he is in fact mentally incapable, the donor has no power to authorise the attorney to participate in transactions (such as making gifts) not authorised by the power. In effect, the 1985 Act requires it to be assumed that the donor has no capacity even though he may still have capacity.

4.7.3 Attorney may apply to the Court of Protection

When an application for registration has been made or when the power has been registered, the attorney also has what is, potentially, the useful right to apply to the Court of Protection to exercise its powers under s 8(2), the provisions of which are considered in detail in para **5.6**. For the present, it is sufficient to note that the court may authorise the attorney to take action which is not authorised by the power.

4.7.4 Gifts when the power is registered

When the power is registered, the attorney's power to make gifts of the donor's property resumes. If the attorney wishes to make a more extensive gift of the donor's assets, perhaps as part of a tax-planning exercise, or wishes to make gifts on an unauthorised occasion or for a non-charitable purpose, an application could be made to the court for an order under s 8(2)(e) which provides that:

> 'Where an instrument has been registered ... the court may ... authorise the attorney to act so as to benefit himself or other persons than the donor otherwise than in accordance with section 3(4) and (5) (but subject to any conditions or restrictions contained in the instrument).'

For details of the court's procedure and requirements on applications for the making of gifts of the donor's property, see procedure note PN9, and Heywood and Massey *Court of Protection Practice* 12th edn (Sweet & Maxwell, 1991).

Chapter 5

THE COURT OF PROTECTION AND ENDURING POWERS

5.1 THE COURT OF PROTECTION

The Enduring Powers of Attorney Act 1985 (the 1985 Act) confers various functions on 'the court', which is defined in s 13(1) as 'the authority having jurisdiction under Part VII of the Mental Health Act 1983'. The authority having that jurisdiction is the Court of Protection.

The scheme introduced by the 1985 Act envisaged the Court of Protection acting:

- first, as the authority concerned with the registering of enduring powers of attorney (EPAs);
- secondly, as the ultimate safeguard for donors of enduring powers; and
- thirdly, in providing support and assistance to attorneys when necessary.

The Act extends the jurisdiction of the court in a number of respects, but leaves untouched its traditional powers in respect of patients under the Mental Health Act 1983. Thus, in a proper case, the court may make a receivership or other order in respect of the donor's property and affairs and decline to register an EPA.

5.2 THE PUBLIC GUARDIANSHIP OFFICE

On 2 January 1987 the Public Trustee and Administration of Funds Act 1986 came into force. This Act created a new organisation, the Public Trust Office, which combined the functions of the former Public Trustee's Office, the Court Funds Office, and the Protection and Receivership Divisions of the Court of Protection.

On 1 July 1994 the Public Trust Office became an executive agency within the Lord Chancellor's Department, and the Court of Protection (Enduring Powers of Attorney) Rules 1994 (SI 1994/3047), which came into force on 22 December 1994, conferred various functions on the Public Trustee in relation to the registration of EPAs.

All executive agencies are subject to a review, which usually takes place every 5 years. The Quinquennial Review of the Public Trust Office was conducted by Miss Ann Chant CB, a former chief executive of the Child Support Agency. Her report, which was published on 18 November 1999, recommended that the Public Trust Office should cease to exist as a separate executive agency.

The Lord Chancellor accepted Miss Chant's recommendation and, on 1 April 2001, the Public Trust Office ceased to exist. The Court Funds Office became part of the Court Service. Trustee and executorship functions were transferred to the Official Solicitor, who was appointed Public Trustee. The Protection and Receivership Divisions have merged to become a new office within the Court of Protection known as the Public Guardianship Office.

The closure of the Public Trust Office necessitated amendments to the rules relating to the registration of enduring powers of attorney, and on 1 April 2001 the Court of Protection (Enduring Powers of Attorney) Rules 2001 (SI 2001/825) came into force. These Rules deleted all references to the Public Trustee and, in effect, revert to the position that existed before the creation of the Public Trust Office executive agency in 1994.

5.3 FUNCTIONS PRIOR TO REGISTRATION

5.3.1 Determining validity of power

An attorney under an enduring power who has reason to believe that the donor is or is becoming mentally incapable may refer to the court for its determination any question as to the validity of the power before making an application for registration. The attorney must comply with directions given to him by the court (s 4(5)).

This procedure may be useful in cases where the attorney is uncertain in his own mind as to whether the donor had mental capacity at the time when the power was granted. A reference to the court would avoid needless notification of relatives, and it would also avoid an attorney feeling obliged to seek to register a power if he had doubts about its validity.

5.3.2 Exercise of court's functions prior to registration

The Law Commission, in its report, *The Incapacitated Principal* (1983) Law Com Paper No 122, para 482, felt that it would occasionally be useful for the court to be able to exercise some of its functions before registration. For example, there might be cases where:

> 'the court's assistance is needed urgently and where it would be unsatisfactory to wait until the registration procedure had been completed. For example, the attorney might need to sell a particular investment quickly but be in doubt whether the instrument gave him authority. In such a case we feel that the court should be able to determine questions as to the meaning or effect of the instrument. There might also be cases where a relative of the donor thought that the donor had become incapable yet the attorney showed no inclination to apply for registration. The court should, we feel, be able to give the attorney directions as to the running of the donor's affairs with a view perhaps to persuading him to apply for registration.'

Section 5 of the 1985 Act, therefore, empowers the court to exercise any of the powers which it would have in relation to a registered power under s 8(2) (see para **5.6**) provided that the following two conditions are satisfied:

(1) The court has reason to believe that the donor of an enduring power may be, or may be becoming, mentally incapable

The court may act where there is doubt or a dispute as to whether the donor's mental deterioration is sufficiently serious. The court's information may come from any source. The application may be made by the attorney or by any other interested person. The court's powers arise only when there is reason to believe that the donor is or is becoming mentally incapable. It is not the court's function to involve itself in the running of an unregistered power while the donor is clearly capable, and the Court of Protection has no jurisdiction in a dispute between a capable donor and his attorney (Law Com Paper No 122, para 4.79).

(2) The court is of the opinion that it is necessary, before the instrument creating the power is registered, to exercise any power with respect to the power of attorney or the attorney appointed to act under it which would become exercisable under s 8(2) on its registration

This condition is tightly drawn so as to give effect to the Law Commission's recommendation that:

> 'the exercise of these functions in advance of registration would be unusual since few matters would be so urgent that they could not await registration. Indeed, we recommend that the court should not use this jurisdiction before registration unless it is of the opinion that this is in fact necessary' (Law Com Paper No 122, para 4.82).

The use of the word *necessary* was intended to indicate a very high degree of desirability. It seems unlikely that the court would be prepared to act prior to registration unless the case was one of real urgency, or one in which the registration process was likely to be lengthy. Thus, for example, in an application to effect a sale before an application for registration has been made, the court will require evidence that the donor may be, or be becoming, mentally incapable, and it will have to be satisfied of the need for the action proposed. In particular, it has been said that if the application is to sell the donor's house, the court will require to be satisfied that there is no reasonable likelihood of the donor returning to live there (PD Lewis, the former Assistant Public Trustee, (1987) LSG 1219 and 3568).

There will, no doubt, be many cases in which the power to act prior to registration will usefully be invoked. For example, where the donor has been suddenly incapacitated, and action is urgently needed in connection with his affairs. It is true that the attorney will in such circumstances have power, without applying to the court, to take action to prevent loss to the donor's estate (s 1(2)(b); see para **4.6.1**), but this may not be sufficient for the reasons set out above.

5.4 FUNCTIONS ON APPLICATION FOR REGISTRATION

The court's powers and duties on application for registration have been considered in Chapter 3 (see paras **3.5–3.11**).

5.5 FUNCTIONS WITH RESPECT TO REGISTERED POWERS

The policy of the 1985 Act is that the court needs to have *powers* after registration because the donor is no longer in a position to give instructions himself but, essentially, it is the attorney who is to be in charge. Registration will in most cases make little difference to the attorney's authority and duties (Law Com Paper No 122, para 4.59).

In particular, it was not intended that the court should act in the same manner as if a receiver had been appointed for the donor, and it is not under any duty to investigate an attorneyship unless it has reason to do so. The Law Commission emphasised that the court would not be expected to exercise its powers to investigate the running of the attorneyship or scrutinise the attorney's management of the donor's affairs as a matter of routine or on a spot-check basis (Law Com Paper No 122, para 4.83).

5.6 COURT'S FUNCTIONS AFTER REGISTRATION

5.6.1 Court's functions

Section 8 of the 1985 Act gives the Court of Protection wide powers to supervise the conduct of an attorney and to see that he is exercising his powers of management and administration properly. It is specifically provided that:

(1) The court may determine any question as to the meaning or effect of the instrument (s 8(2)(a))

This, in effect, gives the court power to rule on the true construction of the instrument.

(2) The court may give certain directions

(a) Directions as to the management or disposal by the attorney of the property and affairs of the donor (s 8(2)(b)(i))

This is an important power which gives the court general authority to authorise transactions which could not otherwise be carried out, and to give directions in cases where the attorney is doubtful as to the propriety of any action – for example, if he is concerned that there is or may be a conflict of interest between himself and the donor.

(b) Directions as to the rendering of accounts by the attorney and the production of records kept by him for that purpose (s 8(2)(b)(ii))

Technically, every attorney has a duty to keep accounts of transactions involving the donor's money (*Gray v Haig* (1854) 20 Beav 219). In practice, however, the parties may agree to other arrangements and this is no doubt common, for example, where the attorney is the donor's spouse. The scheme of the 1985 Act is that the attorney under a registered enduring power (unlike a receiver) is not required as a matter of routine to prepare accounts in a special form. To impose such a requirement would, as the Law Commission recognised, not only be a burden to the attorney but also an expensive charge on the donor's estate. Accordingly, the matter is to be left to the discretion of the court. Consistent with its view that court involvement in the running of an enduring power is to be 'very much more the exception than the rule' (Law Com Paper No 122, para 4.78), the Law Commission stated that it would not expect the court to call for accounts unless it had reason for believing that there was something wrong with the attorneyship, and that the attorney should certainly not be required to file annual accounts as a matter of routine (ibid, para 4.83(iii)). In the light of these indications of the policy on which the Act was based, it seems reasonable to believe that the court would be circumspect in ordering production of accounts.

The power of the court extends to requiring the attorney to produce records kept by him for the purpose of rendering accounts. An illustration of such an order can be found in *Re C (Power of Attorney)* [2000] 2 FLR 1.

(c) Directions as to the remuneration or expenses of the attorney, whether or not in default of or in accordance with any provision made in the instrument (s 8(2)(b)(iii))
The Law Commission said that it was desirable that an enduring power should state whether or not an attorney is to be remunerated and, if so, on what basis (Law Com Paper No 122, para 4.83(iv)); a view endorsed by The Law Society (see para **10.2**). However, the court can authorise remuneration. Even if the instrument contains a charging clause, the court has power to authorise additional remuneration, or to direct remuneration at a lower level than is provided for in the instrument. Awarding a fixed annual fee might prove unsatisfactory in the event of inflation or, indeed, 'if it assumed a large volume of work which never materialised ...' (ibid, para 4.83(iv)).

Although the Commission accepted that an attorney who was authorised to charge might wish to apply to the court if there was a substantial and unforeseen increase in his duties, it expressed the view that the court should be circumspect in considering such requests: 'One relevant factor ... would be the likelihood and relative desirability of the attorney disclaiming the power (in favour, perhaps, of receivership) if his request were rejected' (ibid, para 4.83(iv)).

The court is also given a specific power to direct the repayment of excessive remuneration (s 8(2)(b)(iii)).

(3) The court may require the attorney to furnish information or produce documents or things in his possession as attorney (s 8(2)(c))
This power enables the court to carry out any investigation which it considers appropriate. It also empowers the court to require the attorney to hand over the donor's property.

(4) The court may give any consent or authorisation to act which the attorney would have to obtain from a mentally capable donor (s 8(2)(d))
This power is exercised in two main classes of cases. First, there are cases where the power itself requires that the donor's consent be obtained: for example, to the sale of the family home. In such a case, the donor himself could act prior to registration, but it is specifically provided that no consent given by him after registration shall confer any right (s 7(1)(c)). This is so, even if the power has been registered before the donor became mentally incapable.

The second case in which an application for the giving of consent may be brought under this head is where there is a conflict of interest between the donor and the attorney in the exercise of a power. An example of such a conflict might be where the attorney wished to buy the donor's property, albeit at full value, for himself or for a member of his family (see, generally, *Re Thompson's Settlement* [1985] 2 All ER 720). In such cases, as a matter of general agency law, the consent of the principal would be required to such a transaction, but an incapable donor could not give a valid consent (Law Com Paper No 122, para 4.83 and fn 195).

(5) *The court may, subject to any conditions or restrictions in the instrument creating the power, authorise the attorney to act beyond the statutory powers relating to maintenance and gifts so as to benefit himself or persons other than the donor (s 8(2)(e))*

The restrictions on the attorney's authority to benefit persons other than the donor himself have already been discussed in paras **4.4** and **4.5**. The court may, however, relax these restrictions and give the attorney more extensive power to benefit others (including himself). In an appropriate case, it could, for example, authorise gifts intended to minimise the ultimate impact of inheritance tax on the donor's estate, similar to its jurisdiction under Part VII of the Mental Health Act 1983 (see below).

The enduring power itself cannot authorise the conferring of any benefit outside the scope of that permitted by the 1985 Act and, even if it purports to do so, an application would still have to be made to the court for leave to act on it.

The enduring power may prohibit or restrict the exercise of the statutory powers, or make their exercise subject to conditions, and the court has no power in this jurisdiction to override the instrument in these respects.

The court's powers are, therefore, comparatively narrow, and there may be cases in which it will be more appropriate to invoke its powers in relation to patients under Part VII of the Mental Health Act 1983. These include a wide general power to direct the settlement or gift of any of the patient's property, and to authorise the making of a will on his behalf (Mental Health Act 1983, s 96(1)(d) and (e)). There is no jurisdiction under the 1985 Act to override conditions or restrictions on the power to benefit persons other than the donor which have been included in the instrument (see *Re R (Enduring Power of Attorney)* [1991] 1 FLR 128).

(6) *The court may relieve the attorney wholly or partly from any liability which he has or may have incurred on account of a breach of his duties as attorney (s 8(2)(f))*

This power, which enables the Court of Protection to relieve an attorney from any liability for breach of duty, is comparable to the power of the court under s 61 of the Trustee Act 1925 to relieve a trustee from liability. The Trustee Act 1925 only empowers the court to grant relief if the trustee 'has acted honestly and reasonably, and ought fairly to be excused the breach of trust and for omitting to obtain the directions of the court'. The Court of Protection's powers in respect of attorneys are, by contrast, unrestricted.

5.6.2 Wills

As already pointed out (at para **4.2.2**) the powers conferred by a power of attorney cannot extend to the execution of a will on behalf of the donor. However, s 96(1)(e) of the Mental Health Act 1983 empowers the court to authorise the execution of a statutory will or codicil for a patient. This power may be exercised to permit the execution of a will or codicil on behalf of the donor of an enduring power, provided that the power is registered or in the process of being registered. Medical evidence must be produced to establish that: (a) the donor is incapable, by reason of mental disorder, of managing and administering his property and affairs (so, in effect, he is a 'patient' for the purposes of the Mental Health Act 1983); and (b) the donor lacks testamentary capacity.

An application for an order for the execution of a statutory will may be made by any of the persons listed in r 18 of the Court of Protection Rules 2001 (SI 2001/824), which specifically includes 'an attorney acting under a registered enduring power of attorney'. Rule 18 also confers *locus standi* on: existing beneficiaries under the donor's will; relatives who would be entitled on his intestacy; anyone for whom the donor might be expected to provide if he were not mentally disordered; and any other person whom the court may authorise to make such an application. See, generally, procedure notes PN9 and PN9A issued by the court.

5.7 CANCELLATION OF A REGISTERED POWER

Once a power has been registered the attorney may operate it, and third parties may deal with him, on the footing that both the power and the attorney's authority under it are valid and subsisting (s 9) (see para **8.3**). In effect, registration verifies the validity of the instrument as an enduring power (Law Com Paper No 122, para 4.88).

In some cases, it may be desirable to cancel the registration, and the 1985 Act enables the court to do so in certain specified circumstances.

5.7.1 Confirmation of donor's revocation

Once the power has been registered, the donor, even if he then has the mental capacity to revoke the power, may not do so unless and until the court exercises its power to confirm the revocation (ss 7(1)(a) and 8(3)). On confirming the revocation of the power, the court must cancel the registration of the power (s 8(4)(a)). Revocation is considered in detail in Chapter 6.

5.7.2 Exercise of Mental Health Act 1983 powers

The court must cancel the registration if it gives a direction revoking the power on exercising any of its functions under Part VII of the Mental Health Act 1983 (1985 Act, s 8(4)(b)).

Occasionally, an attorney under a power chooses to apply for his own appointment as receiver under the Mental Health Act 1983 (the 1983 Act). In such circumstances, the application will be accepted if the court considers him suitable to act in that capacity. It has been pointed out by the former Assistant Public Trustee, PD Lewis, at (1987) LSG 1219 that 'this may not be what the donor wished, but an attorney, even though he has executed the EPA, cannot be required to act as attorney under it' (see para **9.1**).

The fact that the court exercises its powers under the 1983 Act does not automatically mean that it will give a direction revoking the enduring power. For example, when it authorises the execution of a statutory will on behalf of the donor, the court exercises its powers under s 96(1)(e) of that Act, but it is unlikely that it would order that the enduring power be revoked. In an unreported decision, *Re C*, on 23 January 1996, the nominated judge, Rattee J, considered a reference where the donor of a registered EPA had imposed a restriction on the attorney, his wife, prohibiting her from entering into any individual transaction involving a sum exceeding £50,000. An opportunity arose for the donor to acquire the freehold of his home in central London, but the purchase price was in excess of £50,000. The judge granted the wife's application to be appointed as an ad hoc receiver under the 1983 Act for the purpose of acquiring the freehold, without revoking the EPA. This facility is sometimes referred to as *switching jurisdictions* (Law Commission *Mental Incapacity* (1995) Law Com Paper No 231, para 7.5).

5.7.3 Donor mentally capable

We have seen that a power may be registered even though the donor is, in fact, mentally capable, but is *becoming* mentally incapable (see para **3.2.4**). However, if the court is subsequently satisfied that the donor *is and is likely to remain mentally capable*, it must then cancel the registration (s 8(4)(c)). The Law

Commission suggested that 'this would involve a complete recovery rather than a return to, say, the *becoming incapable* level' (Law Com Paper No 122, p 47).

The court will require:

– written confirmation from the donor that he agrees to the cancellation of the registration;
– written confirmation from the donor that he is not seeking to revoke the EPA; and
– the original of any medical report or certificate (it being a basic rule that primary evidence is preferred to secondary evidence, such as a photocopy). Medical evidence is required because the court needs to be *satisfied* that the donor is and is likely to remain mentally capable.

If the registration is cancelled under this provision, the power will remain operative unless and until the donor revokes it. Should the donor once again become incapable, the power may again be registered.

5.7.4 Death, bankruptcy, etc

Under s 8(4)(d) of the 1985 Act, the court must cancel the registration:

> 'on being satisfied that the power has expired or has been revoked by the death or bankruptcy of the donor or the death, mental incapacity or bankruptcy of the attorney or, if the attorney is a body corporate, its winding up or dissolution.'

Once again, the court will require primary evidence of the event which has caused the power to be revoked.

5.7.5 Power not valid at time of registration

Registration, in effect, confirms that the power was valid and subsisting at the time when it was registered. If this assumption is subsequently found to be false, for example, by proof that the donor had effectively revoked the power prior to registration, the court must cancel the registration (s 8(4)(e)).

5.7.6 Fraud or undue pressure

The court must cancel the registration if it is satisfied that fraud or undue pressure was used to induce the donor to create the power (s 8(4)(f); and see para **3.7.4**). It will also, by order, revoke the power (s 8(5)).

5.7.7 Attorney unsuitable

Finally, the court must cancel the registration on being satisfied that, having regard to all the circumstances and in particular the attorney's relationship to or connection with the donor, the attorney is unsuitable to be the donor's attorney (s 8(4)(g); and see para **3.7.4**). Again, in such a case the court will, by order, revoke the power (s 8(5)).

5.7.8 Delivering up the instrument to be cancelled

On the cancellation of registration, the instrument creating the power must be delivered up to be cancelled, save in the exceptional case where the cancellation is based on the court being satisfied of the donor's continuing capacity (s 8(6)).

5.8 COURT OF PROTECTION PROCEDURE

The Court of Protection has an important part to play in relation to EPAs and, for a full account of its procedure, reference should be made to Heywood and Massey *Court of Protection Practice* 12th edn (Sweet & Maxwell, 1991). This section is concerned only with those procedural aspects which relate particularly to EPAs.

The court's powers are governed by:

— the 1983 Act, Part VII; and
— the 1985 Act.

The court's procedures are governed by, inter alia:

— the Court of Protection Rules 2001 (SI 2001/824); and
— the Court of Protection (Enduring Powers of Attorney) Rules 2001 (SI 2001/825) (the 2001 Rules).

Certain provisions of the 1983 Act are specifically applied by s 10 of the 1985 Act to donors of and attorneys under EPAs, whether or not they would be *patients* for the purposes of the 1983 Act. Where the court, after considering medical evidence, is satisfied that a person is incapable, by reason of mental disorder, of managing and administering his property and affairs, that person is referred to as a *patient* (1983 Act, s 94(2)). The provisions of the 1983 Act specifically applied by s 10 of the 1985 Act are as follows.

5.8.1 Lord Chancellor's Visitors

Section 103 of the 1983 Act deals with the functions of visitors, and the effect of applying this provision to the EPA legislation is that the court may direct that a donor or attorney be visited by one of the Lord Chancellor's Visitors for the purpose of investigating mental capacity. A visitor's report cannot be disclosed except to the court or a person authorised by it.

5.8.2 Powers of the judge

Section 104 of the 1983 Act deals with the powers of the judge. This expression extends to the Master of the Court of Protection and, in certain circumstances, to a nominated officer (1983 Act, s 94(1) and (1A), and the 2001 Rules, r 4). Under this provision, the court has the same powers as the High Court to secure the attendance of witnesses and the production of documents.

5.8.3 Appeals and rules of procedure

Section 105 of the 1983 Act deals with appeals, which are considered in detail in para **5.13**. Section 106 deals with rules of procedure.

5.9 APPLICATIONS TO THE COURT

The 2001 Rules provide that an application to the court may, generally, be by letter unless the court directs that the application should be formal (r 8(1)), in which case it should be made in Form EP3. There are two exceptions to this general principle:

- an application to dispense with notice to a relative, co-attorney or the donor must be made in Form EP3 (r 6(2));
- an application to register an enduring power must be made in Form EP2 (r 7).

5.9.1 Production of instrument creating power

The original instrument creating the power must accompany an application to register (Form EP2). If the attorney wishes to make an application to the court before lodging the application to register the power (eg under 1985 Act, ss 4(5) or 5 (see paras **5.3.1–5.3.2**)), the original enduring power of attorney must accompany the first application (*Practice Direction – Mental Health Enduring Powers of Attorney: Applications Prior to Registration* [1986] 2 All ER 42).

5.9.2 Applications by letter

An application by letter must include the name and address of the applicant, the name and address of the donor if the applicant is not the donor, the form of relief or determination required and the grounds for the application (r 8(2)).

5.9.3 Directions for hearing

When the court receives an application, whether in one of the prescribed forms or by letter, it may decide either that no hearing shall be held, in which case the application will be dealt with by way of written representations, or it may fix an appointment for the application to be heard (r 10(2)). The court may give such directions as it thinks proper with regard to any matter arising in the course of an application (r 10(3)). Notification of an appointment for directions or hearing shall be given by the applicant to the attorney (if he is not the applicant), to any objector and to any other person directed by the court to be notified (r 10(4)).

5.9.4 Consolidation of proceedings

The court may consolidate any applications for registration or relief or any objections to registration if it considers that the proceedings relating to them can more conveniently be dealt with together (r 11). This might arise, for example, where there were simultaneous applications for and objections to the registration of EPAs created by a husband and a wife, or competing applications for the registration of an enduring power and the appointment of a receiver.

5.10 HEARINGS

If the court decides that a hearing should take place, the procedure is governed by Part VI of the Court of Protection Rules 2001 (SI 2001/824) and Part III of the Court of Protection (Enduring Powers of Attorney) Rules 2001 (SI 2001/825). References to rules per se are to the Court of Protection (Enduring Powers of Attorney) Rules 2001 (the 2001 Rules).

5.10.1 Hearing in chambers

Every application will be heard in chambers unless, in the case of an application for a hearing by a judge, the judge directs otherwise (Court of Protection Rules 2001, r 37(1)). The court will give such directions as it thinks fit concerning the privacy of applications (ibid, r 37(2)).

5.10.2 Representation

The applicant, the attorney (if he is not the applicant) and any person given notice of the appointment or hearing may attend or be represented (r 10(5)). The court also has a general power to determine what persons are entitled to attend (Court of Protection Rules 2001, r 38). If two or more persons appearing at a hearing are represented by the same legal representative, the court may, if it thinks fit, require any of them to be separately represented (ibid, r 39).

5.10.3 Notice of hearing

The applicant must give the stipulated period of notice of any hearing. The stipulated periods are as follows.

— *Ten* clear days' notice of the hearing of certain kinds of application must be given to the attorney, the donor, every relative entitled to receive notice of an application to register (see para **3.3.5**), any co-attorney, and such other persons who appear to the court to be interested as the court may specify. The applications in question are: (i) applications to dispense with notice to the donor; (ii) applications to dispose of the donor's property prior to registration, and (iii) objections to registration of an enduring power (r 14(1)(a)).
— *Seven* clear days' notice must be given in the case of the hearing of any other application (r 14(1)(b)).

For the above purposes, notice is given if the applicant sends a copy of the application, endorsed by the court with the hearing date, to the person concerned (r 14(4)). Rule 5 makes provision for the computation of these periods of time. The court may extend or abridge these periods upon such terms as it thinks fit, and, notwithstanding, in the case of an extension, that the time limited by the 1985 Act and 2001 Rules has expired (r 14(3)).

5.11 SERVICE

Any document required by the 2001 Rules to be given to the donor must be given to him *personally* (r 15(1); and see para **3.3.2**). Documents required to be given to other persons are served by sending them by first-class post, through a document exchange, by fax or by other electronic means (r 15(2)).

There is also provision for service on a solicitor. Where a solicitor acting for the person to be given any document (other than the donor) endorses on that document or on a copy a statement that he accepts the document on behalf of that person, the document shall be deemed to have been duly sent to that person and to have been received on the date on which the endorsement was made (r 16).

There is also provision for substituted service. Where it appears to the court that it is impracticable for any document to be given to any person other than the donor by sending it to him by first-class post, the court may give such directions as it thinks fit for the purpose of bringing the document to that person's notice (r 17).

5.12 MISCELLANEOUS PROVISIONS

5.12.1 Witness summonses

The 2001 Rules prescribe a form of witness summons, Form EP6 (which is set out in Appendix 4 to this book). A witness summons may also require the witness to bring with him and produce at the hearing specified documents (r 20).

5.12.2 Leave to bring an application

Unless the application is by a person who has been served with notice of intention to register an EPA, leave is required for the making of an application for relief specified in the 1985 Act (r 21).

5.12.3 Evidence

The general rule is that evidence is given by affidavit (Court of Protection Rules 2001, r 27(1)). However, notwithstanding this general rule, the court may accept and act upon a statement of facts or such other evidence, whether oral or written, as it considers sufficient, although not given under oath, and whether or not it would otherwise be admissible in a court of law (ibid, r 28(1)). Evidence which has been used in any proceedings relating to the donor may be used at any subsequent stage of those proceedings or in any other proceedings (eg receivership proceedings) before the court (r 18). This general principle is subject to the court directing otherwise.

5.12.4 Searches and copies of documents

Registration of an enduring power, as we have seen, affects the rights of the donor. Third parties may, therefore, wish to ascertain whether or not a power granted by him has been registered. Again, a third party proposing to deal with the attorney may wish to satisfy himself that a power granted by a donor he knows to be mentally incapable has been registered so that he can be satisfied as to its validity and the authority of the attorney to act.

Accordingly, on payment of the prescribed fee, any person may apply for an official search to be made of the register (r 13). The current fee is £25 (r 26 and Sch 2). The application is made on Form EP4. The court will then state whether an EPA has been registered, whether an application for registration is pending, or whether the registration has been cancelled. The search certificate is in Form EP5. Both forms are set out in Appendix 4 to this book.

A third party may also be interested in the contents of a registered power, for example, whether it contains any restrictions on the attorney's authority. The court may supply any person with an office copy of a registered power, if satisfied that he has good reason for requesting a copy and that it is not reasonably practicable to obtain a copy from the attorney (r 13(2)). An application is made on Form EP4 (set out in Appendix 4 to this book) which requires the applicant to show that he satisfies those conditions.

In deciding how far it is necessary or desirable to inquire into the matters discussed above, the provisions of the 1985 Act conferring protection on attorneys and on those dealing with them should be borne in mind (see Chapter 8).

The general principle is that documents filed in the court are not open to inspection without leave of the court, and no copy of any such document or extract is to be taken or issued to any person without leave (r 19(3)). However, there are two exceptions. First, any person who has filed an affidavit or other document shall, unless the court otherwise directs, be entitled on request to be supplied by the court with a copy of it (r 19(1)). Secondly, an attorney or his solicitor may have a search made for, and may inspect and request a copy of, any document filed in proceedings relating to the EPA under which the attorney has been appointed (r 19(2)).

5.13 REVIEWS AND APPEALS

5.13.1 Review of a decision not made on a hearing

Any person who is aggrieved by a decision of the court which was not made at an attended hearing may apply to the court within 14 days of the date on which the decision was given to have the decision reviewed by the court (r 23(1)). On the hearing of the application, the court may either confirm or revoke the previous decision or make or give any other order or decision it thinks fit (r 23(2)). Anyone who is aggrieved by an order or decision made or given on the hearing of the application for review may appeal to a nominated judge (see below).

5.13.2 Appeal from a decision made on a hearing

The right of appeal is conferred by s 105 of the Mental Health Act 1983 and s 10(1)(c) of the 1985 Act. Anyone who is aggrieved by an order or decision of the court made on a hearing may, within 14 days from the date of entry of the order or, as the case may be, from the date of the decision, appeal to a nominated judge (r 24(1)). The appellant must, within those 14 days, serve notice of appeal in Form EP7 (see Appendix 4 to this book) on every person who is 'directly affected' by the decision, and on any other person whom the court may direct. The appellant must also lodge a copy of the notice of appeal at the court (r 24(2)). The time and place at which the appeal is to be heard is fixed by the court, and an officer of the court will arrange for notice of the time and place fixed to be sent to the appellant, who must then *immediately* send notice of it to everyone who has been served with the notice of appeal (r 24(3)). No further evidence can be filed in support of or in opposition to the appeal without leave of the court (r 24(4)).

5.13.3 Appeal to the Court of Appeal

An appeal lies to the Court of Appeal from any decision of a nominated judge, whether given in the exercise of his original jurisdiction or on the hearing of an appeal (Mental Health Act 1983, s 105(2)).

5.13.4 Reference to a judge

The Court of Protection has power to refer to a judge any proceedings or any question arising in any proceedings which ought, by virtue of any enactment or in its opinion, to be considered by the judge (Court of Protection Rules 2001, r 40). The court might make a reference, for example, where it considered that it would be helpful for a decision to be reported on a particular aspect of the EPA legislation.

5.14 FEES

The 2001 Rules make provision for the payment of fees (r 26 and Sch 2). A fee of £75 is payable on lodging an application for registration of an EPA. This fee is payable on lodging the application, rather than on the registration of the power. If the application is unsuccessful, or the registration does not proceed for any reason, the fee is not recoverable.

The person by whom any fee is payable shall, unless it is for a search of the register, or unless the court directs otherwise, make the payment out of the assets of the donor (r 26(3)).

5.15 COSTS

Public funding is not available for Court of Protection proceedings. All costs incurred in relation to matters involving EPAs are in the discretion of the court (Court of Protection Rules 2001, r 84(1)). Usually, they are awarded out of the donor's estate (*Re Cathcart* [1893] 1 Ch 466). However, in disputed cases there may be circumstances in which some other order will be made, especially if the court is satisfied that an applicant or objector has acted unreasonably or has been motivated by self-interest rather than by the donor's best interests.

Chapter 6

REVOCATION, DISCLAIMER AND TERMINATION OF ENDURING POWERS

6.1 INTRODUCTION

6.1.1 The common law

At common law, there are three main ways in which a power of attorney may come to an end.

(1) Revocation by act of donor

First, the power may be revoked by the donor. Normally, he may do so in any circumstances and without obtaining any consent. Revocation may be express (in which case it will usually be by deed), or it may be implied by the doing of an act which is incompatible with the continued operation of the power.

(2) Disclaimer by attorney

Secondly, the power may be terminated by renunciation or disclaimer on the part of the attorney. At common law the attorney is (in the absence of any provision to that effect in the instrument creating the power) under no duty to act and, in principle, may disclaim at any time.

(3) Operation of law

Thirdly, the power may come to an end by operation of law, for example, where the donor dies or becomes mentally incapable (*Drew v Nunn* (1879) 4 QBD 661).

6.1.2 Policy of the 1985 Act

The fundamental principle underlying the Enduring Powers of Attorney Act 1985 (the 1985 Act) is that an enduring power of attorney (EPA) should not come to an end solely by reason of the donor's loss of mental capacity, and this aspect of revocation need not be further considered here. However, the

Act had to make a number of special provisions dealing with disclaimer and revocation in other circumstances for two reasons. First, it is possible that the donor of a power will seek to revoke it at a time when the attorney believes that the donor has become or is becoming mentally incapable. Secondly, the attorney might wish to disclaim his appointment under the power, and this might leave the donor without anyone to look after his affairs in circumstances in which the donor could be exposed to risk.

We consider, first, the rules governing the revocation of an enduring power by the donor; secondly, the rules governing disclaimer; and, finally, the position on termination by operation of law.

6.2 REVOCATION

An EPA may be revoked in one of three ways: first, automatically; secondly, by act of the donor; and, finally, by the court.

6.2.1 Automatic revocation

An EPA is revoked by the bankruptcy of the attorney whatever the circumstances of the bankruptcy (s 2(10)). This reflects the position at common law (*Marwick v Hardingham* (1880) 15 ChD 339). A power coupled with an interest is an exception to this rule.

6.2.2 Revocation by act of the donor

Until an application for registration has been made, the donor may revoke the power in exactly the same way as he can at common law. If he does so, and an application is subsequently made for the registration of the power, the fact that the power created by the instrument no longer subsists is a ground on which the donor or anyone else may validly object to registration (s 6(5)(b)). If this ground of objection is established, the court will refuse the application for registration (s 6(6)).

After registration, no revocation of a power by the donor is valid unless and until the court confirms the revocation under the procedure mentioned below (s 7(1)(a)). The reason for this was explained by the Law Commission, in its report, *The Incapacitated Principal* (1983) Law Com Paper No 122, para 4.72, as follows:

> 'The significance of this recommendation lies in the importance we attach to the ability of the attorney and third parties to rely on the fact of registration as verifying the validity of the instrument. Much of this reliance would be jeopardised if the donor were permitted to make

informal revocations of his registered power. The attorney and third parties would often be uncertain whether the revocations were effective; that is, whether the donor retained sufficient capacity to revoke. We suspect that in many cases third parties would play safe and refuse to deal with the attorney further. This might not be in the donor's interests especially since the third parties might be wary of dealing directly with him as well. We therefore feel that, in these cases, the attorney and third parties should be entitled to act on the strength of the registered power until such time as the donor's purported revocation had been confirmed by the court.'

This provision effectively deprives a donor who still retains mental capacity but is 'becoming incapable' of the right to revoke, even though he could have done so if the power had not been registered. The Law Commission said:

'A desire to revoke after registration might be perfectly legitimate but would, perhaps, be more likely to be attributable to a measure of mental incapacity rendering the continuation of the power more beneficial to the donor than its revocation' (Law Com Paper No 122, para 4.73).

If a donor wishes to revoke a registered power, he must apply to the court to confirm the revocation (s 7(1)(a)). The court will confirm the revocation only if it is satisfied that the donor: (a) has done whatever is necessary in law to effect an express revocation of the power; and (b) was mentally capable of revoking a power of attorney when he did so. It is immaterial whether or not he is still capable at the time when the court considers the application (s 8(3)).

The expression 'whatever is necessary in law to effect an express revocation of the power' is not defined in the 1985 Act. The most satisfactory way of expressly revoking a power is for the donor to execute a deed of revocation. However, what is important is not so much the method used to revoke the power, but the notice given to the attorney. On its own, revocation is insufficient, because the attorney's authority under the power does not cease until he is given notice of the revocation (*Re Oriental Bank ex parte Guillemin* (1885) 28 ChD 634).

6.2.3 A later EPA does not necessarily revoke an earlier one

In *Re E (A Donor)* [2000] 3 WLR 1974 it was held that the execution of a later EPA does not automatically revoke an earlier EPA. The facts were as follows. Mrs E had three daughters, X, Y and Z. In 1992 she made an EPA appointing Y and Z jointly to be her attorneys. In 1997 she executed another EPA appointing all three daughters to act jointly as her attorneys. However, the words 'save that any two of my attorneys may sign' were inserted by hand after the printed word 'jointly'. X applied unilaterally to register the 1997 power, but the application was rejected because the condition that two of the three attorneys could act was incompatible with a joint appointment for the purposes of s 11(1) of the 1985 Act. Y and Z then applied to register the 1992 power. X, who was not on the best of terms with her sisters, objected to registration inter alia on the ground that the 1992 power no longer subsisted, having been revoked by the donor's mere execution of the 1997 power. The Master of the Court of Protection dismissed the objection because there was no evidence that the donor had *animus revocandi*, and that in the 1997 power the donor was confirming the appointment of Y and Z as her attorneys and attempting unsuccessfully to add another attorney. X appealed.

On 21 February 2000, Arden J (as she then was) dismissed the appeal and (at 394G–395F), held as follows:

'I accept the appellant's submission that the 1997 power takes effect as an ordinary power even if it cannot take effect as an EPA. The 1997 power is therefore capable of being used prior to the donor becoming mentally incapable. However, in my judgment, the 1992 power has not been revoked by the execution of the 1997 power and the reasons for my conclusion are as follows.

The general law of agency in my judgment shows that to amount to revocation by conduct, the conduct must be inconsistent with the continuation of the agency. Contrary to the appellant's submission, this in my judgment means more than that the conduct should be reasonably understood as amounting to revocation. To be *inconsistent*, it must be unambiguous in its effect. …

The onus is on the appellant to show that the 1992 power has been revoked. Accordingly, she has to show that the donor must have intended to revoke the 1992 power. It is not enough to show that the donor must have forgotten about the 1992 power or made no reference to it. Indeed if she had forgotten about it that would suggest that she did not intend to revoke it. As the passages cited by the Master from the Law Commission's report show, it is not the policy of the 1985 Act to prohibit successive EPAs. …

There is no contemporaneous evidence as to the donor's intentions, or even any later evidence from her as to what she intended. All that is known is that she did not expressly revoke the 1992 power when she executed the 1997 power. …

I do not consider that it is clear that the 1997 power revokes the 1992 power. There is no reason why the donor should not want to preserve the possibility that the 1992 power might be used if for some reason the 1997 power could not be used. She did not know that the 1997 power was not valid as an EPA when she signed it, but there is no reason why she should not have wanted to cover the situation that it might be invalid. To have several simultaneous powers would be a legitimate and understandable wish, and not an irrational one as suggested by the appellant.'

6.2.4 Capacity to revoke an EPA

The meaning of the expression *mentally capable of revoking a power of attorney* is not entirely clear. It has been held that the same degree of capacity is required to revoke a will as to make one (*Re Sabatini* (1970) 114 SJ 35), and it could be argued that the same principle applies to an enduring power. Indeed, in some common law jurisdictions, the relevant legislation provides that 'a person is capable of revoking a continuing power of attorney if he or she is capable of giving one' (Ontario, Substitute Decisions Act 1992, s 8(2)). Accordingly, if the donor of the power has *Re K; Re F* capacity (see para **2.2.2**) at the time of revocation, he would be mentally capable of revoking the power of attorney, regardless of whether he is mentally capable of managing and administering his property and affairs generally.

However, it could also be argued that the revocation of an EPA is an entirely different transaction from the creation of such a power. 'The mental capacity required by the law in respect of any instrument is relative to the particular transaction which is being effected by means of the instrument, and may be described as the capacity to understand the nature of that transaction when it is explained' (*Gibbons v Wright* (1954) 91 CLR 423 at 438, per Dixon CJ).

The creation and revocation of an enduring power are different transactions involving different thought processes. The discretion exercised by the court when initially appointing a person to manage the finances of an incapacitated person is different from the discretion it exercises when removing a manager who is already in place (*Holt v Protective Commissioner* (1993) 31 NSWLR 227 at 241, New South Wales Court of Appeal). In such a case, it has to be shown that either: (a) the manager is incompetent or has acted unlawfully or improperly or that there is a conflict of interest or duty; or (b) it is otherwise in the protected person's best interests to remove the installed manager. The thought process behind the revocation of an EPA is similar, and usually involves a change in circumstances or some measure of dissatisfaction with the existing attorney or the manner in which he has performed his duties.

At first instance, the Court of Protection has preferred this second line of authority, and has held (in *Re S* (unreported), Master Lush, 13 March 1997) that for it to be satisfied that a donor understands the nature and effect of the transaction of revoking a power, it has to be shown that, having received in broad terms and simple language an explanation of the nature and effect of the transaction, the donor understands:

— who the attorneys are;
— what authority they have;
— why it is necessary or expedient to revoke the power; and
— the foreseeable consequences of revoking the power.

One of the foreseeable consequences of revoking the power, in a case where the power is already registered, would be that the revocation will not be valid unless and until it is confirmed by the Court of Protection.

6.2.5 Revocation by the court

The court may revoke an enduring power in two circumstances:

(1) Valid objection

The court is obliged to revoke the power created by the instrument if it is satisfied that: (a) fraud or undue pressure was used to induce the donor to create the power; or (b) having regard to all the circumstances, the attorney is unsuitable to be the donor's attorney (s 6(5)(d), (e) and (6)). On doing so, it will cancel the registration of the instrument (s 8(4)(f), (g) and (5)). For the position regarding an 'unsuitable' attorney who has been appointed to act jointly and severally with others, see para **7.4.4**.

(2) On exercising powers under the Mental Health Act 1983

The court may give a direction revoking the power on exercising any of its powers (principally that of appointing a receiver) under Part VII of the Mental Health Act 1983 (1983 Act) and, on doing so, it will cancel the registration of the instrument (1985 Act, s 8(4)(b)). The court does not always revoke the power on exercising its powers under the 1983 Act. For example, if the attorney applied to the court for a statutory will to be executed on behalf of the donor, although the order would be made under s 96(1)(e) of the 1983 Act, it is unlikely that the court would direct that the enduring power be revoked.

6.3 DISCLAIMER

An attorney normally has an unrestricted right to disclaim or renounce a power of attorney, but this is not true of an enduring power. Section 2(12) of the 1985 Act provides that 'no disclaimer of an enduring power, whether by deed or otherwise, shall be valid unless and until the attorney gives notice of it to the donor'.

As the Law Commission stated, the reason for such notification is to 'alert the capable donor to the fact that he could no longer rely on the attorney to act for him: the donor would thereby be able to consider making alternative arrangements' (Law Com Paper No 122, para 4.32).

It is not necessary for a notice of disclaimer to be made by deed; nor is it necessary for the attorney to give his reasons for disclaiming. If the attorney is one of two or more attorneys who have been appointed jointly (rather than jointly and severally), the remaining attorneys will no longer have the authority to act under the enduring power.

6.3.1 Notice to the court required after onset of incapacity

If an attorney has reason to believe that the donor is or is becoming mentally incapable, the attorney cannot disclaim simply by giving notice to the donor. Instead, the attorney must give notice of the disclaimer to the court, and the disclaimer is not valid unless and until he has done so (s 4(6)). The same is true if the power is registered (s 7(1)(b)).

Notification to the court may be made by letter (Court of Protection (Enduring Powers of Attorney) Rules 2001 (SI 2001/825) (the 2001 Rules), r 8(1)). Where an attorney seeks to disclaim, the disclaimer shall not take effect earlier than the day on which the notice of disclaimer is received at the court (r 10(7)).

6.3.2 Right to disclaim is preserved

The effect of these provisions is not to prevent the attorney disclaiming. It is merely to ensure that the court is notified. As the Law Commission said, 'the donor should not be abandoned, once he is no longer capable, without alternative arrangements for his welfare being made ... and it would be for the court to decide whether a receivership or other order should be made for the donor' (Law Com Paper No 122, para 4.55). The Commission envisaged that 'few attorneys would disclaim lightly ... especially since they would often be close relatives and feel a strong moral obligation to continue' (ibid, para 4.56).

6.4 TERMINATION BY OPERATION OF LAW

An enduring power will come to an end on the death or bankruptcy of the donor, or the death, mental incapacity, or bankruptcy of the attorney.

Section 8(4)(d) of the 1985 Act provides for the cancellation of the registration of an enduring power if the court is satisfied that 'the power has expired or been revoked by the death or bankruptcy of the donor or the death, mental incapacity or bankruptcy of the attorney or, if the attorney is a body corporate, its winding up or dissolution'. Rule 25(2)(c) of the 2001 Rules provides that the court may cancel the registration of an enduring power revoked by the bankruptcy of the attorney.

6.5 TERMINATION BY EFFLUXION OF TIME

If an EPA is granted for a limited period of time, it will come to an end on the expiry of that period. Section 8(4)(d) of the 1985 Act provides that the court must cancel the registration of the power if it is satisfied that the power has expired.

Chapter 7

APPOINTMENT OF MORE THAN ONE ATTORNEY

7.1 INTRODUCTION

7.1.1 Appointments under ordinary powers

Donors of powers of attorney commonly appoint two or more attorneys to act. The attorneys may be *joint* attorneys (in which case all of them must join together in a transaction), or they may be *joint and several* attorneys (in which case each attorney may act by himself, with the same effect as if all the attorneys had joined in the transaction).

Sometimes, a power of attorney appoints *successive* attorneys – for example, the instrument might appoint Adam to be the donor's attorney but provide that, if Adam ceased for any reason to be an attorney, then Ben should assume his powers instead. Alternatively, an ordinary (non-enduring) power might give Adam *the right to appoint another attorney* to act in his place. It is possible (although the Law Commission thought that it was rarely done (see *The Incapacitated Principal* (1983) Law Com Paper No 122, fn 211)) to appoint an *alternative* attorney, ie someone who will act if the donor's first choice is unable to take up the appointment.

7.1.2 Application to enduring powers

It seems probable that the case for appointing more than one attorney is stronger for enduring powers than ordinary powers because an enduring power may be seen as likely to have a potentially longer lifespan than an ordinary power.

The Enduring Powers of Attorney Act 1985 (the 1985 Act) contains a number of complicated provisions dealing with such appointments. In particular, special provision has to be made because of the essential difference between joint powers, on the one hand, and joint and several powers, on the other. As the Law Commission stated:

> 'Any matter affecting the capacity of an attorney under a joint power to operate his power affects all his co-attorneys also since they cannot act without him. Where, however, the power is joint and several the incapacity of one will not, generally, prejudice the capacity of the other attorneys. This difference creates a measure of complexity for some aspects of our proposed EPA scheme since the validity of the power and the attorney's authority under it may differ according to whether the power is joint or joint and several. Furthermore, the very fact that more than one attorney has been appointed raises questions which cannot necessarily be answered by applying to such cases our recommendations as they apply to sole attorneys' (Law Com Paper No 122, para 4.94).

7.2 ONLY JOINT OR JOINT AND SEVERAL APPOINTMENTS PERMITTED

7.2.1 Appointment of substitute attorneys not permitted

Section 11(1) of the 1985 Act provides that an instrument which appoints more than one person to be an attorney cannot create an enduring power unless the attorneys are appointed to act jointly *or* jointly and severally. This provision is intended to prevent an instrument which provides for one or more attorneys who would replace the original attorneys should he or they cease to act from qualifying as an enduring power of attorney (EPA).

The decision to exclude such powers from the scheme was taken on the grounds that:

> 'the benefit to be gained by including successive EPAs ... would be out of all proportion to the complexity that such powers would create in relation to some of the more detailed areas of our scheme. In any event, successive EPAs are rendered largely unnecessary because a joint and several EPA would permit the continuation of the EPA in the event of one of the attorneys ceasing to act' (Law Com Paper No 122, p 50, fn 214).

The 1985 Act also expressly provides that a power of attorney which gives the attorney a *right* to appoint a substitute or successor cannot be an enduring power (s 2(9)).

It is not clear that the legislation has given effect to the Law Commission's view that it should not be possible within the EPA scheme to provide for the appointment of an *alternative* attorney: one who can act only if the donor's first choice is unable to take up the attorneyship. It would seem to be at least open to argument that an enduring power which appoints 'A or, if A is unable to take up office as my attorney, B' is not 'an instrument which appoints more than one person to be an attorney' within the meaning of the prohibition contained in s 11(1) of the 1985 Act, and it is understood that the Court of

Protection takes this view (PD Lewis, formerly the Assistant Public Trustee, (1986) LSG 3566 at 3567).

7.2.2 Attorneyship cannot run with title

Although, in general, a power of attorney given to secure a proprietary interest may be given to the person entitled to the interest and to persons deriving title under him (s 4(2) of the Powers of Attorney Act 1971), such a power could not be an enduring power because of the provisions of s 2(9) of the 1985 Act. However, this is unlikely to be of practical importance, since such powers would not in any event be revoked by the incapacity of the donor.

7.2.3 A way of providing for a succession of attorneys

It may be possible to create what the Law Commission described (Law Com Paper No 122, p 50, fn 214) as the 'effect of successiveness' within the EPA scheme. A donor could grant enduring powers in separate instruments with the result that the authority of an attorney under one power would commence only upon the termination of the authority under another power.

7.2.4 Joint, and joint and several attorneys

It has already been pointed out that there is a crucial difference between these two types of appointment, and it is necessary to consider how the 1985 Act applies to each. However, the first question for the adviser is whether the donor wishes to appoint joint attorneys, or whether he prefers that they should also be able to act severally.

The main advantage of appointing *joint and several* attorneys is the obvious one that action may have to be taken when one of the attorneys is abroad, or is for some other reason unable or unwilling to act. The advantage of making the appointment *joint* is that the donor has an added measure of security against dishonesty or even imprudence. However, the death, disclaimer or bankruptcy of any joint attorney will effectively terminate the power.

7.3 JOINT ATTORNEYS

Generally speaking, the 1985 Act applies to joint attorneys collectively as it applies to a single attorney (s 11(2)). Hence, all the attorneys come under a duty to apply for registration if they have reason to believe that the donor is or is becoming mentally incapable (s 4(1)) (see para **3.2**). Presumably, the duty arises if only one attorney has 'reason to believe', but it is not easy to see how the other attorneys could come under such a duty if they were unaware of the facts which have created it. The 1985 Act is modified in its application to joint attorneys in a number of minor respects.

7.3.1 Time when attorney must satisfy conditions as to age and solvency

A power of attorney is not an enduring power unless, when he executes the instrument creating it, the attorney is an individual who has attained 18 years of age and is not bankrupt (s 2(7)). The relevant time for determining whether those conditions are satisfied in respect of joint appointments is the time when the second or last attorney executes the instrument (Sch 3, para 1).

Thus, if the donor appoints his wife and two children to be *joint* attorneys, the instrument will be capable of taking effect as an enduring power, notwithstanding the fact that one child was under 18 at the time when his mother and the elder child executed it, provided that the younger child was 18 or over when he executed it. However, it would seem that, unless and until he does execute the instrument, it cannot take effect as an enduring power.

7.3.2 Substitute attorneys

If the power purports to give *any* of the joint attorneys the right to appoint a substitute or successor, it cannot be an enduring power (s 2(9), Sch 3, para 2).

7.3.3 Attorney's bankruptcy

An enduring power will be revoked if *any* joint attorney becomes bankrupt (s 2(10), Sch 3, para 2). It will not be saved as respects the attorneys who were not affected by the bankruptcy.

7.3.4 Court's pre-registration powers

The court's pre-registration functions under s 5 of the 1985 Act (see para **5.3.2**) are exercisable with respect to *any* attorney under the power (Sch 3, para 3).

7.3.5 Valid grounds of objection

The fact that *any* of the attorneys under a joint power are unsuitable to be the donor's attorney, having regard to all the circumstances and, in particular, the attorney's relationship to or connection with the donor, is a valid ground of objection (s 6(5)(e), Sch 3, para 4). If this ground of objection is made out, the court must refuse the application to register, notwithstanding the fact that the other named attorneys would still be perfectly good appointments. The court has no power to authorise the appointment of another attorney in place of the one found to be unsuitable.

7.3.6 Powers of the court once the power is registered

The powers of the court after registration (eg the power to require the attorney to furnish information or produce documents) are exercisable in respect of *any* attorney under the power (s 8(2), Sch 3, para 5) (see para **5.6.1**). Similar provisions apply to the court's duty to cancel the registration of the instrument if, for example, it is satisfied that, having regard to all the circumstances and, in particular, the attorney's relation to or connection with the donor, the attorney is unsuitable to be the donor's attorney (s 8(4); Sch 3, para 6) (see para **5.7.7**).

7.4 JOINT AND SEVERAL ATTORNEYS

The legislation cannot and does not adopt a general principle that it applies to joint and several attorneys collectively as it applies to a single attorney. For many purposes, each attorney must be considered separately, and the 1985 Act is modified in the following respects in the case of joint and several attorneys.

7.4.1 One attorney failing to satisfy qualifications for appointment

If one of a number of joint and several attorneys does not satisfy the requirements for the creation of enduring powers, for example, because he is a minor at the time of execution, then the power will be invalid in his case, but valid in respect of the others (s 11(4)). It would seem that if a power is thereby invalidated in respect of an attorney, it may nevertheless be effective to create an *ordinary* power of attorney in his favour (s 11(4)) (see para **2.1.2**).

7.4.2 Registration procedure

Whereas all attorneys under a *joint* power have to join in the application to register, it is open to attorneys under a *joint and several* power to make *either* a joint application *or* for one or more of them to make the application (s 11(5)) (see Law Com Paper No 122, para 4.97). If the instrument is then registered, the registration will be effective in respect of all the attorneys.

Notice to co-attorneys

Where an attorney intends to register an enduring power, notice of his intention (Form EP1) must be given to any other attorney or attorneys who have not joined in the application (s 11(5)(b), Sch 1, para 7).

Pending the initial determination of the application, an attorney who has not joined in the application (as well as those who have) may act as provided in ss 1(2) or 5 of the 1985 Act (s 11(5)(a)) (see para **4.6**).

7.4.3 Objections to registration

An objection may be taken on a ground relating to an attorney who has not applied for registration as well as one who has (s 11(5)(c)). However, the court will not *refuse to register* the instrument on the ground that an objection to an attorney or power is established if an enduring power subsists as respects some attorney who is not affected (s 11(6)). In such a case, the registration will be qualified, and that fact will be noted on the register and on the instrument, and the qualification will be sealed (Court of Protection (Enduring Powers of Attorney) Rules 2001 (SI 2001/825) (the 2001 Rules), r 12(4)).

7.4.4 Cancellation

In the same way, if a ground on which the court must cancel registration is made out in the case of a joint and several power, the court must not cancel the power if the enduring power nevertheless subsists 'as respects some attorney who is not affected thereby' (s 11(7)). For example, the court may be satisfied that one attorney is unsuitable to be the donor's attorney (s 8(4)(g)) (see para **3.7.4**) but not so satisfied in respect of the others (s 8(7)). A qualification will be noted on the register and on the instrument and sealed (2001 Rules, r 12(4)).

7.4.5 Bankruptcy of attorney

An enduring power is revoked by the bankruptcy of the attorney, whatever the circumstances of the bankruptcy (s 2(10)). In the case of a joint and several power, the bankruptcy of an attorney will cause that person to cease to be an attorney, but will have no effect on the capacity of the others to continue to act. It is only when the last remaining attorney under the power becomes bankrupt that the power is revoked (s 2(10), Sch 3, para 7).

7.4.6 Disclaimer

Generally speaking, no disclaimer of a power is valid once an attorney has reason to believe that the donor is or is becoming mentally incapable unless and until the attorney gives notice of it to the court (s 4(6)). As regards joint powers, this applies to any attorney but, in the case of joint and several powers, it applies only to those attorneys who themselves have reason to believe that the donor is or is becoming mentally incapable (Sch 3, para 8).

7.5 ATTORNEY'S LIABILITY FOR WRONGS OF CO-ATTORNEY

Although the 1985 Act makes no specific provision in this respect, at common law an attorney is not liable for any loss or harm caused by the wrongful act or omission of a co-attorney, unless he authorised or was otherwise party or privy to such wrongful act or omission (see *Bowstead and Reynolds on Agency* 16th edn (Sweet & Maxwell, 1995)).

Chapter 8

PROTECTION OF THIRD PARTIES

8.1 INTRODUCTION

8.1.1 Consequences of revocation – the common law

There are two main risks arising from the possibility that a power of attorney may have been revoked or terminated. First, a third party dealing with the attorney may find that a transaction is invalid because the attorney no longer had authority to carry it out. Such invalidity may, of course, affect his title and that of others subsequently relying on the validity of the transaction. Secondly, an attorney who purports to act under the authority conferred by a power of attorney which is no longer valid may himself be liable to a third party who relied on that authority for breach of an implied warranty that he continued to have the authority conferred by the power (*Yonge v Toynbee* [1910] 1 KB 215).

8.1.2 Protection – the Powers of Attorney Act 1971

The Powers of Attorney Act 1971 (the 1971 Act), accordingly, conferred some protection on attorneys and those dealing with them. The policy of the Enduring Powers of Attorney Act 1985 (the 1985 Act) is that attorneys and third parties acting pursuant to an enduring power should, in principle, have the same protection as is conferred by law in the case of ordinary powers, but it was necessary to confer certain additional protection (see para **8.3**).

8.2 APPLICATION OF THE 1971 ACT TO ENDURING POWERS

An enduring power of attorney (EPA) is a power of attorney for the purposes of the protection conferred by ss 5 and 6 of the 1971 Act. The scope of this protection is as follows.

8.2.1 Protection for innocent attorney

An attorney who acts in pursuance of any power of attorney at a time when it has been revoked does not, by reason of the revocation, incur any liability to the donor of the power or to a third party for breach of an implied warranty of authority, provided that, at that time, he did not know that the donor had revoked the power, or that an event had occurred which caused it to be revoked (1971 Act, s 5(1) and (5)).

8.2.2 Protection for innocent third party

In favour of a third party dealing with the attorney, any transaction is as effective as if the power continued in operation, notwithstanding that it may have been revoked by the donor, or that he may have died or become incapable or bankrupt or, in the case of a body corporate, been wound up or dissolved, *unless* the third party at the time of the transaction had knowledge that the power had been revoked by the donor or of an event which caused it to be revoked (1971 Act, s 5(2) and (5)).

8.2.3 What constitutes knowledge of revocation of enduring power?

Whether or not there is knowledge of revocation is of crucial importance for the purpose of the protection discussed above. Under the 1985 Act, the donor's purported revocation of a power which has been registered will not be valid unless and until the court confirms the revocation (s 7(1)(a)) (see para **6.2.2**). For the purposes of the protection conferred by s 5 of the 1971 Act, knowledge of the confirmation of the revocation is knowledge of revocation of the power but knowledge of the unconfirmed revocation is not (1985 Act, s 9(5)).

8.2.4 Presumption that third party had no knowledge

For these purposes, where the interest of a purchaser (as defined in s 205(1) of the Law of Property Act 1925) depends on the third party's knowledge, it is to be conclusively presumed that the third party had no such knowledge if:

– the transaction by the attorney was completed within 12 months of the date on which the power came into operation; or
– before, or within 3 months after, the completion of the purchase the third party makes a statutory declaration that he had no such knowledge (1971 Act, s 5(4)).

8.3 ADDITIONAL PROTECTION UNDER THE 1985 ACT

The additional protection given by the 1985 Act covers three situations:

- where an instrument was intended to create an enduring power but failed to do so;
- where the attorney's powers are restricted pending the registration of the instrument; and
- where the donor never had capacity to grant a power of attorney.

8.3.1 Where the instrument fails to create an enduring power

The 1985 Act provides protection for the attorney and persons dealing with him in cases where: (a) an instrument 'framed in a form prescribed under section 2(2)' of the Act creates a power which is not a valid enduring power; and (b) the power is revoked by the mental incapacity of the donor (Sch 2, para 1).

(1) Protection for attorney
In such a case, an attorney who acts in pursuance of the power shall not, by reason of the revocation, incur any liability (either to the donor or to any other person) unless at the time of acting he knew: (a) that the instrument did not create a valid enduring power; and (b) that the donor has become mentally incapable (Sch 2, para 2).

(2) Protection for third parties
In these circumstances, and subject to the same two provisions, any transaction between the attorney and another person shall, in favour of that person, be as valid as if the power had then been in existence (Sch 2, para 3).

(3) Presumption in favour of validity
For the purpose of determining whether a transaction is valid by virtue of these provisions, it is to be conclusively presumed in favour of the purchaser that the transaction was valid if: (a) the transaction between that person and the attorney was completed within 12 months of the date on which the instrument was registered; or (b) that person makes a statutory declaration, before or within 3 months after the completion of the purchase, that he had no reason at the time of the transaction to doubt that the attorney had authority to dispose of the property which was the subject of the transaction (s 9(4)). These provisions mirror those contained in the 1971 Act (see para **8.2.4**).

(4) Circumstances in which protection is available

The Law Commission envisaged that an instrument intended to create an enduring power might fail to do so by reason of a drafting error, and that the protection described in the preceding paragraphs would then be available (see *The Incapacitated Principal* (1983) Law Com Paper No 122, p 49, fn 207). However, it will be noted that the protection applies only where an instrument is 'framed in' the prescribed form and, if an instrument is so framed, it is not easy to see how any drafting error could have the effect of creating an ordinary but not an enduring power. It seems more probable that the provisions would be applicable in cases in which the power cannot be an enduring power for some reason not connected with the drafting – as, for example, where the attorney executes the power while he is a minor (s 2(7)(a)) (see para **2.3.3**).

8.3.2 Protection where the attorney's powers are restricted pending registration

The protection conferred by s 5 of the 1971 Act arises only when the power has been revoked, and an enduring power will not be revoked by the donor's supervening mental incapacity (1985 Act, s 1(1)(a)). However, as explained in para **4.6.1**, the donee's authority to act under the power will be severely restricted when such incapacity occurs unless and until the power is registered (s 1(2)).

The 1985 Act therefore provides that the protection for the attorney and persons dealing with him, conferred by s 5 of the 1971 Act, shall in those circumstances be available as it would if the power had been revoked (s 1(1)(c)). For practical purposes, it can be said that the protection will be available if the third party concerned did not know of the incapacity.

The fact that the authority of an attorney is restricted pending registration could give rise to another difficulty. This is because a person dealing with an attorney must normally be concerned to ensure that the attorney is acting within the scope of his authority. Such a person might, in the absence of any provision dealing with the matter, have been put on inquiry as to whether or not the attorney's acts were within the powers to maintain and prevent loss conferred by s 1(2) of the 1985 Act (see para **4.6.1**).

It is true that if the third party were unaware of the onset of the donor's mental incapacity, he would be protected by the provision explained above, but the 1985 Act provides some protection even if he does know. Provided the third party does not know that the attorney is acting otherwise than in accordance with his restricted authority, he is entitled to assume that the attorney is acting in accordance with it (s 1(3)). In practice, therefore, a third party should not need to raise requisitions as to whether or not the action in question is within the attorney's statutory power to maintain the donor and others and to prevent loss to the donor's estate.

8.3.3 Protection where the donor never had capacity to grant a power of attorney

The protection conferred on attorneys and third parties by the 1971 Act is not available if the power never existed – for example, because the donor lacked capacity at the time when he purported to grant it. The Law Commission, therefore, proposed that a bona fide attorney and purchaser should be able to rely on the fact of registration as having 'verified the validity' of an instrument as an enduring power once it had been registered as such (Law Com Paper No 122, para 4.88). Such persons should, in principle, be able to assume that the enduring power was validly created and was still subsisting, and registration should confer protection against any irregularities that there might have been.

Section 9(2) of the 1985 Act accordingly provides that where an instrument which did not create a valid enduring power has been registered, an attorney who acts in pursuance of the power should not incur any liability (either to the donor or to any other person) by reason of the non-existence of the power unless, at the time of acting, he knew that either:

(1) the instrument did not create a valid enduring power; or
(2) an event had occurred which, if the instrument had created a valid enduring power, would have had the effect of revoking it; or
(3) if the instrument had created a valid enduring power it would have expired before that time.

Similar protection is available to those dealing with the attorney. Section 9(3) provides that any transaction between the attorney and another person shall, in favour of that person, be as valid as if the power had then been in existence, unless at the time of the transaction that person had knowledge of any of the matters mentioned above.

Chapter 9

THE DUTIES OF AN ATTORNEY UNDER AN ENDURING POWER

9.1 INTRODUCTION

Whereas a *power* authorises the attorney to act, a *duty* requires him to act in a particular way. The duties of an attorney under an enduring power are similar to those of an attorney under an ordinary power. The following summary draws heavily on the Law Commission's report, *The Incapacitated Principal* (1983) (Law Com Paper No 122), which formed the basis of the Enduring Powers of Attorney Act 1985 (the 1985 Act).

9.2 NO DUTY TO ACT

In the absence of any contractual provision to the contrary, an attorney does not generally have any duty to act. The Law Commission considered whether such a duty should be imposed in respect of enduring powers, but decided against it for the following reasons.

> '(Our provisional view) was that the attorney should be under a "duty of prudent management" once he became aware that the donor was incapable. Thus he would be bound to do for the donor everything which he should reasonably be expected to do having regard to the donor's incapacity. The precise nature and extent of the duty would depend on all the circumstances including the skills and qualifications of the attorney.
>
> Having reconsidered this matter, however, we have decided against including any duty to act as part of our recommendations. Whilst a duty to act has strong theoretical attractions, we soon discovered that it would bring with it a number of problems which were soluble only at the expense of considerable additional complexity to our proposed EPA scheme.
>
> One problem was deciding the nature and extent of the duty. It would, we thought, have to cover attending not only to the donor's property and affairs but also to his needs and those of his dependants. The attorney would be expected to bear in mind the manner in which the

donor would have managed his affairs had he then been capable. The duty had to be fairly comprehensive if it was worth having at all. But this gave rise to the next problem.

The duty would be onerous and compliance would at times be difficult. This would be particularly the case where several attorneys had been appointed each of whom might have different ideas as to the manner in which the donor would have run his affairs. There seemed to be a clear risk that the prospect of such a duty to act would either deter people from becoming an attorney under an EPA or, if they were already an attorney, encourage them to disclaim.

A related further problem was that of sanctions where the attorney was in breach of his duty to manage the donor's affairs. Difficult questions began to arise about the measure of damages and remoteness. Could, for example, the donor's dependants sue the attorney and, if so, what could they claim?

We then asked ourselves whether such a duty would often be realistic or necessary. It seemed to us that the duty would be unrealistic in the cases where the attorney was a close relative of the donor – an elderly spouse perhaps. And it would often be unnecessary in cases where the attorney was a professional person who will be paid for his services and who accepts a contractual obligation to act once the donor was no longer capable.

Accordingly, we do not recommend that the attorney be subject to a statutory duty to act. The problems that such a duty would solve would, we feel, be heavily outweighed by those it would create. And we are well aware of the risks of discouraging the acceptance of EPA attorneyships.

In our view, the prospects of a donor's affairs being run after his incapacity are dependent not so much upon duties and sanctions but rather upon his choice of attorney at the outset' (Law Com Paper No 122, paras 4.67–4.69).

An enduring power of attorney (EPA) does not, therefore, impose a duty on the attorney to act, but merely authorises him to act if he wishes. Once he starts acting, however, the attorney will assume a number of duties and will be required to act in a particular way.

9.3 DUTY TO ACT WITHIN THE SCOPE OF THE POWER

The primary duty is to act only within the scope of the actual authority conferred by the power. If he fails in this duty, and the donor thereby suffers loss, the attorney will usually be liable to compensate him. Similarly, he will generally be liable to the donor if he purports to act at a time when the power has been revoked, unless he was unaware of the revocation (Law Com Paper No 122, para 2.13).

Once the power is registered, the attorney's duty to act within its scope can be overridden by the Court of Protection. Under s 8(2) of the 1985 Act the court can give directions with respect to the management or disposal of the donor's property by the attorney, and authorise the attorney to act so as to benefit himself or other persons otherwise than in accordance with the limitations imposed by s 3(4) and (5). This jurisdiction can be invoked prior to registration, but only if the court has reason to believe that the donor is or is becoming mentally incapable, and it considers that it is necessary to exercise its powers under s 8(2) before the power is registered (s 5).

9.4 DUTY OF CARE

An attorney owes a duty of care to the donor in carrying out his functions under the power. The required standard of care depends on whether the attorney is acting gratuitously, whether he is being paid, or whether he is a professional person, such as a solicitor or accountant.

–   If he is not being paid, he must use such care and skill as he would do in the management of his own affairs. He must, however, use such skill as he does in fact possess, or has held himself out as possessing.
–   If he is being paid for his services, he must apply such skill in the performance of his undertaking as is reasonably necessary for the proper performance of the duties undertaken by him.
–   If he undertakes these duties in the course of his profession, he must display normal professional competence (*Hart & Hodge v Frame, Son & Co* (1839) 6 Cl & Fin 193. See, generally, *Bowstead and Reynolds on Agency* 16th edn (Sweet & Maxwell, 1995) and Law Com Paper No 122, para 2.14).

9.5 DUTY NOT TO DELEGATE

It is a basic principle of the law of agency that an agent cannot delegate his authority. This may be expressed as a duty on the part of the attorney to perform his functions under the power *personally*. Such a duty is imposed because of the discretion and trust reposed in the attorney by the donor. There are, however, exceptions to this general rule, and an implied power to delegate may arise in any of the following circumstances:

–   if the act delegated is of a purely ministerial nature and does not involve or require any confidence or discretion (*Rossiter v Trafalgar Life* (1859) 27 Beav 377);
–   where delegation is usual practice in the trade, profession or business of either the donor or the attorney (*De Bussche v Alt* (1878) 8 ChD 286 at 310);
–   through necessity or unforeseen circumstances (*Gwilliam v Twist* [1895] 2 QB 84); or

– where power to delegate may be implied from the parties' conduct (*De Bussche v Alt*, above).

Like any other agent, an attorney acting under an enduring power has an implied power to delegate any of his functions to which the donor would not expect him to attend to personally. Any wider power of delegation has to be provided for expressly in the instrument (Law Com Paper No 122, para 4.22).

9.6 DUTY NOT TO TAKE ADVANTAGE OF HIS POSITION

In carrying out his functions under the power, the attorney owes the donor duties of a fiduciary nature. He must avoid conflicts between his responsibilities to the donor and his own personal interests. Thus, he must refrain from entering into transactions in which such a conflict might arise unless the donor, with full knowledge of all the material circumstances, gives his consent. Nor can the attorney, without such consent, use his position as an attorney to acquire any benefit for himself, whether or not this would be at the donor's expense (*Parker v McKenna* (1874) LR 10 Ch App 96).

This duty is affected by the provisions of s 3(4) and (5) of the 1985 Act, which respectively confer on the attorney a power to provide for the needs of persons other than the donor (including himself) and a limited power to make gifts to persons related to or connected with the donor (including himself) (see paras **4.4** and **4.5**).

9.7 DUTY OF GOOD FAITH

The attorney acting under an enduring power must act in good faith in the exercise of his authority. There is one aspect of this duty which is particularly relevant to registered powers. A disposal by the attorney of any of the donor's assets might affect the entitlement of the persons interested in the donor's estate after his death. The Law Commission, having identified the problem, felt that there was nothing it could usefully recommend to prevent this happening. It concluded, however, that 'if bad faith were established we have no doubt that the court would consider terminating the EPA by making a receivership or similar order' (Law Com Paper No 122, paras 4.63–4.64; see also *Re Dorman (deceased)* [1994] 2 FLR 52, ChD).

9.8 DUTY TO KEEP ACCOUNTS

An attorney is expected to keep and be constantly ready to produce correct accounts of all his dealings and transactions on the donor's behalf (*Gray v Haig* (1855) 20 Beav 219). He also has a duty to produce to the donor, or to anyone appointed by the donor, all books and documents he has relating to the donor's affairs (*Dadswell v Jacobs* (1887) 34 ChD 278). Where an enduring power has been registered, the Court of Protection can give directions with respect to the rendering of accounts and the production of records kept by the attorney (s 8(2)(b)(ii)).

9.9 DUTY TO KEEP DONOR'S MONEY AND PROPERTY SEPARATE

The attorney should keep the donor's money and property separate from his own and other people's money and property (*Henry v Hammond* [1913] 2 KB 515). It is, of course, open to the parties to agree other arrangements. For example, a husband and wife, who were respectively the donor and attorney under an enduring power, might agree to keep their money in a joint bank account (Law Com Paper No 122, p 6, fn 33).

9.10 DUTY OF CONFIDENTIALITY

Like any other agent, an attorney acting under an enduring power has a duty to keep the donor's affairs confidential, unless the donor consents to their disclosure. This duty continues even after the power has come to an end (*Amber Size and Chemical Co Ltd v Menzel* [1913] 2 Ch 239).

9.11 DUTY TO APPLY FOR REGISTRATION OF THE POWER

There is an important exception to the general principle that an attorney has no specific duty to act under the 1985 Act. The attorney has a duty to apply to the Court of Protection for registration if he has reason to believe that the donor is or is becoming mentally incapable (s 4(1)) (see paras **3.2–3.4**). This duty is acknowledged by the attorney when he signs Part C of the prescribed form of enduring power (reproduced in Appendix 5 to this book).

9.12 DUTY TO COMPLY WITH DIRECTIONS OF THE COURT

If the attorney has reason to believe that the donor is or is becoming mentally incapable, before making an application for the registration of the power, he may refer any question as to the validity of the power to the Court of Protection. The attorney must comply with any direction given by the court on that determination (s 4(5)).

Once the power has been registered the court has specific functions (s 8(1)) (see para **5.6**). These include a power to give directions with respect to the rendering of accounts and the production of records by the attorney; and to require the attorney to furnish information or produce documents or things in his possession as attorney (s 8(2)(b)(ii) and (c)). The attorney has a duty to comply with such directions.

9.13 DUTY NOT TO DISCLAIM WITHOUT NOTIFYING THE DONOR OR THE COURT

A disclaimer of an unregistered enduring power is invalid unless and until the attorney gives notice of it to the donor (s 2(12)). Once an application has been made for the power to be registered, and as long as it remains registered, the attorney cannot disclaim unless and until he gives notice to the court (ss 4(6) and 7(1)(b)). See, generally, para **6.3.1**. Thus, although an attorney appointed under an enduring power has no specific duty to manage the donor's affairs, indirectly he could be put in a position in which he is required to make a choice: either act, or renounce the right to act.

9.14 DUTY TO ACT IN THE BEST INTERESTS OF AN INCAPACITATED DONOR

In 1995, the Law Commission published a report entitled *Mental Incapacity* (Law Com Paper No 231) which proposed wide-ranging reforms of the law relating to decision-making on behalf of mentally incapacitated adults. Its proposals were based on the fundamental principle that anything done for, and any decision made on behalf of, a person without capacity must be done or made in that person's best interests. The Commission's draft Bill, if enacted, will make this a statutory duty. At present, to act in the best interests of someone without capacity is a matter of good practice, but otherwise is probably no more than a strong moral obligation.

In deciding what is in an incapacitated person's best interests, the Law Commission suggested that regard should be had to the following:

- so far as ascertainable, his past and present wishes and feelings;
- so far as ascertainable, the factors which he would consider if he were able to do so;
- the need to permit and encourage him to participate, or to improve his ability to participate, as fully as possible in anything done for and any decision affecting him;
- if it is practicable and appropriate to consult them, the views of anyone engaged in caring for him, or who is interested in his welfare, as to what his wishes and feelings may be and as to what they think would be in his best interests; and
- trying to achieve the purpose for which any action or decision is required in a manner which is less restrictive of his freedom of action (draft Bill, cl 3).

Chapter 10

SOLICITORS AND ENDURING POWERS

10.1 WHO IS THE CLIENT?

10.1.1 Introduction

In 1991, a team of researchers from the Faculty of Law at Bristol University noted a widespread divergence in practice among solicitors as to whether they considered that they were acting for the donor, the attorney or the family generally (*Enduring Powers of Attorney: A Report to the Lord Chancellor* (Lord Chancellor's Department, June 1991) paras 2.5 and 2.6).

10.1.2 The donor is the client

Where a solicitor is instructed to prepare an enduring power of attorney (EPA), the donor is the client (The Law Society *Guide to the Professional Conduct of Solicitors* 9th edn (1999), Principle 24.03, note 1). The attorney is merely the statutory agent of the donor, just as in proceedings under the Mental Health Act 1983 a receiver is the statutory agent of a patient (*Re EG* [1914] 1 Ch 927, CA). The donor remains the client after he has become mentally incapable.

10.1.3 Taking instructions

When asked to prepare an enduring power on written instructions alone, a solicitor should always consider carefully whether these instructions are sufficient, or whether he should see the client personally to discuss them (*Guide to the Professional Conduct of Solicitors*, Principle 12.05).

Where instructions for the preparation of an enduring power are received not from the donor, but from a third party purporting to represent him, a solicitor should obtain written instructions from the donor that he wishes the solicitor to act. In any case of doubt, the solicitor should see the client personally or take other appropriate steps to confirm the instructions. The solicitor must also advise the donor without regard to the interests of the source from which he was introduced.

10.1.4 Court of Protection proceedings

If the donor is within its jurisdiction, the Court of Protection can expressly confirm the solicitor's authority to act for the donor (*Practice Direction: Authority for Solicitors to Act for Patients or Donors*, issued by the Master of the Court of Protection on 9 August 1995; see Appendix 9 to this book).

10.2 REMUNERATION OF SOLICITOR/ATTORNEYS

Some years ago, The Law Society expressed the opinion that where a client appoints a solicitor to be his attorney, the solicitor is entitled to be paid not only for the professional services in preparing the power of attorney, but also for the non-professional services in acting as an attorney (Opinion: 14 March 1958 (1 *Law Society's Digest*, 4th Cum Supp, p 96)). However, The Law Society now recommends that, as a matter of good practice, where a solicitor is appointed as attorney, a professional charging clause should be expressly included in the instrument, and that the factors on which the fees are based should be discussed with the client and agreed at the time of execution of the power (The Law Society *Enduring Powers of Attorney: Guidelines for Solicitors* (1999)). See also para **2.5.3**.

10.3 DUTY NOT TO TAKE ADVANTAGE OF THE CLIENT

A solicitor who holds a power of attorney from a client must not use that power to gain a benefit which, if acting as a professional adviser to that client, he would not be prepared to allow to an independent third party. Similarly, he must not take advantage of the age, inexperience, want of education, business experience or ill-health of the client.

10.4 DISCLAIMER BY SOLICITOR/ATTORNEYS WHEN DONOR'S ASSETS ARE INSUFFICIENT

The Law Society has expressed concern over cases where solicitors, who have agreed to act as an attorney, subsequently disclaim their appointment when the donor's assets prove to be insufficient to make the exercise cost-effective (The Law Society *Enduring Powers of Attorney: Guidelines for Solicitors* (1999)). As was noted in para **9.1**, there is no statutory duty for an attorney to act under an enduring power, and the reason why the Law Commission felt it unnecessary to recommend that there be such a duty was that a professional person who will be paid for his services accepts a contractual obligation to act once the donor is mentally incapable (*The Incapacitated Principal* (1983) Law Com Paper No 122, para 4.68). See also para **6.3.2**.

10.5 DISCLOSURE OF THE DONOR'S WILL TO THE ATTORNEY

Principle 24.03 in the *Guide to the Professional Conduct of Solicitors*, identifies three scenarios.

(1) Where the donor retains capacity and the EPA is unregistered
In this case the donor's instructions must always be sought. This is because the donor's will is confidential to the donor and it cannot be disclosed to anyone without the donor's consent (ibid, Principle 16.01)

(2) Where the EPA is registered and the solicitor is acting for the donor
If the donor has testamentary capacity in accordance with the criteria set out in *Banks v Goodfellow* (1870) LR 5 QB 549, the donor's instructions must be sought. If the donor no longer has testamentary capacity, the solicitor should seek the advice of the Court of Protection or Public Guardianship Office, and indicate whether or not disclosure is in the best interests of the donor.

(3) Where the EPA is registered, but the solicitor holding the will is not currently acting for the donor
If the donor has testamentary capacity, the solicitor must ask the attorney to obtain the donor's consent to disclosure, or may wish to consider obtaining advice from the Court of Protection, the Public Guardianship Office or the Law Society's professional ethics directorate.

Although it may be in the donor's interests for there to be disclosure in order to avoid the possibility of the attorney acting contrary to the donor's wishes in dealing with his property and affairs, there may be circumstances in which it would not be in the donor's interests for disclosure to take place.

When drafting an EPA, it is always advisable to take specific instructions about authorising disclosure of the donor's will to the attorney. Such authorisation might, for example, be subject to the proviso that the donor is or is becoming mentally incapable and the solicitor considers disclosure of the will to be necessary or expedient for the proper exercise of the attorney's functions.

As was noted in para **9.9**, the attorney himself is under a duty to keep the donor's affairs confidential. Thus, if a solicitor discloses the donor's will to the attorney, he should consider obtaining an undertaking from the attorney that he will not divulge the contents to any third party.

Chapter 11

TRUSTEES

11.1 BACKGROUND

11.1.1 Introduction

The essence of a trust is that property is held by the trustees as owners, but that they hold it on behalf of other people, known as beneficiaries. Trustees themselves can be beneficiaries, in which case they have two distinct and separate roles. As a rule – which has gradually become subject to various exceptions – trustees cannot delegate the exercise of their functions. The reasoning behind this rule is that the person who created the trust had specifically selected and entrusted particular people to be the trustees, perhaps for their personal qualities, their unquestionable integrity or their business acumen, and that any delegation by them would be a betrayal of that trust.

11.1.2 Non-statutory powers of delegation

Before trustees were permitted by statute to delegate their functions to someone else, delegation was allowed in three circumstances:

– if the instrument creating the trust authorised it; or
– if the beneficiaries permitted it, provided that they were ascertained and of full age and capacity. This could include authority to delegate in a manner that was not authorised by the instrument creating the trust; or
– if the act delegated was purely ministerial and did not involve the exercise of a discretion, for example, *Re Hetling and Merton's Contract* [1893] 3 Ch 269.

11.1.3 Early statutory powers of delegation

Clearly, in some cases it was difficult or impossible for a trustee to exercise his duties personally, and this became particularly problematic during the First

World War. The Execution of Trusts (War Facilities) Acts 1914 and 1915 authorised trustees who were 'engaged on war service' to delegate their functions 'for the duration'. This power of delegation was placed on a permanent footing by the property legislation in the 1920s (Law of Property Act 1922, s 127A, inserted by the Law of Property (Amendment) Act 1924, Sch 5, para 8).

11.1.4 Trustee Act 1925

Section 23(1) of the Trustee Act 1925 permitted a trustee to employ agents, including solicitors, stockbrokers and bankers. Section 23(2) of that Act allowed a trustee to appoint an attorney to deal with assets outside the United Kingdom.

Section 25 permitted a trustee to delegate his functions generally if he intended to remain out of the United Kingdom for more than a month. Such a delegation was subject to various safeguards, some of which still apply today. For example, the donor/trustee had to give notice to any person who was entitled to appoint a new trustee, and remained liable for the donee's acts and defaults.

11.1.5 Powers of Attorney Act 1971

Section 9 of the Powers of Attorney Act 1971 (the 1971 Act) amended s 25 of the Trustee Act 1925 to allow a trustee to delegate by a power of attorney all or any of his functions as a trustee, personal representative, tenant for life or statutory owner for a period not exceeding 12 months. The amendments contained in s 9 of the 1971 Act have now been superseded by the further amendments in s 5 of the Trustee Delegation Act 1999 (see para **11.2.5**).

Section 10(1) of the 1971 Act provides that, subject to s 10(2), a general power of attorney in the form set out in Sch 1 to the Act, or in a form to the like effect but expressed to be made under the Act, shall operate to confer on the donee of the power (and, if there is more than one donee, on the donees acting jointly, or jointly and severally, as the case may be) authority to do on behalf of the donor anything which he can lawfully do by an attorney.

Section 10(2) of the Act, however, provides that the general authority conferred by s 10(1) does not apply to functions which the donor has as a trustee, personal representative, tenant for life or statutory owner within the meaning of the Settled Land Act 1925.

11.1.6 *The Incapacitated Principal* (1983)

The Enduring Powers of Attorney Act 1985 (the 1985 Act) implemented most of the recommendations made by the Law Commission in its report, *The Incapacitated Principal* (1983) Law Com Paper No 122. A draft Bill, almost identical to that which was eventually enacted, was published in the appendix to that report.

The Law Commission's intention was that the donor of an enduring power of attorney (EPA) should not be able to delegate his functions as trustee by means of an enduring power. It stated:

> 'It follows ... that the EPA scheme would be inappropriate for some types of power. ... We would exclude powers granted by trustees pursuant to s 25 of the Trustee Act 1925. Under that section a trustee may delegate the exercise of his functions for a period of up to 12 months. Clearly little practical value could attach to setting up an EPA with such a short life (only part of which could represent a period during which the donor would be incapable); in any event, the Trustee Act 1925 itself contains provisions for the replacement of incapable trustees' (Law Com Paper No 122, para 4.2).

For this reason cl 2(8) of the draft Bill, which was later enacted verbatim as s 2(8) of the 1985 Act, specifically provided that 'a power of attorney under section 25 of the Trustee Act 1925 (power to delegate trusts etc. by power of attorney) cannot be an enduring power'. Section 2(8) of the 1985 Act has now been repealed by s 12 of the Trustee Delegation Act 1999.

11.1.7 *Walia v Michael Naughton Ltd*

While the Enduring Powers of Attorney Bill was before Parliament, a case was decided in the Chancery Division which had a profound impact on the legislation ultimately enacted. In *Walia v Michael Naughton Ltd* [1985] 1 WLR 1115, it was held that a general power of attorney in the form specified in s 10(1) of the Powers of Attorney Act 1971 was insufficient for the purpose of delegating the donor's functions as a trustee of land that he owned jointly with others. For that purpose a delegation pursuant to s 25 of the Trustee Act 1925 was required.

The then Lord Chancellor, Lord Hailsham of St Marylebone, was concerned about the effect of the decision in *Walia* on the EPA scheme in relation to the co-ownership of a home. The typical scenario he envisaged is where a married couple jointly hold their matrimonial home as trustees on trust for sale for themselves as beneficiaries.

> 'Most married couples nowadays hold the matrimonial home upon trust for sale, so that the inability of the attorney under an enduring power to dispose of trust property would have widespread effect and reduce the efficacy of the scheme contained in the bill' (*Hansard* (HL), cols 548–549 (24 June 1985)).

11.1.8 Enduring Powers of Attorney Act 1985, s 3(3)

To overcome the problems identified by *Walia v Michael Naughton Ltd*, s 3(3) of the 1985 Act was hastily drafted. It provided that:

> 'Subject to any conditions or restrictions contained in the instrument, an attorney under an enduring power, whether general or limited, may (without obtaining any consent) execute or exercise all or any of the trusts, powers or discretions vested in the donor as trustee and may (without the concurrence of any other person) give a valid receipt for capital or other money paid.'

11.1.9 Section 3(3) – a legislative blunder?

Even before the 1985 Act came into force in March 1986, the provisions of s 3(3) of the Act were the subject of a scathing attack by Richard Oerton in an article 'Trustees and the Enduring Powers of Attorney Act 1985: a Legislative Blunder' (1986) 130 SJ 23.

The main problems with s 3(3) were that:

– it provided none of the safeguards for beneficiaries that are required under s 25 of the Trustee Act 1925;
– the delegation remained operative after the donor had become mentally incapacitated;
– it applied automatically and could occur inadvertently; and
– there was statutory duplication with s 25 of the Trustee Act 1925.

11.1.10 The Law Commission's report

In response to these and similar criticisms, the Law Commission published a consultation paper in April 1991, *The Law of Trusts: Delegation by Individual Trustees* (Law Com Paper No 118), which provisionally recommended two separate regimes: first, a general scheme which would apply to all trusts; and, secondly, a special scheme for cases where the trustees held property on trust for themselves alone.

In January 1994 the Law Commission published a report, *The Law of Trusts: Delegation by Individual Trustees* (Law Com Paper No 220), recommending the repeal of s 3(3) of the 1985 Act. The report contained a draft Trustee Delegation Bill, which was introduced in the House of Lords in December 1998. The Trustee Delegation Act 1999 received Royal Assent in July 1999 and came into force on 1 March 2000.

11.2 TRUSTEE DELEGATION ACT 1999

11.2.1 Exercise of trustee functions by attorney

The general rule is that any trustee functions delegated to an attorney (whether under an ordinary power or enduring power) must comply with the provisions of s 25 of the Trustee Act 1925 (as substituted by the Trustee Delegation Act 1999 (the 1999 Act), s 5).

However, s 1(1) of the 1999 Act provides an important exception to this general rule. An attorney can exercise a trustee function of the donor if it relates to land, or the capital proceeds, or income from land, in which the donor has a beneficial interest. This is, of course, subject to any provision to the contrary contained in either the trust instrument or the power of attorney itself.

11.2.2 Evidence of beneficial interest

Clearly, anyone who purchases land from an attorney needs to be satisfied that the donor has a beneficial interest in the land. Accordingly, s 2 of the 1999 Act provides that an 'appropriate statement', made by the attorney at the time of the sale or up to 3 months thereafter, confirming that the donor had a beneficial interest in the property, shall be conclusive evidence. The Land Registry's Practice Leaflet 32, *Powers of Attorney and Registered Land* (see Appendix 7) suggests that the most convenient place for the attorney to make this written statement will be in the disposition itself. The attorney may:

– include a statement on the following lines in the additional provisions panel of a TR1 or other prescribed form, or in the body of a lease or charge:

   (*Name of attorney*) confirms that (*donor of the power*), has a beneficial interest in the property at the date of this (*transfer, charge, etc.*).

or

– adapt the attestation clause as follows:

   Signed as a deed by (*name of donor of the power*), who has a beneficial interest in the property at the date of this (*transfer, charge, etc.*), acting by (*his/her*) attorney (*name of attorney*) in the presence of.

or

– expand the words of the signature as follows:

   John Smith by his attorney Jane Brown who confirms that the donor has a beneficial interest in the property at the date hereof.

If the applicant for registration cannot produce an appropriate statement pursuant to s 2 of the 1999 Act, the Land Registry will consider other evidence that the donor had a beneficial interest in the property at the relevant time. A statutory declaration to that effect by a responsible person with full knowledge of the facts may be acceptable in some cases.

If an attorney makes a false appropriate statement, he will be liable in the same way as if he had made a false statutory declaration (s 2(4)).

11.2.3 General powers in specified form

Section 3 of the 1999 Act relates to ordinary (rather than enduring) powers of attorney. It provides that an attorney, acting under a general power in the form specified by the Powers of Attorney Act 1971, s 10, may exercise the trustee functions of the donor in relation to land, etc, in which the donor has a beneficial interest. In effect, this section is a statutory reversal of the decision in *Walia v Michael Naughton Ltd* (see para **11.2.4**).

11.2.4 Enduring powers of attorney

Section 4 of the 1999 Act affects enduring powers of attorney, including some that are already in existence. Section 12 and the Schedule to the 1999 Act repeal s 3(3) of the 1985 Act, subject to the following transitional provisions:

- s 3(3) does not apply to any EPA created on or after 1 March 2000, the date on which the 1999 Act came into force;
- s 3(3) will cease to apply to an existing registered EPA if and when the registration is cancelled under s 8(4) of the 1985 Act;
- s 3(3) will cease to apply to an EPA created before 1 March 2000, in respect of which a successful application to register is made before 1 March 2001, if and when the registration of the power is cancelled;
- s 3(3) will cease to apply to an EPA created before 1 March 2000, in respect of which an unsuccessful application to register is made before 1 March 2001, when the application is finally refused (the meaning of which is defined in s 4(5) of the 1999 Act);
- in all other cases, s 3(3) will cease to apply on 1 March 2001 to any EPA created before 1 March 2000, in respect of which no application to register has been made before 1 March 2001.

Where s 3(3) does not apply, or when it ceases to apply, s 1(1) of the 1999 Act will apply instead. In other words, the trustee delegation will be effective only insofar as it relates to land, capital proceeds of a conveyance of land, or income from land in which the donor has a beneficial interest.

11.2.5 Amendments to the Trustee Act 1925, s 25

Any delegation of trust functions (other than those in respect of land, etc, in which the donor has a beneficial interest) must comply with the provisions of s 25 of the Trustee Act 1925, as substituted by s 5 of the 1999 Act, which contains various safeguards. In brief, these are:

- a trustee may, by a power of attorney, delegate his functions as a trustee for a period of 12 months or any shorter period commencing on the date specifed in the instrument, or, if the instrument states no commencement date, on the date of the execution of the instrument by the donor (s 25(2));
- the trustee must, before or within 7 days after giving such a power of attorney, give notice to each of his co-trustees and to any person who has power under the trust instrument to appoint a new trustee (s 25(4));
- the power of attorney must be in the form set out in s 25(6), or in a form to the like effect but expressed to be made under s 25 of the Trustee Act 1925 (s 25(5));
- the donor/trustee remains liable for the acts or defaults of the attorney in the same manner as if they were the acts or defaults of the donor/trustee (s 25(7)).

Section 25 also applies to a personal representative, tenant for life and statutory owner, except that different persons are entitled to receive notice of the delegation (s 25(10)).

The form of trustee delegation set out in s 25(6) is as follows:

> THIS GENERAL TRUSTEE POWER OF ATTORNEY is made on (*date*) by (*name of one donor*) of (*address of donor*) as trustee of (*name or details of one trust*).
>
> I appoint (*name of one donee*) of (*address of donee*) to be my attorney (*if desired, the date on which the delegation commences or the period for which it continues (or both)*) in accordance with section 25 of the Trustee Act 1925.
>
> (*To be executed as a deed*)

The notice to be given by the donor to the persons entitled to receive it pursuant to s 25(4) or (10) must specify:

- the date on which the power comes into operation;
- the duration of the power;
- the donee of the power;
- the reason why the power is given; and
- where only some of the trusts, powers and discretions are delegated, the trusts, powers and discretions that are delegated.

In its unamended form, s 25 of the Trustee Act 1925 provided that the donee of a power of attorney could not (unless it were a trust corporation) be the only other co-trustee of the donor. The new s 25(3) effectively removes that prohibition. The desired objective of there being at least two trustees or a trust corporation at the relevant time is now covered instead by s 7 of the 1999 Act (see para **11.2.7**).

11.2.6 Section 25 powers as enduring powers

Sections 6 and 12 of the 1999 Act repeal s 2(8) of the 1985 Act: the section which stated that a power of attorney granted under s 25 of the Trustee Act 1925 cannot be an enduring power. This means that a donor can now use an EPA to delegate trustee functions. However, the requirements of the amended s 25 (such as duration, notice and wording) will apply to such a delegation. For the reasons stated by the Law Commission in Law Com Paper No 122, para 4.2, there would be little practical value in creating such a power (see para **11.1.6**).

11.2.7 The two-trustee rules

Sections 7, 8 and 9 of the 1999 Act contain a number of miscellaneous provisions concerning attorneys acting for trustees.

The 'two-trustee' rules provide that:

— capital monies arising from land must be paid to, or at the direction of, at least two trustees (Law of Property Act 1925, s 27(2); Settled Land Act 1925, ss 18(1)(c) and 94(1));
— a valid receipt for capital monies must be given otherwise than by a sole trustee (Trustee Act 1925, s 14(2)); and
— a conveyance or deed must be made by at least two trustees in order to overreach any powers or interests affecting a legal estate in land (Law of Property Act 1925, s 2(1)(ii)).

Section 7 of the 1999 Act is designed to clarify and strengthen these rules by providing that they can be satisfied either by two people acting jointly in the same capacity, or by two people acting in different capacities. However, they cannot be satisfied by one person acting in two capacities, ie both as a trustee and as an attorney of the other trustee(s), or as attorney for both or all of the trustees.

For example: A and B jointly own a house. They both appoint their daughter, C, to be their sole attorney. C, acting alone, would not satisfy the two-trustee rules. If, however, A had appointed C, and B had appointed D, to be their respective attorneys, C and D could act together and thereby satisfy the two-trustee rules. The same would apply if A and B had appointed C and D jointly, or jointly and severally, to be their attorneys.

11.2.8 Appointment of additional trustee by the attorney

Section 8 of the 1999 Act inserts some new subsections into the Trustee Act 1925, s 36(6), and enables the attorney under an EPA created on or after 1 March 2000, and subsequently registered, to appoint an additional trustee to satisfy the two-trustee rules.

For example: E and F are husband and wife and jointly own their house. They both appoint each other to be their sole attorney under an enduring power. E becomes mentally incapable and F registers the power. F then wants to sell the house. F can appoint G to be an additional trustee in order to satisfy the two-trustee rules.

11.2.9 Attorney acting for an incapable trustee

Section 22(2) of the Law of Property Act 1925 provides that if there is a trust of land, and the land is vested in an incapable trustee, whether solely or jointly, the incapable trustee must be discharged before the legal estate can be dealt with. Section 9 of the 1999 Act inserted a new subs (3) into s 22 of the Law of Property Act 1925, which provides that the legal estate can be dealt with without the appointment of a new trustee, or the discharge of the incapable trustee, if there is an attorney under an enduring power who is authorised to act for the incapable trustee.

Chapter 12

FINANCIAL ABUSE AND ENDURING POWERS

12.1 EXTENT OF THE PROBLEM

Most attorneys are honest, decent people. However, some take liberties and a few are out-and-out crooks. Financial abuse probably occurs in about 10–15% of cases. Expressed as a percentage this may seem to be a relatively minor problem, and maybe even an acceptable price for to pay for the 85–90% of cases where attorneys act lawfully.

Since the Enduring Powers of Attorney Act 1985 (the 1985 Act) came into force, over 100,000 powers have been registered, and the number of powers being registered each year has now risen to about 12,500. The percentages given above cover a wide range of abuse, from making unauthorised gifts, at one extreme, to criminally masterminded frauds, at the other. Fortunately, criminal abuse accounts for an extremely small minority of cases.

The largest fraud unearthed so far involved a sum of £2 million, most of which had been temporarily deposited by the attorney in a Swiss bank account en route for the United States and ultimately Australia. The donor was a spinster in her nineties, without any known relatives. The attorney of the unregistered power was the proprietor of the residential care home in which she resided, who had also managed to procure a will in his favour.

12.2 POWERS OF THE COURT OF PROTECTION

The powers of the Court of Protection are surprisingly limited in cases where the donor of an enduring power of attorney (EPA) is being financially abused. The court has no criminal jurisdiction, and no jurisdiction to set aside a fraudulent transaction.

- The court can intervene only where the donor of the power is, or is becoming, mentally incapable. Generally, it is not concerned with unregistered powers, which is where most instances of financial abuse occur.

- The court has supervisory powers under s 8(2) of the 1985 Act and can, for example, require an attorney to render accounts, provide information and produce records, documents or things in his possession. A hardened criminal is hardly likely to be intimidated by requests of this kind.

- The court can revoke an EPA, but in many cases this is about as useful as closing the stable door after the horse has bolted.

- The court can appoint a receiver or interim receiver with authority to investigate and report on prior dealings with the donor's assets, but this imposes a considerable burden on an individual to obtain the necessary evidence to pursue the matter to a successful conclusion.

- The court can also authorise the receiver or interim receiver to apply to the Chancery Division of the High Court for appropriate relief. However, this is time-consuming and expensive, and can be justified only if the donor is wealthy (or was, until the attorney started meddling).

12.3 WHY ABUSE OCCURS

It is much easier for financial abuse to occur under an attorneyship than in a receivership under the Mental Health Act 1983. There are several reasons why.

12.3.1 The public domain

A receiver is appointed only when the court, after considering medical evidence, is satisfied that a person is incapable, by reason of mental disorder, of managing and administering his property and affairs. The applicant is required to notify the patient's next-of-kin of the application to appoint a receiver. An EPA, however, usually comes into effect immediately – as soon as it is executed – and the attorney may simply decide not to apply for registration, notwithstanding the supervening incapacity of the donor. Relatives do not need to be informed of the creation of an EPA, and most powers never even enter the public domain. The authors of *Enduring Powers of Attorney: A Report to the Lord Chancellor* (Lord Chancellor's Department, 1991) estimated that only 1 in 20 powers is registered.

12.3.2 No supervision by the court

The court supervises the activities of a receiver but, generally speaking, does not monitor an attorney's dealings. This is the whole point of the 1985 Act. It is meant to provide a less bureaucratic means of managing the affairs of someone who lacks capacity. Section 8(2) of the Act confers on the court a number of functions with respect to registered powers, but these are discretionary rather than mandatory, and it requires a whistle-blower to invoke them.

12.3.3 Unlimited access to income and capital

A receiver has authority to receive the patient's income and to apply it for the patient's maintenance, but no authority to deal with the patient's capital unless specifically authorised to do so by the court. An attorney, however, has unrestricted access to the donor's income and capital.

12.3.4 Gifts

A receiver has to obtain authority from the court before making a gift. Although an attorney has a limited power to make gifts under s 3(5) of the 1985 Act without having to apply for an order or direction, the provisions of the Act are frequently flouted, and the most widespread form of abuse in attorneyship is improper gifting.

12.3.5 No accountability

A receiver is required to produce annual accounts. An attorney does not have to account to anyone as a matter of course, although he has a common law duty to keep accounts and to be ready to produce them on request at any time (*Gray v Haig* (1855) 20 Beav 219; *Dadswell v Jacobs* (1887) 34 Ch D 278). On those occasions when the court has ordered an attorney to furnish accounts, many accounts have been unsatisfactory or unhelpful.

12.3.6 No security

A receiver is required to give security for his defaults (Court of Protection Rules 2001, rr 56–60). An attorney is not required to provide security. In fact, this is impossible to obtain because no insurance company is prepared to cover the risk.

12.3.7 Costs

In a receivership, the costs rules of the Civil Procedure Rules 1998 apply (Court of Protection Rules 2001, r 86). There are no such constraints on attorneyship and, basically, solicitors can charge what they like. Situations have arisen where a solicitor who is the sole attorney has taken advantage of an incapacitated donor by excessive billing, both in frequency and amount. The solicitor has simply rendered the bill to himself as attorney, and paid it from the donor's funds without independent scrutiny.

12.3.8 Copies

Even where a power has been revoked, copies – and perhaps the original itself – could still be at large. It may be impossible to prevent a fraudulent attorney from continuing to use the power.

12.3.9 Forgery

It is extremely simple to forge a donor's and a witness's signature on an EPA form. It is not so easy to forge an order of the court impressed with the court's seal.

12.4 DONORS AT RISK

No formal research has been carried out to identify the donors who are particularly at risk, so what follows is largely intuitive. Generally speaking, people who have no immediate family are more exposed than those with a family. Donors with only one child are at greater risk than those with two or more children. Donors who are moderately affluent seem to be more vulnerable than the extremely rich or extremely poor. Donors who suddenly come into additional wealth through inheritance on the death of a relative are at an increased risk of exploitation and are often made party to a deed of variation, regardless of whether it can be justified on bona fide tax-planning grounds.

An aggravating factor is the expectation of inheritance and the desire to preserve and precipitate it. Some people believe that they have an indefeasible right to inherit another person's estate intact, and in a number of cases the attorneys have disposed of the donor's assets to secure entitlement to public funding for long-term care. The risk of abuse is higher if the attorney lives overseas, and there have been several occasions when the entire assets of a donor who is resident here have been transferred out of the jurisdiction.

The abuser's own characteristics are also important, especially where his financial resources fail to gratify his expectations. In one case, an attorney financed her children's private education wholly from the funds of her incapacitated aunt, who would never have contemplated such expenditure if she were still of sound mind.

Mutual dependency poses a particular problem. Not only is the donor dependent on the attorney as the principal or only carer, but the attorney is also dependent on the donor, especially where they share living accommodation and financial arrangements. In these situations it is hard to distinguish a saint from a sinner.

12.5 SIGNS OF ABUSE

There are some fairly common signs of abuse which arouse suspicion, at least, that the attorney may be exploiting the donor. Among the signs to watch for are as follows:

– unpaid bills, for example accumulated arrears of nursing home or residential care home fees;
– the removal of title deeds from the bank or solicitors' office where they have traditionally been held. Although the Land Registry will challenge any outright gift which has not been authorised by the Court of Protection, it will not automatically query transfers at an undervalue and will, of course, have no knowledge as to whether money actually did change hands;
– the opening of credit card accounts;
– the denial to relatives or friends of access to the donor. This may be active denial on the part of the attorney, or passive denial, where the donor suddenly expresses the wish not to be visited by members of the family or longstanding friends;
– the denial of access to a medical practitioner to see the donor;
– the transfer of assets out of the jurisdiction;
– the fact that the attorney resides outside the jurisdiction;
– unusual or extravagant expenditure by the attorney, for example, expensive cars, holidays, jewellery, and generally living the high life. Often the funds misappropriated by attorneys are dissipated rapidly;
– expenditure that clearly bears no relation to the donor's own requirements in life;
– sudden, unexplained changes in living arrangements, for example, where a younger person moves in to care for an elderly person whom they have only just met or with whom they have had little previous contact.

12.6 DIFFICULTIES IN PURSUING THE ABUSER

Should society punish dishonest attorneys and, if so, how? Is it in the donor's interests for an attorney – who is usually a close relative – to be prosecuted for theft, or for civil proceedings to be commenced which, even if successful, will recover assets that the attorney may inherit anyway? Or is there a greater public interest to which the interests of the donor should yield?

Where the abuser is a member of the victim's family, the police are generally reluctant to investigate what they consider to be a domestic problem or a matter that is better suited to the civil justice system. There is often difficulty in identifying a criminal act (as distinct from one which is merely beyond the scope of the power, for example a gift that is unreasonable having regard to the size of the donor's estate).

Even where the police have investigated the matter thoroughly, the Crown Prosecution Service often declines to prosecute on the grounds that the donor is mentally incapacitated and would not be a reliable witness. In cases where a decision is made to prosecute, the charge is usually one of theft.

Solicitors are generally reluctant to get involved in civil proceedings. Often they have acted for both the donor and the attorney and sense that there may be a conflict of interests. Sometimes they advised the donor to create the power in the first place, and sense that they might be partly responsible for facilitating the abuse. Solicitors may also feel that they have insufficient specialist knowledge to handle a major fraud case, and often the likely benefits of commencing civil proceedings are outweighed by the potential costs.

Additional difficulties are caused by the connivance of family members who stand to gain from the financial abuse, and the psychological pressures exerted by the abuser to get the victim to drop proceedings.

12.7 PREVENTING ABUSE

Professional advisers could be more discriminating when recommending that clients create an enduring power. In some cases, a receivership will be patently preferable to an attorneyship, especially where the client comes from an unreliable or dysfunctional family and has a relatively short-life expectation. The Public Guardianship Office's annual administration fee will be inconsequential compared with the costs of a contested EPA application or proceedings in the Chancery Division.

Because of their involvement when the power is created, professional advisers are at the front line when it comes to risk assessment. They may be better placed than anyone else to gauge a client's vulnerability and could be far more candid with donors when considering the suitability of a proposed attorney. Apart from questions of probity, many attorneys lack the basic skills to manage their own finances – let alone someone else's.

Sole attorneyships provide more scope for abuse than *joint and several* attorneyships, and *joint and several* attorneyships provide a greater opportunity for exploitation than *joint* attorneyships.

Unprofessional conduct must be avoided at the time of creating the power. Many enduring powers are made when the donors are already mentally incapacitated. Consequently, they could be unaware of the implications of their actions and are more likely to be vulnerable to exploitation. Professional advisers should be particularly wary about preparing an enduring power – on instructions from the potential attorney – for a donor for whom they have never previously acted.

Solicitors could offer auditing services to their clients. A clause could be inserted in the power requiring the attorney to produce to the donor's solicitor – on a specified date each year – an account of his dealings during the last 12 months. If the attorney fails to render a satisfactory account, the solicitor could apply for the registration of the power to be cancelled on the grounds of the attorney's unsuitability.

The use of unregistered powers should be discouraged. The donor could lodge the power with his solicitor with strict instructions that it is not to be used until the onset of incapacity. Better still, these instructions could be included in the instrument itself.

Finally – whether in a brochure, in correspondence or in person – when clients are advised about the benefits of EPAs they should also be informed of the risks, particularly the risk that the attorney could misuse his powers.

APPENDICES

APPENDIX 1

POWERS OF ATTORNEY ACT 1971

Note. The Act is printed as amended by the Law of Property (Miscellaneous Provisions) Act 1989. Certain provisions have been omitted because they make textual amendments in, or repeal, other legislation.

1 Execution of powers of attorney

(1)   An instrument creating a power of attorney shall be executed as a deed by the donor of the power.

...

(3)   This section is without prejudice to any requirement in, or having effect under, any other Act as to the witnessing of instruments creating powers of attorney and does not affect the rules relating to the execution of instruments by bodies corporate.

...

3 Proof of instruments creating powers of attorney

(1)   The contents of an instrument creating a power of attorney may be proved by means of a copy which:

(a)   is a reproduction of the original made with a photographic or other device for reproducing documents in facsimile; and

(b)   contains the following certificate or certificates signed by the donor of the power or by a solicitor or stockbroker, that is to say:

(i)   a certificate at the end to the effect that the copy is a true and complete copy of the original; and

(ii)   if the original consists of two or more pages, a certificate at the end of each page of the copy to the effect that it is a true and complete copy of the corresponding page of the original.

(2)   Where a copy of an instrument creating a power of attorney has been made which complies with subsection (1) of this section, the contents of the instrument may also be proved by means of a copy of that copy if the further copy itself complies with that subsection, taking references in it to the original as references to the copy from which the further copy is made.

(3)   In this section 'stockbroker' means a member of any stock exchange within the meaning of the Stock Transfer Act 1963 or the Stock Transfer Act (Northern Ireland) 1963.

(4)   This section is without prejudice to section 4 of the Evidence and Powers of Attorney Act 1940 (proof of deposited instruments by office copy) and to any other method of proof authorised by law.

(5)   For the avoidance of doubt, in relation to an instrument made in Scotland the references to a power of attorney in this section and in section 4 of the Evidence and Powers of Attorney Act 1940 include references to a factory and commission.

4 Powers of attorney given as security

(1)   Where a power of attorney is expressed to be irrevocable and is given to secure:

      (a)   a proprietary interest of the donee of the power; or

      (b)   the performance of an obligation owed to the donee,

then, so long as the donee has that interest or the obligation remains undischarged, the power shall not be revoked:

        (i)   by the donor without the consent of the donee; or

        (ii)   by the death, incapacity or bankruptcy of the donor or, if the donor is a body corporate, by its winding up or dissolution.

(2)   A power of attorney given to secure a proprietary interest may be given to the person entitled to the interest and persons deriving title under him to that interest, and those persons shall be duly constituted donees of the power for all purposes of the power but without prejudice to any right to appoint substitutes given by the power.

(3)   This section applies to powers of attorney whenever created.

5 Protection of donee and third persons where power of attorney is revoked

(1)   A donee of a power of attorney who acts in pursuance of the power at a time when it has been revoked shall not, by reason of the revocation, incur any liability (either to the donor or to any other person) if at that time he did not know that the power had been revoked.

(2)   Where a power of attorney has been revoked and a person, without knowledge of the revocation, deals with the donee of the power, the transaction between them shall, in favour of that person, be as valid as if the power had then been in existence.

(3)   Where the power is expressed in the instrument creating it to be irrevocable and to be given by way of security then, unless the person dealing with the donee knows that it was not in fact given by way of security, he shall be entitled to assume that the power is incapable of revocation except by the donor acting with the consent of the donee and shall accordingly be treated for the purposes of subsection (2) of this section as having knowledge of the revocation only if he knows that it has been revoked in that manner.

(4)   Where the interest of a purchaser depends on whether a transaction between the donee of a power of attorney and another person was valid by virtue of subsection (2) of this section, it shall be conclusively presumed in favour of the purchaser that that person did not at the material time know of the revocation of the power if:

      (a)   the transaction between that person and the donee was completed within twelve months of the date on which the power came into operation; or

      (b)   that person makes a statutory declaration, before or within three months after the completion of the purchase, that he did not at the material time know of the revocation of the power.

(5)   Without prejudice to subsection (3) of this section, for the purposes of this section knowledge of the revocation of a power of attorney includes knowledge of the occurrence of any event (such as the death of the donor) which has the effect of revoking the power.

(6)   In this section 'purchaser' and 'purchase' have the meanings specified in section 205(1) of the Law of Property Act 1925.

(7)   This section applies whenever the power of attorney was created but only to acts and transactions after the commencement of this Act.

6 Additional protection for transferees under stock exchange transactions

(1)   Without prejudice to section 5 of this Act, where:

    (a)   the donee of a power of attorney executes, as transferor, an instrument transferring registered securities; and

    (b)   the instrument is executed for the purposes of a stock exchange transaction,

it shall be conclusively presumed in favour of the transferee that the power had not been revoked at the date of the instrument if a statutory declaration to that effect is made by the donee of the power on or within three months after that date.

(2)   In this section 'registered securities' and 'stock exchange transaction' have the same meanings as in the Stock Transfer Act 1963.

7 Execution of instruments, etc., by donee of power of attorney

(1)   If the donee of a power of attorney is an individual, he may, if he thinks fit:

    (a)   execute any instrument with his own signature,

    (b)   do any other thing in his own name,

by the authority of the donor of the power; and any document executed or thing done in that manner shall be as effective as if executed or done by the donee with the signature, or, as the case may be, in the name, of the donor of the power.

(2)   For the avoidance of doubt it is hereby declared that an instrument to which subsection (3) of section 74 of the Law of Property Act 1925 applies may be executed either as provided in that subsection or as provided in this section.

(3)   This section is without prejudice to any statutory direction requiring an instrument to be executed in the name of an estate owner within the meaning of the said Act of 1925.

(4)   This section applies whenever the power of attorney was created.

...

9 Power to delegate trusts, etc., by power of attorney

(1)   Section 25 of the Trustee Act 1925 (power to delegate trusts, etc., during absence abroad) shall be amended as follows.

(2)   For subsections (1) to (8) of that section there shall be substituted the following subsections:

    '(1)   Notwithstanding any rule of law or equity to the contrary, a trustee may, by power of attorney, delegate for a period not exceeding twelve months the execution or exercise of all or any of the trusts, powers and discretions vested in him as trustee either alone or jointly with any other person or persons.

    (2)   The persons who may be donees of a power of attorney under this section include a trust corporation but not (unless a trust corporation) the only other co-trustee of the donor of the power.

    (3)   An instrument creating a power of attorney under this section shall be attested by at least one witness.

    (4)   Before or within seven days after giving a power of attorney under this section the donor shall give written notice thereof (specifying the date on which the power comes into operation and its duration, the donee of the power, the reason why the power is given and, where some only are delegated, the trusts, powers and discretions delegated) to:

(a)   each person (other than himself) if any, who under an instrument creating the trust has power (whether alone or jointly) to appoint a new trustee; and

(b)   each of the other trustees, if any:

but failure to comply with this subsection shall not, in favour of a person dealing with the donee of the power, invalidate any act done or instrument executed by the donee.

(5)   The donor of a power of attorney given under this section shall be liable for the acts or defaults of the donee in the same manner as if they were the acts or defaults of the donor.'

(3)   Subsections (9) and (10) of the said section 25 shall stand as subsections (6) and (7) and for subsection (11) of that section there shall be substituted the following subsection:

'(8)   This section applies to a personal representative, tenant for life and statutory owner as it applies to a trustee except that subsection (4) shall apply as if it required the notice there mentioned to be given:

(a)   in the case of a personal representative, to each of the other personal representatives, if any, except any executor who has renounced probate;

(b)   in the case of a tenant for life, to the trustees of the settlement and to each person, if any, who together with the person giving the notice constitutes the tenant for life;

(c)   in the case of a statutory owner, to each of the persons, if any, who together with the person giving the notice constitute the statutory owner and, in the case of a statutory owner by virtue of section 23(1)(a) of the Settled Land Act 1925, to the trustees of the settlement.'

(4)   This section applies whenever the trusts, powers or discretions in question arose but does not invalidate anything done by virtue of the said section 25 as in force at the commencement of this Act.

10 Effect of general power of attorney in specified form

(1)   Subject to subsection (2) of this section, a general power of attorney in the form set out in Schedule 1 to this Act, or in a form to the like effect but expressed to be made under this Act, shall operate to confer:

(a)   on the donee of the power; or

(b)   if there is more than one donee, on the donees acting jointly or acting jointly or severally, as the case may be,

authority to do on behalf of the donor anything which he can lawfully do by an attorney.

(2)   This section does not apply to functions which the donor has as a trustee or personal representative or as a tenant for life or statutory owner within the meaning of the Settled Land Act 1925.

11 Short title, repeals, consequential amendments, commencement and extent

(1)   This Act may be cited as the Powers of Attorney Act 1971.

(2)   ...

(3)   ...

(4)   This Act shall come into force on 1 October 1971.

(5)   Section 3 of this Act extends to Scotland and Northern Ireland but, save as aforesaid, this Act extends to England and Wales only.

SCHEDULES

SCHEDULE 1

Section 10

FORM OF GENERAL POWER OF ATTORNEY FOR PURPOSES OF SECTION 10

THIS GENERAL POWER OF ATTORNEY is made this day of

19   by AB of

I appoint CD of

[*or* CD of   and

EF of   jointly *or*

jointly and severally] to be my attorney[s] in accordance with section 10 of the Powers of Attorney Act 1971.

IN WITNESS etc.,

APPENDIX 2

ENDURING POWERS OF ATTORNEY ACT 1985

Enduring powers of attorney

1 Enduring power of attorney to survive mental incapacity of donor

(1)   Where an individual creates a power of attorney which is an enduring power within the meaning of this Act then:

(a)   the power shall not be revoked by any subsequent mental incapacity of his; but

(b)   upon such incapacity supervening the donee of the power may not do anything under the authority of the power except as provided by subsection (2) below or as directed or authorised by the court under section 5 unless or, as the case may be, until the instrument creating the power is registered by the court under section 6; and

(c)   section 5 of the Powers of Attorney Act 1971 (protection of donee and third persons) so far as applicable shall apply if and so long as paragraph (b) above operates to suspend the donee's authority to act under the power as if the power had been revoked by the donor's mental incapacity.

(2)   Notwithstanding subsection (1)(b) above, where the attorney has made an application for registration of the instrument then, until the application has been initially determined, the attorney may take action under the power:

(a)   to maintain the donor or prevent loss to his estate; or

(b)   to maintain himself or other persons in so far as section 3(4) permits him to do so.

(3)   Where the attorney purports to act as provided by subsection (2) above then, in favour of a person who deals with him without knowledge that the attorney is acting otherwise than in accordance with paragraph (a) or (b) of that subsection, the transaction between them shall be as valid as if the attorney were acting in accordance with paragraph (a) or (b).

2 Characteristics of an enduring power

(1)   Subject to subsections (7) to (9) below and section 11, a power of attorney is an enduring power within the meaning of this Act if the instrument which creates the power:

(a)   is in the prescribed form; and

(b)   was executed in the prescribed manner by the donor and the attorney; and

(c)   incorporated at the time of execution by the donor the prescribed explanatory information.

(2)   The Lord Chancellor shall make regulations as to the form and execution of instruments creating enduring powers and the regulations shall contain such provisions as appear to him to be appropriate for securing:

(a) that no document is used to create an enduring power which does not incorporate such information explaining the general effect of creating or accepting the power as may be prescribed; and

(b) that such instruments include statements to the following effect:

(i) by the donor, that he intends the power to continue in spite of any supervening mental incapacity of his;

(ii) by the donor, that he read or had read to him the information explaining the effect of creating the power;

(iii) by the attorney, that he understands the duty of registration imposed by this Act.

(3) Regulations under subsection (2) above:

(a) may include different provision for cases where more than one attorney is to be appointed by the instrument than for cases where only one attorney is to be appointed; and

(b) may, if they amend or revoke any regulations previously made under that subsection, include saving and transitional provisions.

(4) Regulations under subsection (2) above shall be made by statutory instrument which shall be subject to annulment in pursuance of a resolution of either House of Parliament.

(5) An instrument in the prescribed form purporting to have been executed in the prescribed manner shall be taken, in the absence of evidence to the contrary, to be a document which incorporated at the time of execution by the donor the prescribed explanatory information.

(6) Where an instrument differs in an immaterial respect in form or mode of expression from the prescribed form the instrument shall be treated as sufficient in point of form and expression.

(7) A power of attorney cannot be an enduring power unless, when he executes the instrument creating it, the attorney is:

(a) an individual who has attained eighteen years and is not bankrupt; or

(b) a trust corporation.

(8) A power of attorney under section 25 of the Trustee Act 1925 (power to delegate trusts, etc. by power of attorney) cannot be an enduring power.

(9) A power of attorney which gives the attorney a right to appoint a substitute or successor cannot be an enduring power.

(10) An enduring power shall be revoked by the bankruptcy of the attorney whatever the circumstances of the bankruptcy.

(11) An enduring power shall be revoked on the exercise by the court of any of its powers under Part VII of the Mental Health Act 1983 if, but only if, the court so directs.

(12) No disclaimer of an enduring power, whether by deed or otherwise, shall be valid unless and until the attorney gives notice of it to the donor or, where section 4(6) or 7(1) applies, to the court.

(13) In this section 'prescribed' means prescribed under subsection (2) above.

3 Scope of authority, etc., of attorney under enduring power

(1)   An enduring power may confer general authority (as defined in subsection (2) below) on the attorney to act on the donor's behalf in relation to all or a specified part of the property and affairs of the donor or may confer on him authority to do specified things on the donor's behalf and the authority may, in either case, be conferred subject to conditions and restrictions.

(2)   Where an instrument is expressed to confer general authority on the attorney it operates to confer, subject to the restriction imposed by subsection (5) below and to any conditions or restrictions contained in the instrument, authority to do on behalf of the donor anything which the donor can lawfully do by an attorney.

(3)   Subject to any conditions or restrictions contained in the instrument, an attorney under an enduring power, whether general or limited, may (without obtaining any consent) execute or exercise all or any of the trusts, powers or discretions vested in the donor as trustee and may (without the concurrence of any other person) give a valid receipt for capital or other money paid.

(4)   Subject to any conditions or restrictions contained in the instrument, an attorney under an enduring power, whether general or limited, may (without obtaining any consent) act under the power so as to benefit himself or other persons than the donor to the following extent but no further, that is to say:

   (a)   he may so act in relation to himself or in relation to any other person if the donor might be expected to provide for his or that person's needs respectively; and

   (b)   he may do whatever the donor might be expected to do to meet those needs.

(5)   Without prejudice to subsection (4) above but subject to any conditions or restrictions contained in the instrument, an attorney under an enduring power, whether general or limited, may (without obtaining any consent) dispose of the property of the donor by way of gift to the following extent but no further, that is to say:

   (a)   he may make gifts of a seasonal nature or at a time, or on an anniversary, of a birth or marriage, to persons (including himself) who are related to or connected with the donor, and

   (b)   he may make gifts to any charity to whom the donor made or might be expected to make gifts.

provided that the value of each such gift is not unreasonable having regard to all the circumstances and in particular the size of the donor's estate.

Action on actual or impending incapacity of donor

4 Duties of attorney in event of actual or impending incapacity of donor

(1)   If the attorney under an enduring power has reason to believe that the donor is or is becoming mentally incapable subsections (2) to (6) below shall apply.

(2)   The attorney shall, as soon as practicable, make an application to the court for the registration of the instrument creating the power.

(3)   Before making an application for registration the attorney shall comply with the provisions as to notice set out in Schedule 1.

(4)   An application for registration shall be made in the prescribed form and shall contain such statements as may be prescribed.

(5)   The attorney may, before making an application for the registration of the instrument, refer to the court for its determination any question as to the validity of the power and he shall comply with any direction given to him by the court on that determination.

(6)   No disclaimer of the power shall be valid unless and until the attorney gives notice of it to the court.

(7)   Any person who, in an application for registration, makes a statement which he knows to be false in a material particular shall be liable:

  (a)   on conviction on indictment, to imprisonment for a term not exceeding two years or to a fine, or both; and

  (b)   on summary conviction, to imprisonment for a term not exceeding six months or to a fine not exceeding the statutory maximum, or both.

(8)   In this section and Schedule 1 'prescribed' means prescribed by rules of the court.

5 Functions of court prior to registration

Where the court has reason to believe that the donor of an enduring power may be, or may be becoming, mentally incapable and the court is of the opinion that it is necessary, before the instrument creating the power is registered, to exercise any power with respect to the power of attorney or the attorney appointed to act under it which would become exercisable under section 8(2) on its registration, the court may exercise that power under this section and may do so whether the attorney has or has not made an application to the court for the registration of the instrument.

6 Functions of court on application for registration

(1)   In any case where:

  (a)   an application for registration is made in accordance with section 4(3) and (4), and

  (b)   neither subsection (2) nor subsection (4) below applies,

the court shall register the instrument to which the application relates.

(2)   Where it appears to the court that there is in force under Part VII of the Mental Health Act 1983 an order appointing a receiver for the donor but the power has not also been revoked then, unless it directs otherwise, the court shall not exercise or further exercise its functions under this section but shall refuse the application for registration.

(3)   Where it appears from an application for registration that notice of it has not been given under Schedule 1 to some person entitled to receive it (other than a person in respect of whom the attorney has been dispensed or is otherwise exempt from the requirement to give notice) the court shall direct that the application be treated for the purposes of this Act as having been made in accordance with section 4(3), if the court is satisfied that, as regards each such person:

  (a)   it was undesirable or impracticable for the attorney to give him notice; or

  (b)   no useful purpose is likely to be served by giving him notice.

(4)   If, in the case of an application for registration:

  (a)   a valid notice of objection to the registration is received by the court before the expiry of the period of five weeks beginning with the date or, as the case may be, the latest date on which the attorney gave notice to any person under Schedule 1; or

  (b)   it appears from the application that there is no one to whom notice has been given under paragraph 1 of that Schedule; or

(c)   the court has reason to believe that appropriate inquiries might bring to light evidence on which the court could be satisfied that one of the grounds of objection set out in subsection (5) below was established,

the court shall neither register the instrument nor refuse the application until it has made or caused to be made such inquiries (if any) as it thinks appropriate in the circumstances of the case.

(5)   For the purposes of this Act a notice of objection to the registration of an instrument is valid if the objection is made on one or more of the following grounds, namely:

(a)   that the power purported to have been created by the instrument was not valid as an enduring power of attorney;

(b)   that the power created by the instrument no longer subsists;

(c)   that the application is premature because the donor is not yet becoming mentally incapable;

(d)   that fraud or undue pressure was used to induce the donor to create the power;

(e)   that, having regard to all the circumstances and in particular the attorney's relationship to or connection with the donor, the attorney is unsuitable to be the donor's attorney.

(6)   If, in a case where subsection (4) above applies, any of the grounds of objection in subsection (5) above is established to the satisfaction of the court, the court shall refuse the application but if, in such a case, it is not so satisfied, the court shall register the instrument to which the application relates.

(7)   Where the court refuses an application for registration on ground (d) or (e) in subsection (5) above it shall by order revoke the power created by the instrument.

(8)   Where the court refuses an application for registration on any ground other than that specified in subsection (5)(c) above the instrument shall be delivered up to be cancelled, unless the court otherwise directs.

Legal position after registration

7 Effect and proof of registration, etc.

(1)   The effect of the registration of an instrument under section 6 is that:

(a)   no revocation of the power by the donor shall be valid unless and until the court confirms the revocation under section 8(3);

(b)   no disclaimer of the power shall be valid unless and until the attorney gives notice of it to the court;

(c)   the donor may not extend or restrict the scope of the authority conferred by the instrument and no instruction or consent given by him after registration shall, in the case of a consent, confer any right and, in the case of an instruction, impose or confer any obligation or right on or create any liability of the attorney or other persons having notice of the instruction or consent.

(2)   Subsection (1) above applies for so long as the instrument is registered under section 6 whether or not the donor is for the time being mentally incapable.

(3)   A document purporting to be an office copy of an instrument registered under this Act [or under the Enduring Powers of Attorney (Northern Ireland) Order 1987] shall, in any part of

the United Kingdom, be evidence of the contents of the instrument and of the fact that it has been so registered.

(4)   Subsection (3) above is without prejudice to section 3 of the Powers of Attorney Act 1971 (proof by certified copies) and to any other method of proof authorised by law.

8 Functions of court with respect to registered power

(1)   Where an instrument has been registered under section 6, the court shall have the following functions with respect to the power and the donor of and the attorney appointed to act under the power.

(2)   The court may:

    (a)   determine any question as to the meaning or effect of the instrument;

    (b)   give directions with respect to:

        (i)   the management or disposal by the attorney of the property and affairs of the donor;

        (ii)   the rendering of accounts by the attorney and the production of the records kept by him for the purpose;

        (iii)   the remuneration or expenses of the attorney, whether or not in default of or in accordance with any provision made by the instrument, including directions for the repayment of excessive or the payment of additional remuneration;

    (c)   require the attorney to furnish information or produce documents or things in his possession as attorney;

    (d)   give any consent or authorisation to act which the attorney would have to obtain from a mentally capable donor;

    (e)   authorise the attorney to act so as to benefit himself or other persons than the donor otherwise than in accordance with section 3(4) and (5) (but subject to any conditions or restrictions contained in the instrument);

    (f)   relieve the attorney wholly or partly from any liability which he has or may have incurred on account of a breach of his duties as attorney.

(3)   On application made for the purpose by or on behalf of the donor, the court shall confirm the revocation of the power if satisfied that the donor has done whatever is necessary in law to effect an express revocation of the power and was mentally capable of revoking a power of attorney when he did so (whether or not he is so when the court considers the application).

(4)   The court shall cancel the registration of an instrument registered under section 6 in any of the following circumstances, that is to say:

    (a)   on confirming the revocation of the power under subsection (3) above or receiving notice of disclaimer under section 7(1)(b);

    (b)   on giving a direction revoking the power on exercising any of its powers under Part VII of the Mental Health Act 1983;

    (c)   on being satisfied that the donor is and is likely to remain mentally capable;

    (d)   on being satisfied that the power has expired or has been revoked by the death or bankruptcy of the donor or the death, mental incapacity or bankruptcy of the attorney or, if the attorney is a body corporate, its winding up or dissolution;

(e)   on being satisfied that the power was not a valid and subsisting enduring power when registration was effected;

(f)   on being satisfied that fraud or undue pressure was used to induce the donor to create the power; or

(g)   on being satisfied that, having regard to all the circumstances and in particular the attorney's relationship to or connection with the donor, the attorney is unsuitable to be the donor's attorney.

(5)   Where the court cancels the registration of an instrument on being satisfied of the matters specified in paragraph (f) or (g) of subsection (4) above it shall by order revoke the power created by the instrument.

(6)   On the cancellation of the registration of an instrument under subsection (4) above except paragraph (c) the instrument shall be delivered up to be cancelled, unless the court otherwise directs.

Protection of attorney and third parties

9 Protection of attorney and third persons where power invalid or revoked

(1)   Subsections (2) and (3) below apply where an instrument which did not create a valid power of attorney has been registered under section 6 (whether or not the registration has been cancelled at the time of the act or transaction in question).

(2)   An attorney who acts in pursuance of the power shall not incur any liability (either to the donor or to any other person) by reason of the non-existence of the power unless at the time of acting he knows:

(a)   that the instrument did not create a valid enduring power; or

(b)   that an event has occurred which, if the instrument had created a valid enduring power, would have had the effect of revoking the power; or

(c)   that, if the instrument had created a valid enduring power, the power would have expired before that time.

(3)   Any transaction between the attorney and another person shall, in favour of that person, be as valid as if the power had then been in existence, unless at the time of the transaction that person has knowledge of any of the matters mentioned in subsection (2) above.

(4)   Where the interest of a purchaser depends on whether a transaction between the attorney and another person was valid by virtue of subsection (3) above, it shall be conclusively presumed in favour of the purchaser that the transaction was valid if:

(a)   the transaction between that person and the attorney was completed within twelve months of the date on which the instrument was registered; or

(b)   that person makes a statutory declaration, before or within three months after the completion of the purchase, that he had no reason at the time of the transaction to doubt that the attorney had authority to dispose of the property which was the subject of the transaction.

(5)   For the purposes of section 5 of the Powers of Attorney Act 1971 (protection of attorney and third persons where action is taken under the power of attorney in ignorance of its having been revoked) in its application to an enduring power the revocation of which by the donor is by virtue of section 7(1)(a) above invalid unless and until confirmed by the court under section 8(3), above, knowledge of the confirmation of the revocation is, but knowledge of the unconfirmed revocation is not, knowledge of the revocation of the power.

(6)   Schedule 2 shall have effect to confer protection in cases where the instrument failed to create a valid enduring power and the power has been revoked by the donor's mental incapacity.

(7)   In this section 'purchaser' and 'purchase' have the meanings specified in section 205(1) of the Law of Property Act 1925.

Supplementary

10 Application of Mental Health Act provisions relating to the court

(1)   The provisions of Part VII of the Mental Health Act 1983 (relating to the Court of Protection) specified below shall apply to persons within and proceedings under this Act in accordance with the following paragraphs of this subsection and subsection (2) below, that is to say:

(a)   section 103 (functions of Visitors) shall apply to persons within this Act as it applies to the persons mentioned in that section;

(b)   section 104 (powers of judge) shall apply to proceedings under this Act with respect to persons within this Act as it applies to the proceedings mentioned in subsection (1) of that section;

(c)   section 105(1) (appeals to nominated judge) shall apply to any decision of the Master of the Court of Protection or any nominated officer in proceedings under this Act as it applies to any decision to which that subsection applies and an appeal shall lie to the Court of Appeal from any decision of a nominated judge whether given in the exercise of his original jurisdiction or on the hearing of an appeal under section 105(1) as extended by this paragraph:

(d)   section 106 except subsection (4) (rules of procedure) shall apply to proceedings under this Act and persons within this Act as it applies to the proceedings and persons mentioned in that section.

(2)   Any functions conferred or imposed by the provisions of the said Part VII applied by subsection (1) above shall be exercisable also for the purposes of this Act and the persons who are 'within this Act' are the donors of and attorneys under enduring powers of attorney whether or not they would be patients for the purposes of the said Part VII.

(3)   In this section 'nominated judge' and 'nominated officer' have the same meanings as in Part VII of the Mental Health Act 1983.

11 Application to joint and joint and several attorneys

(1)   An instrument which appoints more than one person to be an attorney cannot create an enduring power unless the attorneys are appointed to act jointly or jointly and severally.

(2)   This Act, in its application to joint attorneys, applies to them collectively as it applies to a single attorney but subject to the modifications specified in Part 1 of Schedule 3.

(3)   This Act, in its application to joint and several attorneys, applies with the modifications specified in subsections (4) to (7) below and in Part II of Schedule 3.

(4)   A failure, as respects any one attorney, to comply with the requirements for the creation of enduring powers, shall prevent the instrument from creating such a power in his case without however affecting its efficacy for that purpose as respects the other or others or its efficacy in his case for the purpose of creating a power of attorney which is not an enduring power.

(5) Where one or more but not both or all the attorneys makes or joins in making an application for registration of the instrument then:

    (a) an attorney who is not an applicant as well as one who is may act pending the initial determination of the application as provided in section 1(2) (or under section 5);

    (b) notice of the application shall also be given under Schedule 1 to the other attorney or attorneys; and

    (c) objection may validly be taken to the registration on a ground relating to an attorney or to the power of an attorney who is not an applicant as well as to one or the power of one who is an applicant.

(6) The court shall not refuse under section 6(6) to register an instrument because a ground of objection to an attorney or power is established if an enduring power subsists as respects some attorney who is not affected thereby but shall give effect to it by the prescribed qualification of the registration.

(7) The court shall not cancel the registration of an instrument under section 8(4) for any of the causes vitiating registration specified in that subsection if an enduring power subsists as respects some attorney who is not affected thereby but shall give effect to it by the prescribed qualification of the registration.

(8) In this section:

'prescribed' means prescribed by rules of the court; and

'the requirements for the creation of enduring powers' means the provisions of section 2 other than subsections (10) to (12) and of regulations under subsection (2) of that section.

12 Power of Lord Chancellor to modify pre-registration requirements in certain cases

(1) The Lord Chancellor may by order exempt attorneys of such descriptions as he thinks fit from the requirements of this Act to give notice to relatives prior to registration.

(2) Subject to subsection (3) below, where an order is made under this section with respect to attorneys of a specified description then, during the currency of the order, this Act shall have effect in relation to any attorney of that description with the omission of so much of section 4(3) and Schedule 1 as requires notice of an application for registration to be given to relatives.

(3) Notwithstanding that an attorney under a joint or joint and several power is of a description specified in a current order under this section, subsection (2) above shall not apply in relation to him if any of the other attorneys under the power is not of a description specified in that or another current order under this section.

(4) The power to make an order under this section shall be exercisable by statutory instrument which shall be subject to annulment in pursuance of a resolution of either House of Parliament.

13 Interpretation

(1) In this Act:

'the court', in relation to any functions under this Act, means the authority having jurisdiction under Part VII of the Mental Health Act 1983;

'enduring power' is to be construed in accordance with section 2;

'mentally incapable' or 'mental incapacity', except where it refers to revocation at common law, means, in relation to any person, that he is incapable by reason of mental disorder of managing and administering his property and affairs and 'mentally capable' and 'mental capacity' shall be construed accordingly;

'mental disorder' has the same meaning as it has in the Mental Health Act 1983;

'notice' means notice in writing;

'rules of the court' means rules under Part VII of the Mental Health Act 1983 as applied by section 10;

'statutory maximum' has the meaning given by section 74(1) of the Criminal Justice Act 1982;

'trust corporation' means the Public Trustee or a corporation either appointed by the High Court or a county court (according to their respective jurisdictions) in any particular case to be a trustee or entitled by rules under section 4(3) of the Public Trustee Act 1906 to act as custodian trustee.

(2)   Any question arising under or for the purposes of this Act as to what the donor of the power might at any time be expected to do shall be determined by assuming that he had full mental capacity at the time but otherwise by reference to the circumstances existing at that time.

14 Short title, commencement and extent

(1)   This Act may be cited as the Enduring Powers of Attorney Act 1985.

(2)   This Act shall come into force on such day as the Lord Chancellor appoints by order made by statutory instrument.

(3)   This Act extends to England and Wales only except that section 7(3) and section 10(1)(b) so far as it applies section 104(4) of the Mental Health Act 1983 extend also to Scotland and Northern Ireland.

SCHEDULES
SCHEDULE 1

Section 4(3)

NOTIFICATION PRIOR TO REGISTRATION

PART I

DUTY TO GIVE NOTICE TO RELATIVES AND DONOR

Duty to give notice to relatives

1. Subject to paragraph 3 below, before making an application for registration the attorney shall give notice of his intention to do so to all those persons (if any) who are entitled to receive notice by virtue of paragraph 2 below.

2. (1) Subject to the limitations contained in sub-paragraphs (2) to (4) below, persons of the following classes (referred to in this Act as 'relatives') are entitled to receive notice under paragraph 1 above:

   (a)   the donor's husband or wife;

   (b)   the donor's children;

   (c)   the donor's parents;

   (d)   the donor's brothers and sisters, whether of the whole or half blood;

   (e)   the widow or widower of a child of the donor;

   (f)   the donor's grandchildren;

(g)   the children of the donor's brothers and sisters of the whole blood;

(h)   the children of the donor's brothers and sisters of the half blood;

(i)   the donor's uncles and aunts of the whole blood; and

(j)   the children of the donor's uncles and aunts of the whole blood.

(2)   A person is not entitled to receive notice under paragraph 1 above if:

(a)   his name or address is not known to the attorney and cannot be reasonably ascertained by him; or

(b)   the attorney has reason to believe that he has not attained eighteen years or is mentally incapable.

(3)   Except where sub-paragraph (4) below applies, no more than three persons are entitled to receive notice under paragraph 1 above and, in determining the persons who are so entitled, persons falling within the class (a) of sub-paragraph (1) above are to be preferred to persons falling within class (b) of that sub-paragraph, persons falling within class (b) are to be preferred to persons falling within class (c) of that sub-paragraph; and so on.

(4)   Notwithstanding the limit of three specified in subparagraph (3) above, where:

(a)   there is more than one person falling within any of classes (a) to (j) of sub-paragraph (1) above, and

(b)   at least one of those persons would be entitled to receive notice under paragraph 1 above,

then, subject to sub-paragraph (2) above, all the persons falling within that class are entitled to receive notice under paragraph 1 above.

3. (1) An attorney shall not be required to give notice under paragraph 1 above to himself or to any other attorney under the power who is joining in making the application, notwithstanding that he or, as the case may be, the other attorney is entitled to receive notice by virtue of paragraph 2 above.

(2)   In the case of any person who is entitled to receive notice under paragraph 1 above, the attorney, before applying for registration, may make an application to the court to be dispensed from the requirement to give him notice; and the court shall grant the application if it is satisfied:

(a)   that it would be undesirable or impracticable for the attorney to give him notice; or

(b)   that no useful purpose is likely to be served by giving him notice.

Duty to give notice to donor

4. (1) Subject to sub-paragraph (2) below, before making an application for registration the attorney shall give notice of his intention to do so to the donor.

(2)   Paragraph 3(2) above shall apply in relation to the donor as it applies in relation to a person who is entitled to receive notice under paragraph 1 above.

PART II

CONTENTS OF NOTICES

5. A notice to relatives under this Schedule:

(a) shall be in the prescribed form;

(b) shall state that the attorney proposes to make an application to the Court of Protection for the registration of the instrument creating the enduring power in question;

(c) shall inform the person to whom it is given that he may object to the proposed registration by notice in writing to the Court of Protection before the expiry of the period of four weeks beginning with the day on which the notice under this Schedule was given to him;

(d) shall specify, as the grounds on which an objection to registration may be made, the grounds set out in section 6(5).

6. A notice to the donor under this Schedule:

(a) shall be in the prescribed form;

(b) shall contain the statement mentioned in paragraph 5(b) above; and

(c) shall inform the donor that, whilst the instrument remains registered, any revocation of the power by him will be ineffective unless and until the revocation is confirmed by the Court of Protection.

PART III

DUTY TO GIVE NOTICE TO OTHER ATTORNEYS

7. (1) Subject to sub-paragraph (2) below, before making an application for registration an attorney under a joint and several power shall give notice of his intention to do so to any other attorney under the power who is not joining in making the application; and paragraphs 3(2) and 5 above shall apply in relation to attorneys entitled to receive notice by virtue of this paragraph as they apply in relation to persons entitled to receive notice by virtue of paragraph 2 above.

(2) An attorney is not entitled to receive notice by virtue of this paragraph if:

(a) his address is not known to the applying attorney and cannot reasonably be ascertained by him; or

(b) the applying attorney has reason to believe that he has not attained eighteen years or is mentally incapable.

PART IV

SUPPLEMENTARY

8. (1) For the purposes of this Schedule an illegitimate child shall be treated as if he were the legitimate child of his mother and father.

(2) Notwithstanding anything in section 7 of the Interpretation Act 1978 (construction of references to service by post), for the purposes of this Schedule a notice given by post shall be regarded as given on the date on which it was posted.

SCHEDULE 2

Section 9(6)

FURTHER PROTECTION OF ATTORNEY AND THIRD PERSONS

1. Where:

    (a)   an instrument framed in a form prescribed under section 2(2) creates a power which is not a valid enduring power; and

    (b)   the power is revoked by the mental incapacity of the donor,

paragraphs 2 and 3 below shall apply, whether or not the instrument has been registered.

2. An attorney who acts in pursuance of the power shall not, by reason of the revocation, incur any liability (either to the donor or to any other person) unless at the time of acting he knows:

    (a)   that the instrument did not create a valid enduring power; and

    (b)   that the donor has become mentally incapable.

3. Any transaction between the attorney and another person shall, in favour of that person, be as valid as if the power had then been in existence, unless at the time of the transaction that person knows:

    (a)   that the instrument did not create a valid enduring power; and

    (b)   that the donor has become mentally incapable.

4. Section 9(4) shall apply for the purpose of determining whether a transaction was valid by virtue of paragraph 3 above as it applies for the purpose of determining whether a transaction was valid by virtue of section 9(3).

SCHEDULE 3

Section 11(2), (3)

JOINT AND JOINT AND SEVERAL ATTORNEYS

PART I

JOINT ATTORNEYS

1. In section 2(7), the reference to the time when the attorney executes the instrument shall be read as a reference to the time when the second or last attorney executes the instrument.

2. In section 2(9) and (10), the reference to the attorney shall be read as a reference to any attorney under the power.

3. In section 5, references to the attorney shall be read as including references to any attorney under the power.

4. Section 6 shall have effect as if the ground of objection to the registration of the instrument specified in subsection (5)(e) applied to any attorney under the power.

5. In section 8(2), references to the attorney shall be read as including references to any attorney under the power.

6. In section 8(4), references to the attorney shall be read as including references to any attorney under the power.

PART II

JOINT AND SEVERAL ATTORNEYS

7. In section 2(10), the reference to the bankruptcy of the attorney shall be construed as a reference to the bankruptcy of the last remaining attorney under the power; and the bankruptcy of any other attorney under the power shall cause that person to cease to be attorney, whatever the circumstances of the bankruptcy.

8. The restriction upon disclaimer imposed by section 4(6) applies only to those attorneys who have reason to believe that the donor is or is becoming mentally incapable.

APPENDIX 3

TRUSTEE DELEGATION ACT 1999

Attorney of trustee with beneficial interest in land

1 Exercise of trustee functions by attorney

(1)   The donee of a power of attorney is not prevented from doing an act in relation to –

(a)   land,

(b)   capital proceeds of a conveyance of land, or

(c)   income from land,

by reason only that the act involves the exercise of a trustee function of the donor if, at the time when the act is done, the donor has a beneficial interest in the land, proceeds or income.

(2)   In this section –

(a)   'conveyance' has the same meaning as in the Law of Property Act 1925, and

(b)   references to a trustee function of the donor are to a function which the donor has as trustee (either alone or jointly with any other person or persons).

(3)   Subsection (1) above –

(a)   applies only if and so far as a contrary intention is not expressed in the instrument creating the power of attorney, and

(b)   has effect subject to the terms of that instrument.

(4)   The donor of the power of attorney –

(a)   is liable for the acts or defaults of the donee in exercising any function by virtue of subsection (1) above in the same manner as if they were acts or defaults of the donor, but

(b)   is not liable by reason only that a function is exercised by the donee by virtue of that subsection.

(5)   Subsections (1) and (4) above –

(a)   apply only if and so far as a contrary intention is not expressed in the instrument (if any) creating the trust, and

(b)   have effect subject to the terms of such an instrument.

(6)   The fact that it appears that, in dealing with any shares or stock, the donee of the power of attorney is exercising a function by virtue of subsection (1) above does not affect with any notice of any trust a person in whose books the shares are, or stock is, registered or inscribed.

(7)   In any case where (by way of exception to section 3(1) of the Trusts of Land and Appointment of Trustees Act 1996) the doctrine of conversion continues to operate, any person who, by reason of the continuing operation of that doctrine, has a beneficial interest in the proceeds of sale of land shall be treated for the purposes of this section and section 2 below as having a beneficial interest in the land.

(8)   The donee of a power of attorney is not to be regarded as exercising a trustee function by virtue of subsection (1) above if he is acting under a trustee delegation power; and for this purpose a trustee delegation power is a power of attorney given under –

(a)   a statutory provision, or

(b)   a provision of the instrument (if any) creating a trust,

under which the donor of the power is expressly authorised to delegate the exercise of all or any of his trustee functions by power of attorney.

(9)   Subject to section 4(6) below, this section applies only to powers of attorney created after the commencement of this Act.

2 Evidence of beneficial interest

(1)   This section applies where the interest of a purchaser depends on the donee of a power of attorney having power to do an act in relation to any property by virtue of section 1(1) above.

In this subsection 'purchaser' has the same meaning as in Part I of the Law of Property Act 1925.

(2)   Where this section applies an appropriate statement is, in favour of the purchaser, conclusive evidence of the donor of the power having a beneficial interest in the property at the time of the doing of the act.

(3)   In this section 'an appropriate statement' means a signed statement made by the donee –

(a)   when doing the act in question, or

(b)   at any other time within the period of three months beginning with the day on which the act is done,

that the donor has a beneficial interest in the property at the time of the donee doing the act.

(4)   If an appropriate statement is false, the donee is liable in the same way as he would be if the statement were contained in a statutory declaration.

3 General powers in specified form

In section 10(2) of the Powers of Attorney Act 1971 (which provides that a general power of attorney in the form set out in Schedule 1 to that Act, or a similar form, does not confer on the donee of the power any authority to exercise functions of the donor as trustee etc.), for the words 'This section' substitute 'Subject to section 1 of the Trustee Delegation Act 1999, this section'.

4 Enduring powers

(1)   Section 3(3) of the Enduring Powers of Attorney Act 1985 (which entitles the donee of an enduring power to exercise any of the donor's functions as trustee and to give receipt for capital money etc.) does not apply to enduring powers created after the commencement of this Act.

(2)   Section 3(3) of the Enduring Powers of Attorney Act 1985 ceases to apply to enduring powers created before the commencement of this Act –

(a)   where subsection (3) below applies, in accordance with that subsection, and

(b)   otherwise, at the end of the period of one year from that commencement.

(3)   Where an application for the registration of the instrument creating such an enduring power is made before the commencement of this Act, or during the period of one year from that commencement, section 3(3) of the Enduring Powers of Attorney Act 1985 ceases to apply to the power –

    (a)   if the instrument is registered pursuant to the application (whether before commencement or during or after that period), when the registration of the instrument is cancelled, and

    (b)   if the application is finally refused during or after that period, when the application is finally refused.

(4)   In subsection (3) above –

    (a)   'registration' and 'registered' mean registration and registered under section 6 of the Enduring Powers of Attorney Act 1985, and

    (b)   'cancelled' means cancelled under section 8(4) of that Act.

(5)   For the purposes of subsection (3)(b) above an application is finally refused –

    (a)   if the application is withdrawn or any appeal is abandoned, when the application is withdrawn or the appeal is abandoned, and

    (b)   otherwise, when proceedings on the application (including any proceedings on, or in consequence of, an appeal) have been determined and any time for appealing or further appealing has expired.

(6)   Section 1 above applies to an enduring power created before the commencement of this Act from the time when (in accordance with subsections (2) to (5) above) section 3(3) of the Enduring Powers of Attorney Act 1985 ceases to apply to it.

Trustee delegation under section 25 of the Trustee Act 1925

5 Delegation under section 25 of the Trustee Act 1925

(1)   For section 25 of the Trustee Act 1925 substitute –

'25 Delegation of trustee's functions by power of attorney

(1) Notwithstanding any rule of law or equity to the contrary, a trustee may, by power of attorney, delegate the execution or exercise of all or any of the trusts, powers and discretions vested in him as trustee either alone or jointly with any other person or persons.

(2) A delegation under this section –

    (a)   commences as provided by the instrument creating the power or, if the instrument makes no provision as to the commencement of the delegation, with the date of the execution of the instrument by the donor; and

    (b)   continues for a period of twelve months or any shorter period provided by the instrument creating the power.

(3) The persons who may be donees of a power of attorney under this section include a trust corporation.

(4) Before or within seven days after giving a power of attorney under this section the donor shall give written notice of it (specifying the date on which the power comes into operation and its duration, the donee of the power, the reason why the power is given and, where some only are delegated, the trusts, powers and discretions delegated) to –

(a)   each person (other than himself), if any, who under any instrument creating the trust has power (whether alone or jointly) to appoint a new trustee; and

(b)   each of the other trustees, if any;

but failure to comply with this subsection shall not, in favour of a person dealing with the donee of the power, invalidate any act done or instrument executed by the donee.

(5) A power of attorney given under this section by a single donor –

(a)   in the form set out in subsection (6) of this section; or

(b)   in a form to the like effect but expressed to be made under this subsection,

shall operate to delegate to the person identified in the form as the single donee of the power the execution and exercise of all the trusts, powers and discretions vested in the donor as trustee (either alone or jointly with any other person or persons) under the single trust so identified.

(6) The form referred to in subsection (5) of this section is as follows –

"THIS GENERAL TRUSTEE POWER OF ATTORNEY is made on [*date*] by [*name of one donor*] of [*address of donor*] as trustee of [*name or details of one trust*].

I appoint [*name of one donee*] of [*address of donee*] to be my attorney [*if desired, the date on which the delegation commences or the period for which it continues (or both)*] in accordance with section 25(5) of the Trustee Act 1925.

[*To be executed as a deed*]".

(7) The donor of a power of attorney given under this section shall be liable for the acts or defaults of the donee in the same manner as if they were the acts or defaults of the donor.

(8) For the purpose of executing or exercising the trusts or powers delegated to him, the donee may exercise any of the powers conferred on the donor as trustee by statute or by the instrument creating the trust, including power, for the purpose of the transfer of any inscribed stock, himself to delegate to an attorney power to transfer, but not including the power of delegation conferred by this section.

(9) The fact that it appears from any power of attorney given under this section, or from any evidence required for the purposes of any such power of attorney or otherwise, that in dealing with any stock the donee of the power is acting in the execution of a trust shall not be deemed for any purpose to affect any person in whose books the stock is inscribed or registered with any notice of the trust.

(10) This section applies to a personal representative, tenant for life and statutory owner as it applies to a trustee except that subsection (4) shall apply as if it required the notice there mentioned to be given –

(a)   in the case of a personal representative, to each of the other personal representatives, if any, except any executor who has renounced probate;

(b)   in the case of a tenant for life, to the trustees of the settlement and to each person, if any, who together with the person giving the notice constitutes the tenant for life; and

(c)   in the case of a statutory owner, to each of the persons, if any, who together with the person giving the notice constitute the statutory owner and, in the case of a statutory owner by virtue of section 23(1)(a) of the Settled Land Act 1925, to the trustees of the settlement.'

(2)   Subsection (1) above has effect in relation to powers of attorney created after the commencement of this Act.

(3)   In section 34(2)(b) of the Pensions Act 1995 (delegation by trustees of trustee scheme under section 25 of the Trustee Act 1925), for 'during absence abroad' substitute 'for period not exceeding twelve months'.

6 Section 25 powers as enduring powers

Section 2(8) of the Enduring Powers of Attorney Act 1985 (which prevents a power of attorney under section 25 of the Trustee Act 1925 from being an enduring power) does not apply to powers of attorney created after the commencement of this Act.

Miscellaneous provisions about attorney acting for trustee

7 Two-trustee rules

(1)   A requirement imposed by an enactment –

    (a)   that capital money be paid to, or dealt with as directed by, at least two trustees or that a valid receipt for capital money be given otherwise than by a sole trustee, or

    (b)   that, in order for an interest or power to be overreached, a conveyance or deed be executed by at least two trustees,

is not satisfied by money being paid to or dealt with as directed by, or a receipt for money being given by, a relevant attorney or by a conveyance or deed being executed by such an attorney.

(2)   In this section 'relevant attorney' means a person (other than a trust corporation within the meaning of the Trustee Act 1925) who is acting either –

    (a)   both as a trustee and as attorney for one or more other trustees, or

    (b)   as attorney for two or more trustees,

and who is not acting together with any other person or persons.

(3)   This section applies whether a relevant attorney is acting under a power created before or after the commencement of this Act (but in the case of such an attorney acting under an enduring power created before that commencement is without prejudice to any continuing application of section 3(3) of the Enduring Powers of Attorney Act 1985 to the enduring power after that commencement in accordance with section 4 above).

8 Appointment of additional trustee by attorney

(1)   In section 36 of the Trustee Act 1925 (appointment of trustees), after subsection (6) (additional trustees) insert –

    '(6A) A person who is either –

    (a)   both a trustee and attorney for the other trustee (if one other), or for both of the other trustees (if two others), under a registered power; or

    (b)   attorney under a registered power for the trustee (if one) or for both or each of the trustees (if two or three),

    may, if subsection (6B) of this section is satisfied in relation to him, make an appointment under subsection (6)(b) of this section on behalf of the trustee or trustees.

    (6B) This subsection is satisfied in relation to an attorney under a registered power for one or more trustees if (as attorney under the power) –

(a)   he intends to exercise any function of the trustee or trustees by virtue of section 1(1) of the Trustee Delegation Act 1999; or

(b)   he intends to exercise any function of the trustee or trustees in relation to any land, capital proceeds of a conveyance of land or income from land by virtue of its delegation to him under section 25 of this Act or the instrument (if any) creating the trust.

(6C)   In subsections (6A) and (6B) of this section "registered power" means a power of attorney created by an instrument which is for the time being registered under section 6 of the Enduring Powers of Attorney Act 1985.

(6D)   Subsection (6A) of this section –

(a)   applies only if and so far as a contrary intention is not expressed in the instrument creating the power of attorney (or, where more than one, any of them) or the instrument (if any) creating the trust; and

(b)   has effect subject to the terms of those instruments.'

(2)   The amendment made by subsection (1) above has effect only where the power, or (where more than one) each of them, is created after the commencement of this Act.

9 Attorney acting for incapable trustee

(1)   In section 22 of the Law of Property Act 1925 (requirement, before dealing with legal estate vested in trustee who is incapable by reason of mental disorder, to appoint new trustee or discharge incapable trustee), after subsection (2) insert –

'(3) Subsection (2) of this section does not prevent a legal estate being dealt with without the appointment of a new trustee, or the discharge of the incapable trustee, at a time when the donee of an enduring power (within the meaning of the Enduring Powers of Attorney Act 1985) is entitled to act for the incapable trustee in the dealing.'

(2)   The amendment made by subsection (1) above has effect whether the enduring power was created before or after the commencement of this Act.

Authority of attorney to act in relation to land

10 Extent of attorney's authority to act in relation to land

(1)   Where the donee of a power of attorney is authorised by the power to do an act of any description in relation to any land, his authority to do an act of that description at any time includes authority to do it with respect to any estate or interest in the land which is held at that time by the donor (whether alone or jointly with any other person or persons).

(2)   Subsection (1) above –

(a)   applies only if and so far as a contrary intention is not expressed in the instrument creating the power of attorney, and

(b)   has effect subject to the terms of that instrument.

(3)   This section applies only to powers of attorney created after the commencement of this Act.

Supplementary

11 Interpretation

(1)   In this Act –

'land' has the same meaning as in the Trustee Act 1925, and

'enduring power' has the same meaning as in the Enduring Powers of Attorney Act 1985.

(2)   References in this Act to the creation of a power of attorney are to the execution by the donor of the instrument creating it.

12 Repeals

The enactments specified in the Schedule to this Act are repealed to the extent specified in the third column, but subject to the note at the end.

13 Commencement, extent and short title

(1)   The preceding provisions of this Act shall come into force on such day as the Lord Chancellor may by order made by statutory instrument appoint.

(2)   This Act extends to England and Wales only.

(3)   This Act may be cited as the Trustee Delegation Act 1999.

APPENDIX 4

THE COURT OF PROTECTION (ENDURING POWERS OF ATTORNEY) RULES 2001, SI 2001/825

PART I

Preliminary

1 Title and commencement

These Rules may be cited as the Court of Protection (Enduring Powers of Attorney) Rules 2001 and shall come into force on 1st April 2001.

2 Application

Subject to the provisions of these Rules, the Court of Protection Rules 2001 shall apply to the proceedings under the Enduring Powers of Attorney Act 1985.

3 Interpretation

(1)   In these Rules, unless the context otherwise requires –

expressions used in the Supreme Court Act 1981[4] shall have the same meanings as they have in that Act;

'the Act' means the Enduring Powers of Attorney Act 1985;

'the 1983 Act' means the Mental Health Act 1983;

'the 2001 Rules' means the Court of Protection Rules 2001;

'applicant' includes an objector;

'application' includes an objection;

'attended hearing' means a hearing where one or more of the parties to the proceedings have been invited to attend the court for the determination of the application;

'the court' means the Court of Protection;

'direction' means a direction or authority given under the seal of the court;

'enduring power of attorney' shall be construed in accordance with section 2 of the Act;

'entered' means entered in the register of enduring powers of attorney kept by the court;

'filed' means filed in the court office;

'hearing' means an attended or unattended hearing;

'judge' means the Lord Chancellor or a judge nominated under section 93(1) of the 1983 Act;

'Master' means the Master of the Court of Protection;

'nominated officer' means an officer of the court nominated under section 93(4) of the 1983 Act;

'order' means an order of the court under seal and includes a certificate, direction or authority of the court under seal;

'relative' means one of the persons referred to as relatives and entitled to receive notice under the provisions of paragraphs 1 and 2 of Schedule 1 to the Act;

'seal' means an official seal of the court and 'sealed' shall be construed accordingly.

(2)   In these Rules –

(a)   any reference to a numbered rule or to a numbered Schedule is a reference to the rule of, or the Schedule to, these Rules so numbered in these Rules;

(b)   any reference in a rule to a numbered paragraph is a reference to the paragraph so numbered in the rule in which the reference occurs; and

(c)   a form referred to by a letter alone means the form so designated in Schedule 1 or a form to the same effect with such variations as the circumstances may require and the court may approve and in both cases shall include a Welsh translation of the form.

4 Exercise of court's functions

Where any discretion, power or function is (in whatever words) expressed by these Rules to be exercisable by the court then, subject to the provisions of the Act, that discretion, power or other function may be exercised –

(a)   by a judge;

(b)   by the Master;

(c)   to the extent to which he is authorised to exercise it under section 94 of the 1983 Act, by a nominated officer.

5 Computation of time

(1)   Where a period of time fixed by the Act or by these Rules or by a judgment, order or direction for doing any act expires on a day on which the court office is closed and for that reason cannot be done on that day, the act shall be done in time if done on the next day on which the office is open.

(2)   Where the act is required to be done within a specified period after or from a specified date, the period begins immediately after that date.

(3)   Where any period of time, fixed as mentioned in paragraph (1), is three days or less, any day on which the court office is closed shall not be included in the computation of that period.

PART II

Applications

6 Notice of intention to register

(1)   Notice of the attorney's intention to apply to register an enduring power of attorney shall be given in Form EP1 to the donor and to those relatives entitled to receive such notice and to any co-attorney, all such notices to be served within fourteen days of each other.

(2)   An application to dispense with such notice shall be made in Form EP3 before any application for registration is made and shall be accompanied by the original power of attorney.

7 Time limits

An application to register an enduring power of attorney shall be made in Form EP2 and shall be lodged with the court office not later than 10 days after the date on which –

    (a)   notice has been given to the donor and every relative entitled to receive notice and every co-attorney; or

    (b)   leave has been given to dispense with notice

whichever may be the later.

8 Form of application

(1)   Subject to the provisions of rules 6 and 7 and to the following provisions of this rule, an application may be made by letter unless the court directs that it should be formal, in which case it shall be made in Form EP3.

(2)   Any application made by letter to the court, other than an objection to registration, shall include the name and address of the applicant, the name of the donor if he is not the applicant, the form of relief or determination required and the grounds for the application.

9 Objections to registration

(1)   Any objection to registration shall be made in writing and shall set out –

    (a)   the name and address of the objector;

    (b)   the name and address of the donor if he is not the objector;

    (c)   any relationship of the objector to the donor;

    (d)   the name and address of the attorney; and

    (e)   he grounds for objecting to registration of the enduring power of attorney.

(2)   Any objection to registration received by the court on or after the date of registration shall be treated by the court as an application to cancel the registration.

10 Exercise of the court's powers and functions under the provisions of the 1985 Act

(1)   This rule shall apply to applications made to the court –

    (a)   for relief or for determination of any question under sections 1(1)(b), 4(5), 5, 6(3), 6(4), 8(2), 8(3), 8(4) or 11(5)(c) of the Act; or

    (b)   under paragraphs 2(1), 3(2), 4(2) or 7(1) of Schedule 1 to the Act,

which are not made simultaneously with an application for registration of an enduring power of attorney.

(2)   On receipt of an application, the court may decide either that no hearing shall be held, in which case the application shall be dealt with by written representations, or it may fix an appointment for directions or for the application to be heard.

(3)   The court may at any time, on application or of its own motion, give such direction as it thinks proper with regard to any matter arising in the course of an application.

(4)   Notification of an appointment for directions or a hearing shall be given by the applicant to the attorney (if he is not the applicant), to any objector and to any other person directed by the court to be notified.

(5)   The applicant, the attorney (if he is not the applicant) and any person given notice of the hearing may attend or be represented.

(6)   If it appears to the court that any order for relief should be made or any question determined, the court may make such order or give such directions as it thinks fit, of its own motion.

(7)   Where an attorney seeks to disclaim an enduring power of attorney pursuant to sections 4(6) or 7(1)(b) of the Act, the disclaimer shall not take effect earlier than the day on which the notice of disclaimer is received at the court.

11 Consolidation of proceedings

The court may consolidate any application for registration or relief or any objection to registration if it considers that the proceedings may be dealt with more conveniently together.

12 Registration of an enduring power of attorney

(1)   Where there is no objection to the registration of an enduring power of attorney or any objection has been withdrawn or dismissed, the enduring power of attorney shall be registered and sealed by the court.

(2)   The court shall retain a copy of the registered enduring power of attorney and shall return the original instrument to the applicant attorney.

(3)   Any alterations which appear on the face of the instrument when an application for registration is made shall be sealed.

(4)   Any qualification to registration imposed by reason of section 11(6) or (7) of the Act shall be noted on the register and on the instrument and sealed.

(5)   The date of registration shall be the date stamped by the court on the instrument at the time of its registration.

13 Searches of the register and copies of registered enduring powers of attorney

(1)   On payment of the appropriate fee, any person shall be entitled to request the court in Form EP4 to search the register and to state whether an enduring power of attorney has been registered and the court shall so state in Form EP5.

(2)   The court may supply a person with an office copy of a registered enduring power of attorney if it is satisfied that he has a good reason for requesting a copy and that it is not reasonably practicable to obtain a copy from the attorney.

(3)   For the purposes of this rule, an office copy is a photocopy or a facsimile copy of an enduring power of attorney, marked as an office copy and sealed.

(4)   An office copy of an enduring power of attorney need not contain the explanatory information endorsed on the original power.

PART III

Hearings

14 Notice of hearing

(1)   Except where these rules otherwise provide or the court otherwise directs, the following minimum periods of notice of a hearing shall be given by the applicant –

     (a)   ten clear days in the case of –

         (i)   an application to dispense with notice to the donor;

         (ii)   an application to dispose of the donor's property prior to registration; and

         (iii)   an objection to registration of an enduring power of attorney; and

     (b)   seven clear days in the case of any other application.

(2)   Unless the court otherwise directs, notice of a hearing shall be given to the attorney, the donor, every relative, any co-attorney and to such other persons who appear to the court to be interested as the court may specify.

(3)   The court may extend or abridge the time limited by these Rules or any order or direction for doing any act upon such terms and notwithstanding in the case of an extension that the time so limited has expired.

(4)   For the purpose of this rule, notice of a hearing is given if the applicant sends a copy of the application, endorsed by the court with the hearing date, to the person concerned.

15 Mode of giving documents

(1)   Any document required by these Rules to be given to the donor shall be given to him personally.

(2)   Except where these Rules otherwise provide, any document required by these Rules to be given to any person shall be given to him by –

    (a)   sending it to him by first class post or through a document exchange; or

    (b)   transmitting it to him by fax or other electronic means.

16 Giving documents to a solicitor

Where a solicitor acting for the person to be given any document, other than the donor, endorses on that document, or on a copy of it, a statement that he accepts the document on behalf of that person, the document shall be deemed to have been duly given to that person and to have been received on the date that the endorsement was made.

17 Alternative method of giving documents

Where it appears to the court that it is impracticable for any document to be given to a person in accordance with rule 15(2), the court may give such directions for the purpose of bringing the document to the notice of the person to whom it is addressed as it thinks fit.

18 Use of evidence in subsequent proceedings

Except where the court otherwise directs, evidence which has been used in any proceedings relating to a donor may be used at any subsequent stage of those proceedings or in any other proceedings before the court.

19 Copies of documents in court

(1)   Any person who has filed an affidavit or other document shall, unless the court otherwise directs, be entitled on request to be supplied with a copy of it.

(2)   An attorney or his solicitor may have a search made for and may inspect and request a copy of any document filed in proceedings relating to the enduring power of attorney under which the attorney has been appointed.

(3)   Subject to paragraphs (1) and (2), no documents filed in the court shall be open to inspection without the leave of the court and no copy of any such document or an extract from it shall be taken by or issued to any person without such leave.

20 Summoning of witnesses

Any witness summons required to be issued in any proceedings under these Rules shall be in Form EP6.

21 Leave to bring an application

Any person other than a person who has been served with a notice of intention to register an enduring power of attorney shall apply to the court for leave to make an application for relief specified in the Act.

22 Notification of decision

All persons to whom notice is to be given under rule 10(4) shall be notified by the applicant of the court's decision and shall also be sent by the applicant a copy of any order made or direction given.

PART IV

Reviews and Appeals

23 Review of decision not made on an attended hearing

(1)   Any person who is aggrieved by a decision of the court that was made without an attended hearing may apply to the court within fourteen days of the date on which the decision was given to have the decision reviewed by the court.

(2)   On considering an application for review, the court may either confirm or revoke the previous decision or give any other order or decision which it thinks fit.

(3)   Any person aggrieved by any order or decision of the court made on considering an application for review may apply to the court for an attended hearing.

24 Appeal from decision made on an attended hearing

(1)   Any person aggrieved by an order or decision of the court made on an attended hearing, may, within fourteen days from the date of entry of the order or as the case may be, from the date of the decision, appeal to a nominated judge.

(2)   The appellant shall within fourteen days –

(a)   serve notice of appeal in form EP7 on every person who is directly affected by the decision and on any other person whom the court may direct; and

(b)   lodge a copy of the notice at the court.

(3)   The court shall fix a time and place at which the appeal is to be heard and shall cause notice of the time and place to be sent to the appellant, who shall immediately send notice of it to every person who has been served with notice of the appeal.

(4)   No evidence further to that given at the hearing shall be filed in support of, or in opposition to, the appeal without leave of the court.

PART V

Cancellation of Registration

25 Cancellation of a registered power of attorney

(1)   Where the court is satisfied that one of the circumstances listed in section 8(4) of the Act applies, it shall cancel the registration of the enduring power of attorney in question and send a notice to the attorney requiring him to deliver the original instrument to the court.

(2)   Where the court –

(a)   receives a notice of disclaimer under section 7(1)(b) of the Act;

(b)   is satisfied that the enduring power of attorney has been revoked by the death or bankruptcy of the donor; or

    (c)   is satisfied that the enduring power of attorney has been revoked by the death or bankruptcy of the attorney or, if the attorney is a body corporate, its winding up or dissolution;

it shall cancel the registration of the enduring power of attorney and send notice to the attorney, or, (where appropriate) to his personal representative or to the liquidator or receiver of a body corporate, requiring him or them to deliver the original instrument to the court.

(3)   Where the instrument creating an enduring power of attorney has been lost or destroyed, the attorney shall give to the court written details of that date of such loss or destruction and of the circumstances in which the loss or destruction occurred.

(4)   Where registration has been cancelled for any reason other than that set out in section 8(4)(c) of the Act, the court shall mark the power of attorney as cancelled.

(5)   Any notices issued by the court under this rule may contain a warning that failure to comply with the notice may lead to punishment for contempt of court.

PART VI

Fees

26 Schedule of fees

(1)   Fees shall be payable in accordance with the provisions of Schedule 2.

(2)   The fees specified in column 2 of Schedule 2 shall apply in respect of the corresponding event referred to in column 1.

(3)   The person liable to pay the fee for the registration of a power of attorney shall, unless the court otherwise directs, make the payment out of the assets of the donor.

PART VII

Transitional Provisions

27 (1)   Where any matter is pending before the Public Trustee before the coming into force of these Rules which by virtue of these Rules relates to a function to be exercised by the court, the court shall deal with the matter in accordance with these Rules.

(2)   Where any review or appeal is pending before the Court or the Public Trustee before the coming into force of these Rules, it shall be dealt with in accordance with the provisions of these Rules.

PART VIII

Revocation

28 Revocation of previous Rules

The Court of Protection (Enduring Powers of Attorney) Rules 1994[5] and the Court of Protection (Enduring Powers of Attorney) (Amendment) Rules 1999[6] are hereby revoked.

SCHEDULE 1
Form EP1

Court of Protection
Enduring Powers of Attorney Act

Notice of intention to apply for registration

To...

Of...

This form may be adapted for use by three or more attorneys.	**TAKE NOTICE THAT** I.. of... and I... of...
Give the name and address of the donor.	The attorney(s) of.................................. .... of.. ....
It will be necessary for you to produce evidence in support of your objection. If evidence is available please send it with your objection, the attorney(s) will be given an opportunity to respond to your objection.	intend to apply to the Court of Protection for registration of the enduring power of attorney appointing me (us) attorney(s) and made by the donor on the.......................................
The grounds upon which you can object are limited and are shown at 2 overleaf.	1. If you wish to object to the proposed registration you have 4 weeks from the day on which this notice is given to you to do so in writing. Any objections should be sent to the Court of Protection and should contain the following details: • Your name and address • Any relationship to the donor • If you are not the donor, the name and address of the donor • The name and address of the attorney • The grounds for objecting to the registration of the enduring power

Note. The instrument means the enduring power of attorney made by the donor which it is sought to register.	2. The grounds on which you may object are: • That the power purported to have been created by the instrument is not valid as an enduring power of attorney. • That the power created by the instrument no longer subsists. • That the application is premature because the donor is not yet becoming mentally incapable. • That fraud or undue pressure was used to induce the donor to make the power. • That the attorney is unsuitable to be the donor's attorney (having regard to all the circumstances and in particular the attorney's relationship to or connection with the donor).
The attorney(s) does not have to be a relative. Relatives are not entitled to know of the existence of the enduring power of attorney prior to being given this notice.	

Note. This is addressed only to the donor	3. You are informed that while the enduring power of attorney remains registered, you will not be able to revoke it until the Court of Protection confirms the revocation.

Note. This notice should be signed by every one of the attorneys who are applying to register the enduring power of attorney	Signed......................................Dated................ Signed......................................Dated................

Form EP2

No..................

Court of Protection
Enduring Powers of Attorney Act 1985

| Application for registration |

Note. Give the full name and present address of the donor. If the donor's address on the enduring power of attorney is different give that one too.	**The donor** Name... Address... .... Address on the Enduring Power of Attorney (if different)......... ....
Note. Give the full name(s) and details of the attorney(s)	**The attorney(s)** Name... Address... Age..................Occupation...................................... Relationship to donor (if any)......................................
This form may be adapted for use by three or more attorneys	Name... Address... Age..................Occupation...................................... Relationship to donor (if any)......................................
The date is the date upon which the donor signed the enduring power of attorney	I (we) the attorney(s) apply to register the enduring power of attorney made by the donor under the above Act on the............ ....20....... the original of which accompanies this application. I (we) have reason to believe that the donor is or is becoming mentally incapable.
Notice must be personally given. It should be made clear if someone other than the attorney(s) gives the notice.	I (we) have given notice in the prescribed form to the following: • The donor personally at...................................... .... on the...20..............

	• The following relatives of the donor at the addresses below on the dates given:			
If there are no relatives entitled to notice please say so	Names	Relationship	Addresses	Date

Note. Cross out this section if it does not apply	• The Co-Attorney(s)...................................... At.. On...

A remittance for the registration fee accompanies this application.

Note. The application should be signed by all the attorneys who are making the application.	I (we) certify that the above information is correct and that to the best of my (our) knowledge and belief I (we) have complied with the provisions of the Enduring Powers of Attorney Act 1985 and of all the Rules and Regulations under it. Signed.....................................Dated..................
This must not pre-date the date(s) when the notices were given	Signed.....................................Dated..................

Address to which correspondence relating to the application is to be sent if different to that of the first-named attorney making this application..

....

Form EP3
Court of Protection
Enduring Powers of Attorney Act 1985

In the matter of a power given by

<table>
<tr><td>If this application is being made prior to an application for registration the original enduring power of attorney should accompany this application.</td><td>...(a donor)

to...(attorney)

and...(attorney)

General Form of Application</td></tr>
<tr><td>Note. Give details of the order or directions that you are seeking</td><td>I...

of...

and I..</td></tr>
<tr><td>State under which subsection of the Enduring Powers of Attorney Act 1985 or which rule of the Court of Protection (Enduring Powers of Attorney) Rules 2001 this application is made</td><td>Apply for an order or directions that.............................

....

....

....

....

....</td></tr>
<tr><td>Note. Give details of the grounds on which you are seeking the order or directions</td><td>And for any other directions which are necessary as a result of my/our application.

The grounds on which I/we make this application are:</td></tr>
<tr><td>Evidence in support should accompany this application.</td><td>..

....

....</td></tr>
<tr><td>Note. The application should be signed by all the applicants or their solicitors</td><td>Signed...Dated.................

Signed...Dated.................

Address where notices should be sent..............................

....</td></tr>
</table>

Form EP4

No.......................

Court of Protection
Enduring Powers of Attorney Act 1985

Application for search/office copy

I (we)..

of..

....

apply to be informed by the Court of Protection whether an enduring power of attorney has been registered (or whether registration of an enduring power of attorney is pending) in the

Name of..

Alternative name..

Address (if known)..

....

Alternative address..

....

I (we) enclose the prescribed fee of £...............................

Please supply me (us) with an office copy of the power.

- My/our reasons for requesting a copy from the Court of Protection are...

....

....

- It is not reasonably practicable to obtain a copy from the attorney because...

....

....

Signed..

Dated...

Form EP5

No...................

Court of Protection
Enduring Powers of Attorney Act 1985

Certificate of result of search

Your reference.......................

In reply to your enquiry made on............................

☐ The following enduring power of attorney is registered against the donor's name you give:

Donor's name.......................................

Attorney's name.....................................

Power made by donor on...........................

Registered on.......................................

☐ There is an application pending for registration of the following enduring power of attorney:

Donor's name.......................................

Attorney's name.....................................

Power made by donor on...........................

☐ There was an enduring power of attorney registered against the donor's name you give but the registration has been cancelled:

Donor's name.......................................

Attorney's name.....................................

Power made by donor on...........................

Registered on.......................................

Date cancelled......................................

☐ There is no enduring power of attorney registered against the donor's name (....................) you give.

Signed...

Dated..

Form EP6

No........................

Court of Protection
Enduring Powers of Attorney Act 1985

In the matter of a power given by

....…...a donor

Witness summons

To..

of...

....

you are ordered to attend before

....

at...

....

on the.....................day of.................................20................

at......................o'clock to:

- Give evidence in this matter
- Bring with you and produce at the hearing the documents listed below:

....

....

....

....

....

....

Dated...

This summons was issued at the request of

....

Solicitors for the...

of...

....

Form EP7

No.............................

Court of Protection
Enduring Powers of Attorney Act 1985

In the matter of...

....a donor

Notice of appeal

I (we)..

of..

....

Note. If you are appealing against only part of the order/decision write down which part

Wish to appeal to a judge against the order/decision of the Court

made in this matter on the................................20........

....

....

....

Note. Tick the box that applies.

I (we) intend to ask that the order/decision may be

☐   discharged

☐   varied in the following way:

Note. Give details of the new order/decision you are asking to be made.

....

....

....

Note. The form should be sent to the Court of Protection.

Signed...

Dated..

Solicitors for the appellant(s).......................................

....

of..

....

To the appellant(s): You will be sent notice of the time, date and place of this appeal.

SCHEDULE 2   Rule 26

FEES

Column 1	Column 2
Item	*Fee*
Registration Fee 1. On lodging an application for registration of an enduring power of attorney.	£75.00
Search Fee 2. On application for a search of the register.	£25.00

EXPLANATORY NOTE

(This note is not part of the Rules)

These Rules replace the Court of Protection (Enduring Powers of Attorney) Rules 1994 (as amended).

The rules are supplemental to the Court of Protection Rules 2001 (SI 2001/824) and regulate the procedure in respect of applications under the Enduring Powers of Attorney Act 1985. The principal change made by these Rules is to provide that such applications are to be made to the Court of Protection ('the court') whereas the previous rules provided for the division of functions between the court and the Public Trustee.

The rules continue to contain provisions which –

(a) provide that any function under them expressed to be exercisable by the court may be exercised by a judge, the Master of the court or, in certain case, by an officer of the court (rule 4);

(b) prescribe the form of notice to be given by an attorney of his intention to apply to the court to register an enduring power of attorney (rule 6) and the form of such application (rule 8);

(c) specify the information to be set out in an objection to the registration of an enduring power of attorney (rule 9);

(d) provide for searches to be made of the register of enduring powers of attorney (rule 13);

(e) provide for reviews of, and appeals from, decisions of the court (rules 23 and 24);

(f) provide for the cancellation by the court of the registration of an enduring power of attorney in certain circumstances (rule 25); and

(g) specify the fees payable in connection with an application for the registration of an enduring power of attorney and an application for a search of the register and which remain unchanged at £75 and £25 respectively (Schedule 2).

APPENDIX 5

THE ENDURING POWERS OF ATTORNEY (PRESCRIBED FORM) REGULATIONS 1990, SI 1990/1376

The Lord Chancellor, in exercise of the powers conferred on him by section 2(2) of the Enduring Powers of Attorney Act 1985, hereby makes the following Regulations:

1 Citation and commencement

These Regulations may be cited as the Enduring Powers of Attorney (Prescribed Form) Regulations 1990 and shall come into force on 31st July 1990.

2 Prescribed form

(1)   Subject to paragraphs (2) and (3) of this regulation and to regulation 4, an enduring power of attorney must be in the form set out in the Schedule to these Regulations and must include all the explanatory information headed 'About using this form' in Part A of the Schedule and all the relevant marginal notes to Parts B and C. It may also include such additions (including paragraph numbers) or restrictions as the donor may decide.

(2)   In completing the form of enduring power of attorney –

(a)   there shall be excluded (either by omission or deletion) –

(i)   where the donor appoints only one attorney, everything between the square brackets on the first page of Part B; and

(ii)   one and only one of any pair of alternatives;

(b)   there may also be so excluded –

(i)   the words on the second page of Part B 'subject to the following restrictions and conditions', if those words do not apply;

(ii)   the attestation details for a second witness in Parts B and C if a second witness is not required; and

(iii)   any marginal notes which correspond with any words excluded under the provisions of this paragraph and the two notes numbered 1 and 2 which appear immediately under the heading to Part C.

(3)   The form of execution by the donor or by an attorney may be adapted to provide –

(a)   for a case where the donor or an attorney signs by means of a mark; and

(b)   for the case (dealt with in regulation 3) where the enduring power of attorney is executed at the direction of the donor or of an attorney;

and the form of execution by an attorney may be adapted to provide for execution by a trust corporation.

(4)   Subject to paragraphs (1), (2) and (3) of this regulation and to regulation 4, an enduring power of attorney which seeks to exclude any provision contained in these Regulations is not a valid enduring power of attorney.

3 Execution

(1)   An enduring power of attorney in the form set out in the Schedule to these Regulations shall be executed by both the donor and the attorney, although not necessarily at the same time, in the presence of a witness, but not necessarily the same witness, who shall sign the form and give his full name and address.

(2)   The donor and an attorney shall not witness the signature of each other nor one attorney the signature of another.

(3)   Where an enduring power of attorney is executed at the direction of the donor –

    (a)   it must be signed in the presence of two witnesses who shall each sign the form and give their full names and addresses; and

    (b)   a statement that the enduring power of attorney has been executed at the direction of the donor must be inserted in Part B;

    (c)   it must not be signed by either an attorney or any of the witnesses to the signature of either the donor or an attorney.

(4)   Where an enduring power of attorney is executed at the direction of an attorney –

    (a)   paragraph (3)(a) above applies; and

    (b)   a statement that the enduring power of attorney has been executed at the direction of the attorney must be inserted in Part C;

    (c)   it must not be signed by either the donor, an attorney or any of the witnesses to the signature of either the donor or an attorney.

4 Where more than one attorney is appointed and they are to act jointly and severally, then at least one of the attorneys so appointed must execute the instrument for it to take effect as an enduring power of attorney, and only those attorneys who have executed the instrument shall have the functions of an attorney under an enduring power of attorney in the event of the donor's mental incapacity or of the registration of the power, whichever first occurs.

5 Revocation

The Enduring Powers of Attorney (Prescribed Form) Regulations 1987 are hereby revoked, except that –

    (a)   a power executed in the form prescribed by those Regulations and executed by the donor before 31st July 1991 shall be capable (whether or not seals are affixed to it) of being a valid enduring power of attorney;

    (b)   regulation 3(3) shall apply to a power executed by the donor before 31st July 1991 under the provisions of those Regulations and the form of enduring power of attorney prescribed by those Regulations may be modified accordingly.

SCHEDULE

Regulations 2·and 3

ENDURING POWER OF ATTORNEY

Part A: About using this form

1. **You may choose one attorney or more than one.** If you choose one attorney then you must delete everything between the square brackets on the first page of the form. If you choose more than one, you must decide whether they are able to act:
   - Jointly (that is, they must all act together and cannot act separately) or
   - Jointly and severally (that is, they can all act together but they can also act separately if they wish).

   On the first page of the form, show what you have decided by crossing out one of the alternatives.

2. **If you give your attorney(s) general power** in relation to all your property and affairs, it means that they will be able to deal with your money or property and may be able to sell your nouse.

3. **If you don't want your attorney(s) to have such wide powers,** you can include any restrictions you like. For example, you can include a restriction that your attorney(s) must not act on your behalf until they have reason to believe that you are becoming mentally incapable; or a restriction as to what your attorney(s) may do. Any restrictions you choose must be written or typed where indicated on the second page of the form.

4. **If you are a trustee** (and please remember that co-ownership of a home involves trusteeship), you should seek legal advice if you want your attorney(s) to act as a trustee on your behalf.

5. **Unless you put in a restriction preventing it** your attorney(s) will be able to use any of your money or property to make any provision which you yourself might be expected to make for their own needs or the needs of other people. Your attorney(s) will also be able to use your money to make gifts, but only for reasonable amounts in relation to the value of your money and property.

6. **Your attorney(s) can recover the out-of-pocket expenses** of acting as your attorney(s). If your attorney(s) are professional people, for example solicitors or accountants, they may be able to charge for their professional services as well. You may wish to provide expressly for remuneration of your attorney(s) (although if they are trustees they may not be allowed to accept it).

7. **If your attorney(s) have reason to believe** that you have become or are becoming mentally incapable of managing your affairs, your attorney(s) will have to apply to the Court of Protection for registration of this power.

8. **Before applying to the Court of Protection for registration** of this power, your attorney(s) must give written notice that that is what they are going to do, to you and your nearest relatives as defined in the Enduring Powers of Attorney Act 1985. You or your relatives will be able to object if you or they disagree with registration.

9. **This is a simplified explanation** of what the Enduring Powers of Attorney Act 1985 and the Rules and Regulations say. If you need more guidance, you or your advisers will need to look at the Act itself and the Rules and Regulations. The Rules are the Court of Protection (Enduring Powers of Attorney) Rules 1986 (Statutory Instrument 1986 No. 127). The Regulations are the Enduring Powers of Attorney (Prescribed Form) Regulations 1990 (Statutory Instrument 1990 No. 1376).

10. **Note to Attorney(s)**
   After the power has been registered you should notify the Court of Protection if the donor dies or recovers.

11. **Note to Donor**
   Some of these explanatory notes may not apply to the form you are using if it has already been adapted to suit your particular requirements.

YOU CAN CANCEL THIS POWER AT ANY TIME BEFORE IT HAS TO BE REGISTERED

Part B: To be completed by the 'donor' (the person appointing the attorney(s))

Don't sign this form unless you understand what it means

Please read the notes in the margin which follow and which are part of the form itself.

Donor's name and address.

I _____

of _____

Donor's date of birth.

born on _____

appoint _____

See note 1 on the front of this form. If you are appointing only one attorney you should cross out everything between the square brackets. If appointing more than two attorneys please give the additional name(s) on an attached sheet.

of _____

• [and _____

of _____

Cross out the one which does not apply (see note 1 on the front of this form).

• jointly
• jointly and severally]

to be my attorney(s) for the purpose of the Enduring Powers of Attorney Act 1985

Cross out the one which does not apply (see note 2 on the front of this form). Add any additional powers.

• with general authority to act on my behalf
• with authority to do the following on my behalf:

If you don't want the attorney(s) to have general power, you must give details here of what authority you are giving the attorney(s).

in relation to

Cross out the one which does not apply.

• all my property and affairs:
• the following property and affairs:

Part B: continued

Please read the notes in the margin which follow and which are part of the form itself.
If there are restrictions or conditions, insert them here; if not, cross out these words if you wish (see note 3 on the front of this form).

• subject to the following restrictions and conditions:

If this form is being signed at your direction:–
• the person signing must not be an attorney or any witness (to Parts B or C).
• you must add a statement that this form has been signed at your direction.
• a second witness is necessary (please see below).

Your signature (or mark).

I intend that this power shall continue even if I become mentally incapable

I have read or have had read to me the notes in Part A which are part of, and explain, this form.

Signed by me as a deed _____
and delivered

Date.
Someone must witness your signature.

Signature of witness.

Your attorney(s) cannot be your witness. It is not advisable for your husband or wife to be your witness.

on_____

in the presence of _____

Full name of witness_____

Address of witness _____

_____

_____

A second witness is only necessary if this form is not being signed by you personally but at your direction (for example, if a physical disability prevents you from signing).
Signature of second witness.

in the presence of _____

Full name of witness_____

Address of witness _____

_____

_____

Part C: To be completed by the attorney(s)

Note: 1. This form may be adapted to provide for execution by a corporation
2. If there is more than one attorney additional sheets in the form as shown below must be added to this Part C

Please read the notes in the margin which follow and which are part of the form itself.

Don't sign this form before the donor has signed Part B or if, in your opinion, the donor was already mentally incapable at the time of signing Part B.

If this form is being signed at your direction:–
• the person signing must not be an attorney or any witness (to Parts B or C).
• you must add a statement that this form has been signed at your direction.
• a second witness is necessary (please see below).

Signature (or mark) of attorney.

Date.

Signature of witness.

The attorney must sign the form and his signature must be witnessed. The donor may not be the witness and one attorney may not witness the signature of the other.

A second witness is only necessary if this form is not being signed by you personally but at your direction (for example, if a physical disability prevents you from signing).
Signature of second witness.

I understand that I have a duty to apply to the Court for the registration of this form under the Enduring Powers of Attorney Act 1985 when the donor is becoming or has become mentally incapable.

I also understand my limited power to use the donor's property to benefit persons other than the donor.

I am not a minor

Signed by me as a deed _____
and delivered

on_____

in the presence of _____

Full name of witness_____

Address of witness _____

_____

_____

in the presence of _____

Full name of witness_____

Address of witness _____

_____

_____

EXPLANATORY NOTE

(This note is not part of the Regulations)

These Regulations prescribe a revised form of an enduring power of attorney, the explanatory information endorsed on it and the manner in which it is to be executed.

In particular these Regulations make amendments consequent upon the coming into force on 31st July 1990 of provisions in the Law of Property (Miscellaneous Provisions) Act 1989 (c.34) which change the law relating to deeds and their execution.

APPENDIX 6

THE ENDURING POWER OF ATTORNEY (WELSH LANGUAGE PRESCRIBED FORM) REGULATIONS 2000, SI 2000/289

The Lord Chancellor, in exercise of the powers conferred upon him by section 2 of the Enduring Powers of Attorney Act 1985 as extended by section 26(3) of the Welsh Language Act 1993, makes the following Regulations:

1   These Regulations may be cited as the Enduring Powers of Attorney (Welsh Language Prescribed Form) Regulations 2000 and shall come into force on 1st March 2000.

2   The form of words in the Schedule to these Regulations may be used instead of that set out in the Schedule to the Enduring Powers of Attorney (Prescribed Form) Regulations 1990.

SCHEDULE

ATODLEN

ATWRNEIAETH BARHAUS

Rhan A: Ynghylch defnyddio'r ffurflen hon

1. **Cewch ddewis un atwrnai neu fwy nag un.** Os mai un atwrnai a ddewiswch, rhaid i chi ddileu popeth rhwng y bracedi sgwâr ar dudalen gyntaf y ffurflen. Os dewiswch chi fwy nag un, rhaid i chi benderfynu a ydyn nhw'n gallu gweithredu:

- Ar y cŷd (hynny yw, rhaid iddyn nhw i gyd weithredu gyda'i gilydd ac ni chânt weithredu ar wahân) neu
- Ar y cyd ac ar wahân (hynny yw, cânt oll weithio gyda'i gilydd ond cânt hefyd weithredu ar wahân os ydyn nhw'n dymuno gwneud hynny).

Ar dudalen gyntaf y ffurflen, nodwch eich penderfyniad chi trwy groesi un o'r dewisiadau allan.

2. **Os rhowch chi bŵer cyffredinol i'ch atwrnai** yng nghyswllt eich holl eiddo a'ch busnes, mae hynny'n golygu y byddan nhw'n gallu delio gyda'ch arian a'ch eiddo ac, o bosib, yn gallu gwerthu eich tŷ.

3. **Os nad ydych chi'n dymuno i'ch atwrnai feddu ar bwerau mor eang**, cewch gynnwys unrhyw gyfyngiadau a fynnwch chi. Er enghraifft, cewch gynnwys cyfyngiad na chaiff ei atwrnai(eiod) weithredu ar eich rhan nes bod ganddyn nhw sail dros gredu bod yn feddyliol analluog; neu gyfyngiad ynghylch yr hyn y caiff eich atwrnai(eiod) ei wneud. Rhaid ysgrifennu neu deipio unrhyw gyfyngiadau y dewiswch eu nodi yn y man priodol ar ail dudalen y ffurflen.

4. **Os ydych chi'n ymddiriedolwr** (a chofiwch hefyd bod cyd-berchnogi cartref yn golygu eich bod yn ymddiriedolwr), dylech ofyn am gyngor cyfreithiol os ydych chi'n dymuno i'r atwrnai(eiod) weithredu fel ymddiriedolwr ar eich rhan.

5. **Oni bai eich bod yn cynnwys cyfyngiad i rwystro hynny**, bydd eich atwrnai(eiod) yn gallu defnyddio eich arian neu'ch eiddo i wneud darpariaeth y gellid disgwyl i chi eich hun ei gwneud at eu hanghenion eu hunain neu at anghenion pobl eraill. Bydd eich atwrnai(eiod) hefyd yn gallu defnyddio eich arian fel rhoddion, ond dim ond am symiau rhesymol yng nghyswllt gwerth eich arian a'ch eiddo.

6. **Caiff eich atwrnai(eiod) adennill y mân-gostau** o weithredu fel atwrnai(eiod) ar eich rhan. Os yw eich atwrnai(eiod) yn weithwyr proffesiynol, er enghraifft cyfreithwyr neu gyfrifwyr, mae'n bosib y gallan nhw godi am eu gwasanaethau proffesiynol hefyd. Mae'n bosib y byddwch yn dymuno gwneud darpariaeth arbennig ar gyfer rhoi cydnabyddiaeth am waith eich atwrnai(eiod) (er, os ydyn nhw'n ymddiriedolwyr, mae'n bosib na fydd ganddyn nhw'r hawl i'w derbyn).

7. **Os yw eich atwrnai(eiod) o'r farn eich bod**, neu eich bod ar fin bod, yn feddyliol analluog i gadw trefn ar eich busnes, bydd yn rhaid i'ch atwrnai(eiod) gyflwyno cais i'r Llys Nodded er mwyn cofrestru ei bŵer.

8. **Cyn cyflwyno cais i'r Llys Nodded ar gyfer cofrestru'r pŵer hwn**, bydd yn rhaid i'ch atwrnai(eiod) roi rhybudd ysgrifenedig o'u bwraid, i chi ac i'ch perthnasau agos, yn ôl diffiniad Deddf Atwrneiaeth Barhaus 1985. Byddwch chi neu'ch perthnasau yn gallu gwrthwynebu os ydych chi, neu os ydyn nhw, yn anghytuno gyda'r cofrestriad hwn.

9. **Mae hwn yn esboniad syml** o'r hyn sydd gan Ddeddf Atwrneiaeth Barhaus 1985 a'r Rheolau a'r Rheoliadau i'w ddweud. Os oes angen rhagor o arweiniad arnoch, bydd gofyn i chi, neu'ch cynghorwyr, edrych ar y Ddeddf ei hun ac ar y Rheolau a'r Rheoliadau. Y Rheolau yw Rheolau y Llys Nodded (Atwrneiaeth Barhaus) 1986 (Offeryn Statudol 1986 Rhif 127). Y Rheoliadau yw Rheoliadau Atwrneiaeth Barhaus (Ffurf Benodedig) 1990 (Offeryn Statudol 1990 Rhif 1376).

10. **Nodyn i'r Atwrnai(eiod)**
Ar ôl cofrestru'r pŵer, dylech roi gwybod i'r Llys Nodded os yw'r rhoddwr yn marw neu'n gwella.

11. **Nodyn i'r Rhoddwr**
Mae'n bosib na fydd rhywfaint o'r nodiadau esboniadol yn berthnasol i'r ffurflen y byddwch chi'n ei defnyddio os yw eisoes wedi'i haddasu i gyd-fynd â'ch gofynion penodol chi.

CEWCH GANSLO'R PŴER HWN UNRHYW BRYD CYN BOD YN RHAID EI GOFRESTRU

Rhan B: I'w llenwi gan y rhoddwr (y sawl sy'n penodi'r atwrnai(eiod)).

Peidiwch â llofnodi'r ffurflen hon nes eich bod yn deall beth mae hynny'n ei olygu

A fyddech gystal â darllen y nodiadau isod ar ymyl y dudalen sy'n rhan o'r ffurflen ei hun.

Enw a chyfeiriad y Rhoddwr.

Yr wyf fi _____

o _____

Dyddiad geni y Rhoddwr.

a anwyd ar _____

yn penodi _____

Gweler nodyn 1 ar flaen y ffurflen hon. Os mai dim ond un atwrnai yr ydych yn ei benodi, dylech ddileu popeth arall sy'n ymddangos rhwng y bracedi sgwâr trwy'i groesi allan. Os ydych chi'n penodi mwy na dau atwrnai, nodwch yr enw(au) ar y ddalen sydd ynghlwm.

o _____

• [ac _____

o _____

Dilëwch ba un bynnag sy'n amherthnasol trwy'i groesi allan (gweler nodyn 1 ar flaen y ffurflen hon).

• ar y cyd
• ar y cyd ac ar wahân]
i fod yn atwrnai (eiod) at ddibenion Deddf Atwrneiaeth Barhaus 1985
• gydag awdurdod cyffredinol i weithredu ar fy rhan
• gydag awdurdod i wneud y canlynol ar fy rhan

Dilëwch ba un bynnag sy'n amherthnasol trwy'i groesi allan (gweler nodyn 2 ar flaen y ffurflen hon). Nodwch unrhyw bwerau ychwanegol.

Os nad ydych chi'n dymuno i'r atwrnai(eiod) feddu ar bŵer cyffredinol, rhaid nodi yma fanylion yr awdurdod yr ydych yn ei roi i'r atwrnai(eiod).

yng nghyswllt
• fy holl eiddo a'm busnes
• yr eiddo a'r busnes canlynol:

Dilëwch ba un bynnag sy'n amherthnasol trwy'i groesi allan.

Rhan B: parhad

A fyddech gystal â darllen y nodiadau isod ar ymyl y dudalen sy'n rhan o'r ffurflen ei hun. Os oes yna unrhyw gyfyngiadau neu amodau, nodwch y rheiny yma; os nad oes, croeswch y geiriau hyn allan os ydych chi'n dymuno (gweler nodyn 3 ar flaen y ffurflen hon).

- yn amodol ac y cyfyngiadau a'r amodau isod:

Os yw'r ffurflen hon yn cael ei llofnodi yn unol â'ch cyfarwyddiadau chi:—
- rhaid i'r sawl sy'n ei llofnodi beidio â bod yn atwrnai nac yn dyst (i Rannau B nac C).
- rhaid i chi ychwanegu datganiad sy'n dweud fod y ffurflen hon wedi'i llofnodi ar eich cyfarwyddiadau chi.
- rhaid wrth ail dyst (gweler isod).

Fy mwriad yw i'r pŵer hwn barhau hyd yn oed os byddaf, un diwrnod, yn feddyliol analluog.

Yr wyf wedi darllen, neu darllenodd rywun i mi, nodiadau Rhan A sy'n rhan o'r ffurflen hon, ac yn cynnig esboniad ohoni.

Eich llofnod chi (neu farc).

Llofnodwyd gennyf fi fel gweithred _____ a chyflwynwyd

Dyddiad.
Rhaid i rywun fod yn dyst i'ch llofnod.

ar _____

Llofnod y tyst.

ym mhresenoldeb _____

Enw llawn y tyst _____

Ni chaiff eich atwrnai(eiod) fod yn dyst(ion) i chi. Ni chynghorir i'ch gŵr neu'ch gwraig fod yn dyst i chi.

Cyfeiriad y tyst _____

_____

_____

Dim ond os nad ydych chi'n llofnodi'r ffurflen hon yn bersonol, ond eich bod wedi rhoi cyfarwyddiadau i rywun arall ei lofnodi ar eich rhan, (er enghraifft, os yw anabledd corfforol yn eich rhwystro rhag llofnodi) y bydd yn rhaid i chi gael ail dyst. Llofnod yr ail dyst.

ym mhresenoldeb _____

Enw llawn y tyst _____

Cyfeiriad y tyst _____

_____

_____

Rhan C: I'w llenwi gan yr atwrnai(eiod)

Nodyn:
1. Gellir addasu'r ffurflen hon i ganiatáu ar gyfer cyflawni gan gorfforaeth.
2. Os oes mwy nag un atwrnai, rhaid rhoi dalennau ychwanegol yn unol â'r ffurf isod, at Ran C.

A fyddech gystal â darllen y nodiadau isod ar ymyl y dudalen sy'n rhan o'r ffurflen ei hun.

Peidiwch â llofnodi'r ffurflen hon nes bod y rhoddwr wedi llofnodi Rhan B neu os oedd y Rhoddwr, yn eich barn chi, eisoes yn feddyliol analluog adeg llofnodi Rhan B.

Deallaf fod gennyf ddyletswydd i gyflwyno cais i'r Llys am i'r ffurflen hon gael ei chofrestru o dan Ddeddf Atwrneiaeth Barhaus 1985 pan fo'r rhoddwr ar fin bod yn feddyliol analluog neu eisoes yn y cyflwr hwnnw.

Deallaf hefyd fod fy mhŵer i ddefnyddio eiddo'r rhoddwr er budd unrhyw un, ar wahân i'r rhoddwr, wedi'i gyfyngu.

Os yw'r ffurflen hon yn cael ei llofnodi yn unol â'ch cyfarwyddiadau chi:—
• rhaid i'r sawl sy'n ei llofnodi beidio â bod yn atwrnai nac yn dyst (i Rannau B nac C).
• rhaid i chi ychwanegu datganiad sy'n dweud fod y ffurflen hon wedi'i llofnodi ar eich cyfarwyddiadau chi.
• rhaid wrth ail dyst (gweler isod).

Nid wyf dan oed

Llofnod (neu farc) yr atwrnai.

Llofnodwyd gennyf fi fel gweithred _____ a'i chyflwyno

Dyddiad.

ar _____

Llofnod y tyst.

ym mhresenoldeb _____

Enw llawn y tyst _____

Rhaid i'r atwrnai lofnodi'r ffurflen a rhaid cael tyst i'w lofnod. Ni chaiff y rhoddwr fod yn dyst ac ni chaiff un atwrnai fod yn dyst i lofnod y llall.

Cyfeiriad y tyst _____

_____

_____

Dim ond os nad ydych chi'n llofnodi'r ffurflen hon yn bersonol, ond eich bod wedi rhoi cyfarwyddiadau i rywun arall ei llofnodi ar eich rhan, (er enghraifft, os yw anabledd corfforol yn eich rhwystro rhag llofnodi) y bydd yn rhaid i chi gael ail dyst. Llofnod yr ail dyst.

ym mhresenoldeb _____

Enw llawn y tyst _____

Cyfeiriad y tyst _____

_____

_____

EXPLANATORY NOTE

(This note is not part of the Rules)

These regulations prescribe a Welsh language form for an enduring power of attorney. It is a translation of the form contained in the Enduring Powers of Attorney (Prescribed Form) Regulations 1990.

APPENDIX 7

LAND REGISTRY PRACTICE LEAFLET 32

Powers of Attorney and Registered Land

A   What the Land Registry needs to know

B   Types of power of attorney

    1.   General powers under section 10 of the Powers of Attorney Act 1971

    2.   Other general and special powers

    3.   Security powers

    4.   Enduring powers

    5.   Trustee Act powers

    6.   Power given by all the trustees to a beneficiary under section 9 of the Trusts of Land and Appointment of Trustees Act 1996.

C   Joint Proprietors – receipts for capital money

D   Joint Proprietors – evidence that the donor of a power had a beneficial interest

E   Powers more than 12 months old – evidence of non-revocation

F   Evidence of the Power

G   Checklists

    1.   Power given by a sole proprietor (not a trustee)

    2.   Power given by one of joint proprietors dated before 1 March 2000

    3.   Power given by one of joint proprietors dated after 29 February 2000

    4.   Power given to beneficiaries by all the joint proprietors of the land

Annex   Statutory declaration/certificate as to non-revocation

A What the Land Registry needs to know

When we are registering a document signed by an attorney, we need to be sure that the document binds the individual or company on whose behalf it was signed. We do this by checking that the power of attorney

- was validly executed as a deed;
- was still in force at the date of the document;
- authorised the attorney to take the action in question; and
- was, where necessary, made under the correct statutory provision.

There are cases where, even though the power does not meet these requirements, the person who relied on the document can assume that the power was correctly made or that it was still in force at the time it was used. In those cases we may need confirmatory evidence from that person.

When an individual executes a deed, it must be clear that the document is signed as a deed and the signature must be made in the presence of a witness who attests the signature. Practice Advice Leaflet No.6 deals in detail with execution of deeds by different types of legal person. Copies are available from any district land registry.

This leaflet takes account of the changes in the law made by the Trustee Delegation Act 1999, in force from 1 March 2000.

This leaflet does not cover the more complex issues involved when a power of attorney is granted under the law of another jurisdiction. In such a case we may require an opinion as to the matters specified above from a lawyer qualified in that jurisdiction.

B Types of power of attorney

1. General powers under section 10 of the Powers of Attorney Act 1971

The 1971 Act provides a short form of general power of attorney that can be used by a sole beneficial owner of land. It operates to give the attorney authority to do anything that the donor can lawfully do by an attorney. However, powers in that form dated before 1 March 2000 are never suitable for dealing with land of which the donor is a joint proprietor. And those dated after 29 February 2000 may only be used by a joint proprietor if the donor has a beneficial interest in the land. The death, bankruptcy or mental incapacity of the donor will automatically revoke the power. The donor may also revoke it at any time.

2. Other general and special powers

A person wishing to appoint an attorney does not have to use the form set out in the 1971 Act. The only strict requirement is that the donor must execute the power as a deed. The donor may use any form of wording, giving the attorney either general authority to act or limited powers, for example in connection with a particular transaction or dealings with specified property. A power that does not follow any of the statutory forms may be used on behalf of a donor who is a joint proprietor only if

- it is dated after 29 February 2000; and
- the donor has a beneficial interest in the land; and
- there is no indication in the power that the donor did not intend the attorney to exercise trustee functions.

Unless it is a security power the donor may revoke such a power and the death, bankruptcy or mental incapacity of the donor will automatically revoke it.

3. Security powers

A security power is a power of attorney that is expressed to be irrevocable and is given to secure

- a proprietary interest of the attorney; or
- the performance of an obligation owed to the attorney.

While the donee has the interest or until the obligation is discharged the donor can only revoke the power with the attorney's consent and the death, bankruptcy or mental incapacity of the donor does not revoke it.

4. Enduring powers

An enduring power of attorney is one made by an individual under the Enduring Powers of Attorney Act 1985. It must be in the form prescribed under that Act at the date that the power was granted. An enduring power is not revoked by the donor's mental incapacity. But the attorney must apply to register the power with the Court of Protection if there is reason to believe that the donor is becoming mentally incapable. After the power is registered the donor can only revoke it if the Court confirms that he or she is mentally capable of doing so. The bankruptcy or death of the donor will automatically revoke the power whether or not it is so registered. The bankruptcy of the attorney will also revoke the power.

Enduring powers dated after 29 February 2000 may only be used on behalf of a donor who is a joint proprietor if

- the donor has a beneficial interest in the land; and

- there is no indication in the power that the donor did not intend the attorney to exercise trustee functions.

There are transitional provisions in the 1999 Act for enduring powers dated before 1 March 2000. Until 1 March 2001 such a power may be used on behalf of any donor who is a joint proprietor. From 1 March 2001 an enduring power dated before 1 March 2000 may only be so used if

- the donor has a beneficial interest in the land; and

- there is no indication in the power that the donor did not intend the attorney to exercise trustee functions

Or

- the power is registered with the court following an application made to the Court before 1 March 2001;

Or

- an application made to the Court for registration of the power before 1 March 2001 has not been finally refused.

An attorney under an enduring power can make gifts and confer benefits on behalf of the donor only in very limited circumstances – see section 3(4) and (5) of the 1985 Act. We will usually refuse to register a transfer involving a gift or benefit that is executed under an enduring power unless the Court has authorised the transfer under section 8 (2) (e) of the Act.

5. Trustee Act powers

Section 25 of the Trustee Act 1925 allows a trustee to grant a power of attorney delegating his or her functions as a trustee to the attorney. The original section 25 was substantially amended by the Powers of Attorney Act 1971 and, with effect from 1 March 2000, the Trustee Delegation Act 1999 has substituted a new section 25.

The new section 25 provides a short form of power by which a single donor can delegate trustee functions under a single trust to a single donee. Trustees can use other forms. The short form would not, for example, be appropriate where the donor wishes to delegate functions under several trusts to one attorney or wishes to limit the range of functions to be delegated.

A Trustee Act power can be granted only for a period of up to twelve months. For powers granted before 1 March 2000 that period commenced on the date of the power. For those granted after 29 February 2000 the twelve months period may start at a later date specified in the power.

A Trustee Act power can always be used, while in force, to execute dispositions of land on behalf of a donor who is a joint proprietor, whether or not the donor has a beneficial interest in the land. Before 1 March 2000 a trustee could not grant such a power to an attorney who was also the only other trustee under the trust. The 1999 Act has removed that limitation. However, where there are only two trustees, it will always be sensible to appoint a third party. This is because, as explained in part D below, a trustee who is also acting as attorney for the only other co-trustee will not be able to give valid receipts for capital money.

6. Power given by all the trustees to a beneficiary under section 9 of the Trusts of Land and Appointment of Trustees Act 1996

All the trustees of a trust of land can together appoint a beneficiary or the beneficiaries to exercise their functions in relation to the land. But the attorney cannot give a receipt for capital money, so the trustees would, in any event, need to join in any disposition of the land where such a receipt was required. This type of power is, therefore, likely to be encountered rarely in the context of dispositions of registered land. It could only be used effectively when no capital money is passing, e.g. on the grant of a rack rent lease.

Where this form of power is used for a registered disposition we need a statutory declaration from the person(s) who dealt with the attorney that they:

- acted in good faith; and

- had no knowledge at the time of completion of the transaction that the attorney was not a person to whom the functions of the trustees in relation to the land to which the application relates could be delegated under section 9 of the 1996 Act. – see rule 82B of the Land Registration Rules 1925.

Alternatively, we will accept a certificate to the same effect from a solicitor or licensed conveyancer. The combined form of the statutory declaration and certificate, set out in the Annex to this leaflet, covers the above points as well as the evidence we need if this form of power is over twelve months old at the date of the disposition.

C   Joint Proprietors – receipts for capital money

For dispositions dated after 29 February 2000, section 7 of the Trustee Delegation Act 1999 provides that a receipt for capital money will overreach beneficial interests only if an attorney acts with at least one other person. This means that a receipt clause in a disposition by joint proprietors is not acceptable if it is signed only by one person both as proprietor and as attorney for the other proprietor(s). Nor is it acceptable for one person to sign as attorney for all the proprietors.

If such a document is lodged we will return it for execution by the donor of the power. If the document is not re-executed we will enter a joint proprietor restriction on the register to protect any beneficial interests that may still subsist.

There is an exception to this rule under the transitional provisions of the Trustee Delegation Act 1999, described in paragraph B4 above. This applies where an enduring power of attorney dated before 1 March 2000 still covers all trustee functions, even though the donor of the power may have no beneficial interest in the land.

D   Joint Proprietors – evidence that the donor of a power had a beneficial interest

All joint proprietors hold the registered legal estate as trustees. Until 1 March 2000 this meant that a joint proprietor always had to appoint an attorney by a power under the Trustee Act 1925 or the Enduring Powers of Attorney Act 1985 if the attorney was to be able to execute dispositions of registered land. The Trustee Delegation Act 1999, in force on that date, has

relaxed this rule where the joint proprietor has a beneficial interest in the land.

The 1999 Act allows a general or an enduring power of attorney dated after 29 February 2000 to be used in relation to trust property if, at the time it is used, the donor of the power owns a beneficial interest in that property. The same rule will apply to enduring powers of attorney dated before 1 March 2000 once the transitional provisions mentioned in paragraph B4 above have expired.

A written statement by the attorney given within three months of the date of the document confirming that the donor had a beneficial interest in the property is, in favour of a purchaser, conclusive evidence that the power could be used (section 2 (2) Trustee Delegation Act 1999).

The most convenient place for the attorney to make this written statement will be in the disposition itself. The attorney may

- include a statement on the following lines in the additional provisions panel of a TR1 or other prescribed form, or in the body of a lease or charge:

    "(Name of attorney) confirms that *(donor of the power)* has a beneficial interest in the property at the date of this *(transfer, charge etc.)"*

    Or

- adapt the attestation clause as follows:

    "Signed as a deed by *(name of donor of the power)*, who has a beneficial interest in the property at the date of this *(transfer, charge etc.)*, acting by *(his/her)* attorney *(name of attorney)* in the presence of"

    Or

- expand the words of signature as follows:

    "John Smith by his attorney Jane Brown who confirms that the donor has a beneficial interest in the Property at the date hereof"

The written statement can also be made separately as long as it is dated within three months of the date of the document.

If an applicant for registration cannot produce such a statement we will consider other evidence that the donor had a beneficial interest at the relevant time. A statutory declaration to that effect by a responsible person with full knowledge of the facts may be acceptable in some cases. But if the applicant does not produce sufficient evidence of the donor's beneficial entitlement the document will need to be executed by the donor of the power.

E   Powers more than 12 months old – evidence of non-revocation

A purchaser from a person who has dealt with an attorney is entitled to assume that the power of attorney has not been revoked if the transaction in question took place within twelve months of the date when the power came into operation.

This general presumption about non-revocation does not apply to powers of attorney that are more than twelve months old. Under rule 82A of the Land Registration Rules 1925, if your application to the Registry relies on such a power you must produce evidence of non-revocation. This evidence will be either

- a statutory declaration as to non-revocation in the appropriate form made by the person dealing with the attorney; or

- a certificate to the same effect given by that person's solicitor or licensed conveyancer.

The form of statutory declaration and certificate set out in the Annex to this leaflet covers all the information that we might require. You may photocopy it or reproduce it on your own word processor.

Trustee Act powers of attorney can only operate for twelve months. We will not, therefore, need evidence of non-revocation for these powers.

F   Evidence of the Power

The Registry will need to see either the original or a sufficient copy of any power of attorney that you are relying on to establish that a document lodged with your application is validly executed. We will retain the evidence lodged in our files. If, therefore, you need to keep the original you should lodge a copy with your application.

Section 3 of the Powers of Attorney Act 1971 prescribes a strict method of proving the contents of a power of attorney. To follow this procedure a solicitor, notary public or stockbroker must certify

- at the end of a photocopy of the power that it is a true and complete copy of the original; and

- on each page of the photocopy, if the power includes more than one page, that the page is a true and complete copy of the corresponding page of the original.

In practice, we will usually accept a photocopy that is certified, by a solicitor or licensed conveyancer, to be a true copy of the original power. However, in any case of doubt, we would need to ask you to produce either the original or the more formal certified copy mentioned above.

G   Checklists

The following checklists are set out below:

1. Power given by a sole proprietor (not a trustee)

2. Power given by one of joint proprietors dated before 1 March 2000

3. Power given by one of joint proprietors dated after 29 February 2000

4. Power given to beneficiaries by all the joint proprietors of the land

We hope that the checklists will help you, in the cases that they cover, to lodge the correct documents and evidence with your applications. Unless you can answer "yes" to all the questions that apply, the donor of the power will need to execute the document personally before we can register it.

1.   Power given by a sole proprietor (not a trustee)

- Are you able to lodge the original or a certified copy of the power?

- Is the power validly executed as a deed?

- Is the power wide enough to cover what the attorney has done?

- If the power was more than 12 months old when the attorney signed the document are you able to lodge the additional evidence that we need? - see part E.

2.   Power given by one of joint proprietors dated before 1 March 2000

- Are you able to lodge the original or a certified copy of the power?

- Is the power validly executed as a deed?

- Is the power a Trustee Act power? – see paragraph B5

Or

- Is the power an enduring power and was the transfer or other document dated before 1 March 2001 (or within the transitional period if registered with the court)? – see paragraph B4.

Or

- Is the power an enduring power and did the donor have a beneficial interest in the property, there being no intention, expressed in the power, of excluding functions that the donor held as a trustee? – see paragraph B4 and part D

- Is the power wide enough to cover what the attorney has done?

For documents signed by the attorney after 29 February 2000

- Has at least one other proprietor of the land (or a third party as attorney on that proprietor's behalf) also given any necessary receipt for capital money?

Or

Is the power an enduring power dated before 1 March 2000 and was the document dated before 1 March 2001 (or within the transitional period if registered with the court)? – see paragraph B4

- If the power was more than 12 months old when the attorney signed the document are you able to lodge the additional evidence that we need? – see part E.

3. Power given by one of joint proprietors dated after 29 February 2000

- Are you able to lodge the original or a certified copy of the power?

- Is the power validly executed as a deed?

- Is the power made under the Trustee Act 1925? – see paragraph B5.

Or

Did the donor of the power have a beneficial interest in the property, there being no intention, expressed in the power, of excluding functions that the donor held as a trustee? – see paragraphs B1, B2 and B4 and part D.

- Is the power wide enough to cover what the attorney has done?

- Has at least one other proprietor of the land (or a third party as attorney on that proprietor's behalf) also given any necessary receipt for capital money? – see part C.

- If the power was more than 12 months old when the attorney signed the document are you able to lodge the additional evidence that we need? – see Part E.

4. Power given to beneficiaries by all the joint proprietors of the land

- Are you able to lodge the original or a certified copy of the power?

- Is the power validly executed as a deed?

- Is the power made under the Trusts of Land and Appointment of Trustees Act 1996? – see paragraph B6.

- Is the power wide enough to cover what the attorney has done?

- If the transaction involved the payment of capital money did the trustees join in to give a receipt?

- If the power was more than 12 months old when the attorney signed the document are you able to lodge the additional evidence that we need? – see Part E.

Peter Collis, Chief Land Registrar
HM Land Registry
February 2000

© Crown Copyright.

Annex

Statutory declaration/certificate as to non-revocation for powers more than 12 months old at the date of the disposition for which they are used

Date of power of attorney ....

Donor of power of attorney ....

I/We...

of ....

do solemnly and sincerely declare, or certify, that at the time of completion of the

.... to me/us/my client, I/we/my client had no knowledge

either

*   of a revocation of the power

*   of the death or bankruptcy of the donor or, if the donor is a corporate body, its winding up or dissolution

*   of any incapacity of the donor where the power is not a valid enduring power

*   if the power is in the form prescribed for an enduring power

    –   of the bankruptcy of the attorney

    –   of an order or direction of the Court of Protection which revoked the power

    –   that the power was not in fact a valid enduring power

*   if the power was given under section 9 of the Trusts of Land and Appointment of Trustees Act 1996

    –   of an appointment of another trustee of the land in question

    –   of any other event which would have had the effect of revoking the power

    –   of any lack of good faith on the part of the person(s) who dealt with the attorney

    –   that the attorney was not a person to whom the functions of the trustees could be delegated under section 9

or if the power is expressed to be given by way of security

    –   that the power was not in fact given by way of security

    –   of any revocation of the power with the consent of the attorney

    –   of any other event which would have had the effect of revoking the power.

Where a Certificate is given

Signature of Solicitor/Licensed Conveyancer .... Date ....

Where a Statutory Declaration is made

And I/We make this solemn declaration conscientiously believing the same to be true and by virtue of the provisions of the Statutory Declarations Act 1835.

Signature of Declarant(s) .... Date ....

DECLARED at .... before me, a person entitled to administer oaths,

Name ....

Address ....

Qualification .... Signature ....

Please note a certificate can only be given by a solicitor or licensed conveyancer who has knowledge of the relevant facts. If such a certificate cannot be given, the person(s) who dealt with the attorney (e.g. the transferee(s) in the case of a transfer signed by an attorney on behalf of the transferor) must make the statutory declaration.

APPENDIX 8

NON-CONTENTIOUS PROBATE RULES 1987 (EXTRACT)

Rules 31 and 35 extracted from SI 1987/2024.

31 Grants to attorneys

(1)   Subject to paragraphs (2) and (3) below, the lawfully constituted attorney of a person entitled to a grant may apply for administration for the use and benefit of the donor, and such grant shall be limited until further representation be granted, or in such other way as the registrar may direct.

(2)   Where the donor referred to in paragraph (1) above is an executor, notice of the application shall be given to any other executor unless such notice is dispensed with by the registrar.

(3)   Where the donor referred to in paragraph (1) above is mentally incapable and the attorney is acting under an enduring power of attorney, the application shall be made in accordance with r 35.

35 Grants in case of mental incapacity

(1)   Unless a registrar otherwise directs, no grant shall be made under this rule unless all persons entitled in the same degree as the incapable person referred to in paragraph (2) below have been cleared off.

(2)   Where a registrar is satisfied that a person entitled to a grant is by reason of mental incapacity incapable of managing his affairs, administration for his use and benefit, limited until further representation be granted or in such other way as the registrar may direct, may be granted in the following order of priority –

(a)   to the person authorised by the Court of Protection to apply for a grant;

(b)   where there is no person so authorised, to the lawful attorney of the incapable person acting under a registered enduring power of attorney;

(c)   where there is no such attorney entitled to act, or if the attorney shall renounce administration for the use and benefit of the incapable person, to the person entitled to the residuary estate of the deceased.

(3)   Where a grant is required to be made to not less than two administrators, and there is only one person competent and willing to take a grant under the foregoing provisions of this rule, administration may, unless a registrar otherwise directs, be granted to such person jointly with any other person nominated by him.

(4)   Notwithstanding the foregoing provisions of this rule, administration for the use and benefit of the incapable person may be granted to such two or more other persons as the registrar may by order direct.

(5)   Notice of an intended application under this rule shall be given to the Court of Protection.

APPENDIX 9

PRACTICE DIRECTIONS

Enduring Powers of Attorney – Grants of Administration (14 March 1986)

1.   The Enduring Powers of Attorney Act 1985 came into force on 10 March 1986. The Act provides that an enduring power of attorney, within the meaning of the Act, is not revoked by the subsequent mental incapacity of the donor, but once the donor has become incapable the rights of the attorney are limited until the power of attorney has been registered with the Court of Protection. Even a registered enduring power of attorney may confer only limited powers on the attorney, so that it will be necessary to ensure that the power covers an application for a grant.

2.   Effect on existing grants:

    (a)   If a sole, or sole surviving, grantee becomes mentally incapable his attorney under an enduring power of attorney is not able to continue the administration on behalf of the grantee in reliance on the power of attorney, whether or not it has been registered with the Court of Protection. Where the attorney subsequently applies for a grant in respect of any unadministered estate the grant to the donor should be lodged with the application for the grant and will be retained by the court.

    (b)   If one of two or more grantees becomes mentally incapable, the attorney under an enduring power of attorney of the incapable administrator similarly will not be able to continue the administration with the capable grantee(s). The grant in these circumstances should be revoked and a fresh grant will be needed to continue the administration.

    (c)   Where a grant has issued to an attorney of a donor for the use and benefit of that donor and the donor becomes mentally incapable, the attorney will be able to continue with the administration, provided that the donor has also appointed the same attorney under a sufficient enduring power of attorney which has been registered with the Court of Protection, even if the power of attorney used on the grant application was a different power of attorney and it has been revoked by the donor's mental incapacity.

3.   Applications for grants after 10 March 1986:

    (a)   Where the donor is mentally capable of managing his affairs, an application for a grant by an attorney may be made, as before, under r 30 of the Non-Contentious Probate Rules 1954 (NCPR) in reliance on a power of attorney which is not an enduring power of attorney. The existing practice and procedure will apply.

    (b)   Where the donor is mentally capable of managing his affairs and the application for a grant is supported by a power of attorney but which has not been registered with the Court of Protection the application may proceed under r 30, NCPR and the existing practice and procedure will apply, save that the original power of attorney should normally be produced on the application. If a copy of the power of attorney certified in accordance with section 3 of the Powers of Attorney Act 1971 is lodged, instead of the original, the oath to lead to the grant should confirm that no application has been made to the Court of Protection for the registration of the enduring power of attorney.

(c)   Where the donor is mentally capable of managing his affairs and the application for the grant is supported by an enduring power of attorney which has been registered with the Court of Protection (the donor's incapacity being impending) it must be sworn in the oath to lead to the grant (and in the affidavit in support of any application for a direction under r 30(2), NCPR) that the donor is mentally capable of managing his affairs. The original power of attorney sealed by the Court of Protection should be produced on the application.

(d)   Where the donor is mentally incapable of managing his affairs and the application for the grant is supported by an enduring power of attorney which has been registered with the Court of Protection it will not be apparent from the fact of registration whether the donor is mentally incapable or whether the incapacity is impending. It must be sworn in the oath to lead to the grant that the donor is mentally incapable of managing his affairs. No other evidence of mental incapacity will be called for. Notice of the application for the grant must be given to the Court of Protection as required by r 33(3), NCPR and although r 33, NCPR does not at present refer to an attorney, under a registered enduring power of attorney, of a person who is by reason of mental incapacity incapable of managing his affairs, such an attorney will normally be considered to be a suitable person to whom to direct the issue of a grant pursuant to an order made under the last line of r 33(1)(b), NCPR. The original power of attorney, sealed by the Court of Protection, should be produced on the application. Practitioners' attention is also drawn to the provisions of r 33(2), NCPR.

4.   Unless there is a relevant restriction in the power of attorney, the limitation to be included in a grant issuing to an attorney under an enduring power of attorney should be 'to AB the lawful attorney of CD for his use and benefit and until further representation be granted', whether the donor is capable and the application is made under r 30, NCPR or whether the donor is mentally incapable and the application is made under r 33, NCPR.

B. P. Tickle

Senior Registrar

Principal Registry of the Family Division

Citations: [1986] 1 FLR 627; [1986] 1 WLR 419; [1986] 2 All ER 41; [1986] Fam Law 198.

Authority to Solicitors to act for Patients or Donors (9 August 1995)

In Court of Protection matters, problems may arise for solicitors in knowing for whom they act.

In the case of *Re EG* [1914] 1 Ch 927, it was established that where a receiver has been appointed, the solicitor acting in the matter is acting for the patient and not for the receiver. The decision leaves undecided the question of who is the patient's solicitor in cases where more than one solicitor has been instructed to make an application for receivership or where a patient himself wishes to instruct another solicitor for a particular area of his affairs, for example, where he remains of testamentary capacity and wishes to instruct a different solicitor to draw up a will for him. Where more than one solicitor has been instructed, perhaps each by a different member of the patient's family, this places the solicitors in a position of uncertainty as to who is acting for the patient on the principle of *Re EG*.

A further difficulty may arise as a result of the case of *Yonge v Toynbee* [1901] 1 KB 215, which decided that the retainer of a solicitor came to an end when the patient lost capacity (as an extension of the general rule that, except in the case of an enduring power of attorney, the mental incapacity of the principal revokes any agency). Nevertheless, incapacitated people may need solicitors to act for them and them alone.

Assuming that a patient or donor is within the jurisdiction of the Court of Protection, the solicitor's authority to act for him can be expressly confirmed by the Court of Protection. Solicitors are also entitled to look upon themselves as acting for a patient or donor and not for the person who has given them instructions (if that is not the patient or donor) from the time that an application which is in order is received by the Court of Protection or the Public Trust Office. This may, for example, be an application for the appointment of a receiver, for an order determining proceedings, for the appointment of a new receiver, for confirmation of the revocation of an enduring power of attorney or for some other relief or authorisation. Where two or more solicitors have been instructed (expressly or by implication) to act for the same patient or donor, preliminary directions should be sought from the Court as to who will be deemed to be the solicitor in the matter.

A solicitor instructed by an applicant for receivership (or by an attorney) will be treated by the Court as the patient's (or donor's) solicitor until an objection to the application, or a competing application, is received by the Court. As soon as this happens, the solicitor instructed by the first applicant must elect whether to continue representing the patient or to represent the first applicant. If the solicitor elects to represent the first applicant, then it is for the Court to decide whether the patient needs separate representation and if so, to instruct a different private solicitor or the Official Solicitor (if he agrees) to act for him. If the solicitor elects to remain as the patient's solicitor, then the first applicant will have to instruct another firm.

Solicitors will no doubt wish to make clear to the person from whom they take initial instructions relating to patients or donors that their client will be the patient or donor and that the solicitors will have a duty of confidentiality to the patient or donor, even if the instructions come from somebody else.

The Court would like applicants and solicitors to be aware that if a reference which is received by the Court in respect of an applicant is not satisfactory, no further inquiry will be made as to the applicant's suitability but the applicant will not be appointed as receiver. This may be considered unfair to the applicant but in the Court's view, the best interests of the patient must come first.

Mrs A B Macfarlane

Master of the Court of Protection

Court of Protection

9 August 1995

APPENDIX 10

ENDURING POWERS OF ATTORNEY GUIDELINES FOR SOLICITORS PREPARED BY THE MENTAL HEALTH AND DISABILITY COMMITTEE – REVISED SEPTEMBER 1999

Introduction

The following guidelines are intended to assist solicitors in advising clients who wish to draw up an enduring power of attorney (EPA). They have been prepared by the Law Society's Mental Health and Disability Committee, after consultation with other Law Society committees and the Professional Ethics Division, in response to queries raised by practitioners.

Different considerations apply in relation to donors who make an EPA as a precautionary measure while they are still in the prime of life, and those who are of borderline mental capacity, where the EPA may need to be registered immediately. These guidelines set out general points for consideration, and their relevance will depend on the particular circumstances of individual cases.

The guidelines are based on the law in England and Wales. It should be noted that there is currently no internationally recognised form of EPA, and additional arrangements must be made for clients who have property in other jurisdictions.

Who is the client?

Where a solicitor is instructed to prepare an EPA, the donor is the client (The Law Society, *The Guide to the Professional Conduct of Solicitors* (8th edition, 1999) Principle 24.03 note 1).

A solicitor must not accept instructions where he or she suspects that those instructions have been given by a client under duress or undue influence (ibid., Principle 12.04).

When asked to prepare an EPA on written instructions alone, a solicitor should always consider carefully whether these instructions are sufficient, or whether he or she should see the client to discuss them (ibid., Principle 24.03 note 2).

Where instructions for the preparation of an EPA are received not from the client (i.e. the prospective donor), but from a third party purporting to represent that client, a solicitor should obtain written instructions from the client that he or she wishes the solicitor to act. In any case of doubt the solicitor should see the client alone or take other appropriate steps, both to confirm the instructions with the donor personally after offering appropriate advice, and also to ensure that the donor has the necessary capacity to make the power (see section 5 below). The solicitor must also advise the prospective donor without regard to the interests of the source from which he or she was introduced (ibid., Principle 12.04 and Principle 24.03, note 2).

Once the EPA has been executed and comes into effect, instructions may be accepted from the attorney but the solicitor continues to owe his/her duties to the donor (ibid., Principle 24.03 , note 1). Before registration of the EPA, it may be advisable for the solicitor, where appropriate, to satisfy him/herself that the donor continues to have capacity and to confirm the instructions with the donor. See also the Practice Statement issued by Mrs A B Macfarlane, former Master of the Court of Protection, on 9 August 1995 (The Law Society's Gazette, 11 October 1995, p. 21 or The Law Society Professional Standards Bulletin No. 15, p. 53), which clarifies solicitors' duties in acting for patients or donors and sets out procedures for dealing with conflicts of interest.

The attorney is the statutory agent of the donor, just as in receivership proceedings the receiver is the statutory agent of the patient (Re E.G. [1914] 1 Ch. 927, CA).

Capacity to make an EPA

The solicitor should be satisfied that, on the balance of probabilities, the donor has the mental capacity to make an EPA. Many EPAs are made when the donors are already losing capacity. Consequently they could be unaware of the implications of their actions and are more likely to be vulnerable to exploitation.

If there is any doubt about the donor's capacity, a medical opinion should be obtained. The solicitor should inform the doctor of the test of capacity laid down in Re K, Re F [1988] 1 All ER 358, 363 (see Appendix A attached, and Assessment of Mental Capacity: Guidance for doctors and lawyers issued by the Law Society and the British Medical Association (1995)). If the doctor is of the opinion that the donor has capacity, he or she should make a record to that effect and witness the donor's signature on the EPA (Kenward v Adams [1975] The Times, 29 November 1975).

Risk of Abuse

The Master of the Court of Protection has estimated that financial abuse occurs in 10 to 15 percent of cases of registered EPAs and even more often with unregistered powers (Denzil Lush, Solicitors Journal, 11th September 1998). When advising clients of the benefits of EPAs, the solicitor should also inform them of the risks of abuse, particularly the risk that the attorney could misuse the power. Throughout these guidelines, an attempt has been made to identify possible risk areas and to suggest ways of preventing abuse, which the solicitor should discuss with the donor. Written information for clients on both the benefits and risks of EPAs, whether in a brochure or correspondence, may also be helpful.

During the initial stages of advising a client, the solicitor should consider the following points:

(i)   There may be circumstances when an EPA may not be appropriate, and a later application for receivership, with oversight of the Court of Protection, may be preferable. This may be adviseable, for example:

- where there are indications of persistent family conflicts suggesting that an EPA may be contested, or

- where the assets are more substantial or complex than family members are accustomed to handle, or

- in cases where litigation may lead to a substantial award of damages for personal injury.

(ii)   The solicitor should consider discouraging the use of an unregistered EPA as an ordinary power of attorney, particularly for vulnerable elderly clients. Instructions to this effect could be included in the instrument itself (see paragraph 5.3 below) or the donor could be advised to lodge the power with the solicitor, with strict instructions that it is not to be used until the donor becomes or is becoming incapable.

Taking instructions

The solicitor should take full and careful instructions from the donor, and ensure that the following matters, where applicable, are considered by the donor when giving instructions.

Choice of attorney
More than one attorney
General or limited authority
When the power is to come into operation
Gifts
Delegation by the attorney
Investment business
Trusteeships held by the donor
Solicitor-attorneys
The donor's property and affairs
Notification of intention to register the EPA
Disclosure of the donor's will
Medical evidence
Safeguards against abuse

Choice of attorney

The choice of attorney is clearly a personal decision for the donor, but it is important for the solicitor to advise the donor of the various options available, and to stress the need for the attorney to be absolutely trustworthy, since on appointment the attorney's actions will be subject to little supervision or scrutiny (see section 4 above). The donor should be advised that the appointment of a sole attorney may provide greater opportunity for abuse and exploitation than appointing more than one attorney (see below).

The solicitor should ask questions about the donor's relationship with the proposed attorney and whether the attorney has the skills required to manage the donor's financial affairs. The donor should also consider the suitability of appointing a family member or someone independent of the family, or a combination of both.

More than one attorney

Where more than one attorney is to be appointed, they must be appointed to act either 'jointly' or 'jointly and severally' (Enduring Powers of Attorney Act 1985, s.11(1)).

One of these two alternatives must be chosen and the other crossed out. Failure to cross out one of these alternatives on the prescribed form makes the power invalid, and this is one of the commonest reasons for the Court of Protection or Public Trust Office refusing to register an EPA.

The differences between a 'joint' and 'joint and several' appointment should be explained to the donor.

- In addition to the explanatory information in the prescribed form to the effect that joint attorneys must all act together and cannot act separately, the donor should be advised that a joint appointment will terminate if any one of the attorneys disclaims, dies, or becomes bankrupt or mentally incapable. However, joint appointments may provide a safeguard against possible abuse, since each attorney will be able to oversee the actions of the other(s).

- Similarly, in addition to the explanatory information in the prescribed form to the effect that joint and several attorneys can all act together but can also act separately if they wish, the donor should be advised that, where there is a joint and several appointment, the disclaimer, death, bankruptcy and incapacity of one attorney will not automatically terminate the power.

The donor may have to make difficult choices as to which family member(s) to appoint as his or her attorney. It is possible to allow some flexibility, as in the following examples:

(i)   The donor may wish to appoint a family member and a professional to act jointly and severally with, for example, the family member dealing with day-to-day matters, and the professional dealing with more complex affairs.

(ii)   The donor may wish to appoint his or her spouse as attorney, with provision for their adult child(ren) to take over as attorney(s) should the spouse die or become incapacitated. One way to achieve this is for the donor to execute two EPAs: the first appointing the spouse as attorney, and the second appointing the child(ren) with a provision that it will only come into effect if the first power is terminated for any reason. Alternatively, the donor could appoint everyone to act jointly and severally, with an informal understanding that the children will not act while the spouse is able to do so.

(iii)   The donor may wish to appoint his or her three adult children as attorneys to act jointly and severally, with a proviso that anything done under the power should be done by at least two of them. This could be achieved by careful wording of the EPA document or by an accompanying statement or letter of wishes, which although not directly enforceable, would provide a clear indication as to how the donor wishes the power to be operated.

General or limited authority

The donor must be clear whether the EPA is to be a general power, giving the attorney authority to manage all the donor's property and affairs, or whether the authority is to extend only to part of his or her property and affairs. Any restrictions to the power should be carefully drafted and should have regard to the provisions of the Enduring Powers of Attorney Act 1985 (see also paragraphs 5.6 and 5.11 below).

The solicitor should also discuss with the donor what arrangements should be made for the management of those affairs which are not covered by the EPA. Donors should be advised that if they leave a 'gap', so that part of their affairs are not covered by the EPA, it may be necessary for the Court of Protection to intervene and appoint a receiver.

When the power is to come into operation

The donor must understand when the power is to come into operation. If nothing is said in the instrument, it will take effect immediately, and can be used as an ordinary power of attorney. The donor should be advised of the risk of abuse of an unregistered power, unless s/he is in a position to supervise and authorise use of the power.

If the donor does not want the power to take effect immediately and would prefer it to be held in abeyance until the onset of his or her incapacity, he or she must expressly say so in the EPA. The donor may also wish to include a specific condition that a statement from a doctor confirming lack of capacity must accompany the application to register the EPA.

In such circumstances, it may be preferable to state that the power will not come into operation until the need arises to apply to register the EPA, rather than state that it will not come into operation until it is registered. Pending completion of the registration formalities, the attorney has limited powers, and it may be better for the attorney to have these powers, rather than none at all.

Gifts

Section 3(5) of the Enduring Powers of Attorney Act 1985 gives the attorney limited authority to make gifts of the donor's money or property:

- The recipient of the gift must be either an individual who is related to or connected with the donor, or a charity to which the donor actually made gifts or might be expected to make gifts if s/he had capacity.

- The timing of the gift must occur within the prescribed parameters. A gift to charity can be made at any time of the year, but a gift to an individual must be of a seasonal nature, or made on the occasion of a birth or marriage, or on the anniversary of a birth or marriage.

- The value of the gift must be not unreasonable having regard to all the circumstances and in particular the size of the donor's estate.

The donor cannot confer wider authority on the attorney than that specified in section 3(5), but it is open to the donor to restrict or exclude the authority which would otherwise be available to the attorney under that subsection. This possibility should be specifically discussed with the donor, since improper gifting is the most widespread form of abuse in attorneyship. The donor may wish to specify in the power the circumstances in which the attorney may make gifts of money or property.

Section 3(5) applies to both registered and unregistered EPAs, but not to those which are in the course of being registered. Where an application to register the EPA has been made, the attorney cannot make any gifts of the donor's property until the power has been registered.

If the EPA is registered, the Court of Protection can authorise the attorney to act so as to benefit himself or others, otherwise than in accordance with section 3(5), provided that there are no restrictions in the EPA itself (Enduring Powers of Attorney Act 1985, s 8(2)(e)).

Solicitors must also take account of Principle 15.05 of the Guide to Professional Conduct (op cit, 1999) concerning gifts to solicitors.

Delegation by the attorney

It is a basic principle of the law of agency that a delegate cannot delegate his or her authority. Alternatively, this could be expressed as a duty on the part of an agent to perform his or her functions personally.

Like any other agent, an attorney acting under an EPA has an implied power to delegate any functions which are of a purely ministerial nature; which do not involve or require the exercise of any confidence or discretion; and which the donor would not expect the attorney to attend to personally.

Any wider power of delegation must be expressly provided for in the EPA itself: for example, transferring the donor's assets into a discretionary investment management scheme operated by a stockbroker or bank.

Investment business

Unless the power is restricted to exclude investments as defined by the Financial Services Act 1986, the attorney may need to consider the investment business implications of his/her appointment. A solicitor who is appointed attorney under an EPA is likely to be conducting investment business and if so, will need to be authorised under the Financial Services Act. In addition, the solicitor will need to consider whether the Solicitors Investment Business Rules 1995 apply.

The Financial Services and Markets Bill due to come into effect in approximately mid-2000, is likely to change the definition of investment business and affect the need for authorisation. The detailed position, at the time of writing, is unclear and solicitors will need to keep this aspect under review.

Trusteeships held by the donor

The solicitor should ask whether the donor holds:

* any trusteeships; and

* any property jointly with others.

Section 3(3) of the Enduring Powers of Attorney Act 1985 has been repealed by the Trustee Delegation Act 1999 with effect from 1st January 2000. Section 4 of the 1999 Act contains detailed transitional provisions which affect existing EPAs, both registered and unregistered.

The general rule is that any trustee functions delegated to an attorney (whether under an ordinary power or an enduring power) must comply with the provisions of section 25 of the Trustee Act 1925, as amended by the 1999 Act.

However, section 1(1) of the 1999 Act provides an exception to this general rule. An attorney can exercise a trustee function of the donor if it relates to land, or the capital proceeds or income from land, in which the donor has a beneficial interest. This is, of course, subject to any provision to the contrary contained in the trust instrument or the power of attorney itself.

Solicitor-attorneys

Where a solicitor is appointed as attorney, or where it is intended that a particular solicitor will deal with the general management of the donor's affairs, it is recommended that the solicitor's current terms and conditions of business (including charging rates and the frequency of billing) be discussed with and approved by the donor at the time of granting the power.

Since the explanatory information on the prescribed form of EPA is ambiguous about the remuneration of professional attorneys, it is recommended that a professional charging clause be included in the power for the avoidance of doubt.

Where a solicitor is appointed sole attorney (or is reasonably likely to become the sole attorney), or where two or more solicitors in the same firm are appointed and there is no external attorney, the donor should be informed of the potential problems of accountability if he or she should become mentally incapacitated. If necessary, arrangements could be made for the solicitor's costs to be approved or audited by an independent third party in the event of the donor's incapacity.

In a number of cases solicitor-attorneys have disclaimed when it became apparent that the donor's assets were insufficient to make the attorneyship cost-effective. The Law Society's view is that, if solicitors intend to disclaim in such circumstances, they should not take on the attorneyship in the first place, or should warn the donor of this possibility at the time of making the power.

Further guidance is given in the Guide to Professional Conduct (op cit, Principle 24.03, Notes 5,6,7). Solicitors are also reminded that any commission earned should be paid to the donor (see Annex 14G of the Guide to Professional Conduct).

The donor's property and affairs

It may be helpful for solicitors to record and retain information relating to the donor's property and affairs, even where they are not to be appointed as an attorney themselves. The Law Society's Personal Assets Log, which is sometimes used when taking will-drafting instructions, could be suitably adapted for this purpose. In addition, there are certain requirements under the Solicitors' Investment Business Rules where solicitors safeguard and administer documents of title to investments e.g. share certificates.

Notification of intention to register the EPA

Solicitors should explain to the donor that the attorney has a duty to notify the donor in person, and at least three members of the donor's family, of his or her intention to register the EPA with the Public Trust Office if the attorney has reason to believe that the donor is, or is becoming mentally incapable.

It may be helpful to obtain a list of the names and addresses of the relatives at the time the EPA is granted. If the donor would like other members of the family, or friends or close associates to be notified in addition to those on the statutory list, details could be included in the EPA itself or in a separate letter.

In any event, solicitors should encourage donors to tell their family that they have made an EPA and perhaps explain why they have chosen the attorney(s). This may help to guard against the possibility of abuse by the attorney and may also reduce the risk of conflict between family members at a later stage.

Disclosure of the donor's will

Solicitors are under a duty to keep their clients' affairs confidential (The Law Society, *The Guide to the Professional Conduct of Solicitors* (8th edition, 1999) Principle 16.01). However, the attorney(s) may need to know about the contents of the donor's will in order to avoid acting contrary to the testamentary intentions of the donor (for example, by the sale of an asset specifically bequeathed, when other assets that fell into residue could be disposed of instead).

The question of disclosure of the donor's will should be discussed at the time of making the EPA, and instructions should be obtained as to whether disclosure is denied, or the circumstances in which it is permitted. For example, the donor may agree that the solicitor can disclose the contents of the will to the attorney, but only if the EPA is registered and the solicitor thinks that disclosure of the will is necessary or expedient for the proper performance of the attorney's functions.

Principle 24.03, note 4 of the Guide (ibid) gives guidance where the EPA is registered and is silent on the subject of disclosure. Advice may also be sought from the Professional Ethics Division or from the Public Trust Office (see section 13 below).

The attorney also has a common law duty to keep the donor's affairs (including the contents of a will) confidential.

Medical evidence

It may be worth asking the donor to give advance consent in writing authorising the solicitor to contact the donor's GP or any other medical practitioner if the need for medical evidence should arise at a later date (for example, on registration of the power; or, after the power has been registered, to assess whether the donor has testamentary capacity).

Safeguards against abuse

Solicitors should discuss with the donor appropriate measures to safeguard against the power being misused or exploited. This could include notifying other family members of the existence of the power, and how the donor intends it to be used.

The solicitor could also consider offering an auditing service, by inserting a clause into the power requiring the attorney to produce to the solicitor, on a specified date each year, an account of his/her actions as attorney during the last 12 months. If the attorney failed to render a satisfactory account, the solicitor could apply for registration of the power to be cancelled on the grounds of the attorney's unsuitability. Again a charging procedure for this service must be agreed with the donor in advance.

Drawing up the EPA

The prescribed form
An EPA must be in the form prescribed by the Enduring Powers of Attorney (Prescribed Form) Regulations in force at the time of its execution by the donor. There have been three sets of regulations and the periods during which they have been in force are:

1986 Regulations – 10 March 1986 to 30 June 1988

1987 Regulations – 1 November 1987 to 30 July 1991

1990 Regulations – 31 July 1991 onwards

Solicitors should ensure that existing EPAs are in the form prescribed on the date they were executed by the donors and that the form they are currently using is the one prescribed by the Enduring Powers of Attorney (Prescribed Form) Regulations 1990 (SI 1990 No.1376).

Provided the prescribed form is used, it does not matter whether it is a printed form from a law stationers or whether it is transcribed onto a word-processor, although a law stationer's form is more easily recognisable by third parties. What is essential, however, is that there should be no unauthorised departure from the prescribed form. So, where the donor is to be offered an EPA which is not on a law stationer's form, the solicitor should be absolutely certain that the form complies with the prescribed form regulations. Use of inaccurate or incomplete word-processed forms are common reasons for refusal to register an EPA.

Part A ('About using this form') and the marginal notes must be included in the EPA because the Enduring Powers of Attorney Act requires the prescribed explanatory information to be incorporated in the instrument at the time of execution by the donor (section 2(1) and 2(2) and Regulation 2(1) of the 1990 Regulations).

Completing the form
Solicitors should ensure that where alternatives are provided on the form (for example for 'joint' or 'joint and several' appointments, or to specify the extent of the authority granted), the required deletions are made by crossing out the options not chosen by the donor.

There is space on the prescribed form to provide details of two attorneys. Where it is intended to appoint three attorneys, the details of the third attorney may be included in the main document, fitted in to the space after the details of the second attorney.

Where more than three attorneys are to be appointed, details of the first two attorneys should be given in the main document, followed by the words 'and (see additional names on attached sheet)' and the details given on a sheet to be attached to the main document marked clearly 'Names of additional attorneys'.

About 10% of EPAs are refused registration because of a defect in the form or the wording of the instrument. In some cases, registration may be possible after the filing of further evidence to overcome the defect. Solicitors who have assisted a donor in drawing up an EPA which is subsequently refused registration because of a defect that is material may be liable for the additional costs of receivership, since at that point the donor may not have the capacity to execute a new EPA.

Executing the power

An EPA must be executed by both the donor and the attorney(s). The donor must execute Part B of the prescribed form. The attorney must execute Part C. Where more than one attorney is appointed, each of them must complete a separate Part C, the additional sheets having been added and secured to the EPA document beforehand. One Part C cannot be 'shared' by more than one attorney.

The donor must execute the EPA before the attorney(s), because the attorney(s) cannot accept a power which has not yet been conferred. However, execution by the donor and attorney(s) need not take place simultaneously. There is no reason why execution by the attorney(s) should not occur at a later date, provided it happens before the donor loses capacity. It is often advisable for the attorney(s) to sign as soon as possible after the donor.

Execution by the donor and the attorney(s) must take place in the presence of a witness, but not necessarily the same witness, who must sign Part B or Part C of the prescribed form, as the case may be, and give his or her full name and address.

There are various restrictions as to who can act as a witness, and in particular:

- the donor and attorney must not witness each other's signature;

- one attorney cannot witness the signature of another attorney;

- the marginal notes to Part B of the prescribed form warn that it is not advisable for the donor's spouse to witness his or her signature – this is because of the rules of evidence relating to compellability; and

- at common law, a blind person cannot witness another person's signature.

If the donor or attorney is physically disabled and unable to sign, he or she may make a mark, and the attestation clause should be adapted to explain this. Alternatively, the donor or an attorney may authorise another person to sign the EPA at his or her direction, in which case it must be signed by that person in the presence of two witnesses, as described in the marginal notes.

Although the Enduring Powers of Attorney (Prescribed Form) Regulations 1990 do not expressly state that, where someone executes the EPA at the direction of the donor or attorney, he or she must do so in the presence of the donor or attorney, it is essential that the power be executed in their presence in order to comply with section 1(3) of the Law of Property (Miscellaneous Provisions) Act 1989.

If the donor is blind, this should be stated in the attestation clause so that, if an application is made to register the EPA, the Public Trust Office can make enquiries as to how the donor was notified of the intention to register.

Copies of an EPA

The contents of an EPA can be proved by means of a certified copy. In order to comply with the provisions of section 3 of the Powers of Attorney Act 1971, a certificate should appear at the end of each page of the copy stating that it is a true and complete copy of the corresponding page of the original. The certificate must be signed by the donor, or a solicitor, or a notary public or a stockbroker.

Notification of intention to register the EPA

When it is necessary to give notice of the attorney's intention to register the power, the prescribed form of notice (Form EP1) must be used. The donor must be personally served with this notice, and the donor's relatives must be given notice by first class post.

It may be helpful, in the case of the relatives, to send the notice with an accompanying letter explaining the circumstances because, in the absence of such an explanation, there may be cause for concern. Giving an appropriate explanation and information at this stage may prevent the application from becoming contentious.

Although there is no statutory requirement to do so, a copy of the EPA could also be sent to the relatives, in view of the fact that one of the grounds on which they can object to registration is that the power purported to have been created by the instrument is not valid as an enduring power.

As stated above, the notice of intention to register (Form EP1) must be given to the donor personally. The notice need not be handed to the donor by the attorney. It can be given to the donor by an agent (perhaps a solicitor) acting on the attorney's behalf, and the name of the person who gives notice to the donor must be stated on Form EP2.

Many attorneys, both relatives and professionals, find it distressing to have to inform donors of the implications of their failing mental capacity. Schedule 1 to the Enduring Powers of Attorney Act 1985 makes provision for the attorney to apply to the Public Trustee for dispensation from the requirement to serve notice on anyone entitled to receive it, including the donor.

However, the Public Trustee is reluctant to grant such a dispensation because it is the donor's right, and the right of entitled relatives, to be informed and to have an opportunity to object to registration. A dispensation is only likely to be granted in relation to the donor where there is clear medical evidence to show that notification would be detrimental to the donor's health, and in the case of relatives, only in exceptional circumstances.

Statutory wills

An attorney cannot execute a will on the donor's behalf because the Wills Act 1837 requires a will to be signed by the testator personally or by someone in his or her presence and at his or her direction.

Where a person lacks testamentary capacity, the Court of Protection can order the execution of a statutory will on his or her behalf. The Court's will-making jurisdiction is conferred by the Mental Health Act 1983 – not the Enduring Powers of Attorney Act 1985 – but can be invoked where there is a registered EPA. An application for an order authorising the execution of a statutory will should be considered by solicitors where there is no will or where the existing will is no longer appropriate due to a change of circumstances. In statutory will proceedings, the Official Solicitor is usually asked to represent the testator.

The Court will require recent medical evidence showing that the donor:

- is incapable, by reason of mental disorder, of managing and administering his or her property and affairs. This evidence should be provided on Form CP3 because, in effect, the Court needs to be satisfied that the donor is a 'patient' for the purposes of the Mental Health Act; and

- is incapable of making a valid will for himself or herself.

The Court's procedure notes PN9 and PN9(A) explain the Court's requirements. Guidance on the relevant tests of capacity can be found in the Law Society/BMA publication *Assessment of Mental Capacity: Guidance for doctors and lawyers* (1995).

Support for attorneys

Section 4(5) of the Enduring Powers of Attorney Act 1985 provides that the attorney may, before making an application for the registration of the EPA, refer to the Court any question as to the validity of the power. However, such an application can only be made when the attorney has reason to believe that the donor is, or is becoming, mentally incapable. The Court will not determine any question as to the validity of an unregistered power in any other circumstances.

Under section 8 of the Act, the Court of Protection has various functions with respect to registered powers. However, the Court should not be seen as being available to 'hold the hand' of the attorney, who should in normal circumstances be able to act in the best interests of the donor, taking advice where necessary from a solicitor or other professional adviser. It should be noted that, although the Court may interpret the terms of an EPA or give directions as to its exercise, it does not have power to extend or amend the terms of the EPA as granted by the donor.

Where abuse is suspected

If solicitors suspect that an attorney may be misusing an EPA or acting dishonestly and the donor is unable to take action to protect him or herself, they should try to facilitate the remedies that the donor would have adopted if able to do so. In the first instance, the Public Trust Office should be notified and guidance sought from the Court of Protection as to how to proceed. This might include:

- an application to the Court of Protection under the Mental Health Act 1983 for an Order giving authority to take action to recover the donor's funds

- an application to the Court for registration of the power to be cancelled on the grounds of the attorney's unsuitability and for receivership proceedings to be instituted.

- involvement of the police to investigate allegations of theft or fraud.

- where residential care or nursing homes are involved, using the local authority complaints procedure or involving the relevant registration authority.

Further Advice

Solicitors may obtain confidential advice on matters relating to professional ethics from the Law Society's Professional Ethics Division (0870 606 2577) and on practice issues from the Practice Advice Service (0870 606 2522). The Mental Health and Disability Committee is also willing to consider written requests from solicitors for comments on complex cases.

Information and advice can also be obtained from the Customer Services Unit of the Public Trust Office (020 7664 7300).

Further reading

Trevor Aldridge, Powers of Attorney, (8th Edition, 1991) Longman

Gordon R Ashton, The Elderly Client Handbook, (1994) The Law Society (2nd Edition due late 1999)

Gordon R Ashton, Elderly People and the Law (1995) Butterworths

Gordon R Ashton (Ed), Butterworths Older Client Law Service (1997) (loose-leaf), Butterworths

Stephen Cretney and Denzil Lush, Enduring Powers of Attorney (4th Edition, 1996) Jordans

Anthony Donelly, Court of Protection Handbook (9th Edition, 1995) FT Law and Tax

Denzil Lush, Elderly Clients: A Precedent Manual (1996) Jordans

Norman Whitehorn, Heywood & Massey: Court of Protection Practice (12th Edition, 1991) Sweet & Maxwell

Law Society: guidelines for solicitors

Law Society, The Guide to the Professional Conduct of Solicitors (8th Edition, 1999)

Law Society/British Medical Association, Assessment of Mental Capacity: Guidance for Doctors and Lawyers (1995) BMA (available from the Law Society Shop, £8.95)

Law Society Mental Health and Disability Sub-Committee, Gifts of Property: Implications for future liability to pay for long-term care (1995) (published in Professional Standards Bulletin No 15, March 1996)

Information for clients

Penny Letts, Managing Other People's Money (2nd Edition, 1998) Age Concern England

Public Trust Office, Enduring Powers of Attorney (1995), available free of charge from the Public Trust Office

Age Concern Factsheet No 22, Legal arrangements for managing financial affairs, available from Age Concern England.

Appendix A

Capacity to make an Enduring Power of Attorney

The implications of Re K, Re F

Capacity to make an Enduring Power of Attorney

A power of attorney signed by a person who lacks capacity is null and void, unless it can be proved that it was signed during a lucid interval. Shortly after the Enduring Powers of Attorney Act 1985 came into force, the Court of Protection received a considerable number of applications to register enduring powers which had only just been created. This raised a doubt as to whether the donors had been mentally capable when they signed the powers. The problem was resolved in the test cases Re K, Re F [1988] Ch 310, in which the judge discussed the capacity to create an enduring power.

Having stated that the test of capacity to create an enduring power of attorney was that the donor understood the nature and effect of the document, the judge in the case set out four pieces of information which any person creating an EPA should understand:

– first, if such be the terms of the power, that the attorney will be able to assume complete authority over the donor's affairs;
– secondly, if such be the terms of the power, that the attorney will be able to do anything with the donor's property which the donor could have done;
– thirdly, that the authority will continue if the donor should be or should become mentally incapable; and
– fourthly, that if he or she should be or should become mentally incapable, the power will be irrevocable without confirmation by the Court of Protection.

It is worth noting that the donor need not have the capacity to do all the things which the attorney will be able to do under the power. The donor need only have capacity to create the EPA.

The implications of *Re K, Re F*

The judge in *Re K, Re F* also commented that if the donor is capable of signing an enduring power of attorney, but incapable of managing and administering his or her property and affairs, the attorney has an obligation to register the power with the Court of Protection straightaway. Arguably, the attorney also has a moral duty in such cases to forewarn the donor that registration is not merely possible, but is intended immediately.

The decision in *Re K, Re F* has been criticised for imposing too simple a test of capacity to create an enduring power. But the simplicity or complexity of the test depends largely on the questions asked by the person assessing the donor's capacity. For example, if the four pieces of basic relevant information described by the judge in *Re K, Re F* were mentioned to the donor and he or she was asked 'Do you understand this?' in such a way as to encourage an affirmative reply, the donor would probably pass the test with flying colours and, indeed, the test would be too simple. If, on the other hand, the assessor were specifically to ask the donor 'What will your attorney be able to do?' and 'What will happen if you become mentally incapable?' the test would be substantially harder. There is no direct judicial authority on the point, but it can be inferred from the decision in *Re Beaney (deceased)* [1978] 1 WLR 770, that questions susceptible to the answers 'Yes' or 'No' may be inadequate for the purpose of assessing capacity.

[Adapted from BMA/Law Society, *Assessment of Mental Capacity: Guidance for Doctors and Lawyers* (1995) BMA]

Appendix B

Checklist of Dos and Don'ts for Enduring Powers of Attorney

In taking instructions:

DO:

- Assess carefully the donor's capacity to make an EPA
- Advise the donor fully on both the benefits and the risks
- Discuss with the donor the suitability of the proposed attorney(s)
- Confirm instructions with the donor personally
- Clarify and specify arrangements relating to:
  - disclosure of the donor's will
  - dealing with investment business
  - making gifts
  - payment of professional charges

DON'T:

- Forget that the donor is your client
- Act on the unconfirmed instructions of third parties
- Allow third parties to control your access to the donor

In preparing the EPA:

DO:

- Use the current prescribed form of EPA
- Clarify when the power is to take effect
- Ensure the power is executed by the donor while still competent

- Ensure the power is signed by the attorney(s) after the donor has signed
- Ensure the signatures of donor and attorney(s) are properly witnessed
- Ensure the power is dated

DON'T:

- Omit Part A of the form or any of the marginal notes
- Fail to make the required deletions where alternatives are offered on the form
- Include restrictions or instructions which are unclear or outside the scope of the Enduring Powers of Attorney Act 1985

In applying for registration:

DO:

- Notify the donor and the required relatives using Form EP1
- Apply for registration within 10 days of the notification of the last person required to be notified
- Enclose the original EPA with the application
- Insert on form EP2 the dates on which the people concerned were notified and the date of the application for registration
- Send the registration fee with the application
- Send medical evidence in support of any application to dispense with the requirement to serve notice on the donor

DON'T:

- Forget that Form EP1 must be given to the donor personally
- Fail to comply with specified time limits

These Guidelines are reproduced here with the kind permission of the Mental Health and Disability Committee of the Law Society.

APPENDIX 11

LEADING ENDURING POWER OF ATTORNEY CASES:

[1988] 2 FLR 15

RE K; RE F (ENDURING POWERS OF ATTORNEY)

Chancery Division

Hoffmann J

27 October 1987

Power of attorney – Mental incapacity – Enduring power of attorney executed by donors understanding nature and effect of power but lacking mental capacity to manage their affairs – Whether execution of power valid – Enduring Powers of Attorney Act 1985 s. 6(5)(a)

In both cases enduring powers of attorney were executed under the Enduring Powers of Attorney Act 1985 at a time when those executing them were capable of understanding the nature and effect of the powers but were not capable by reason of mental disorder of managing their property and affairs. Applications were made to register the powers in accordance with s. 4 of the 1985 Act. In the case of Miss K relatives objected to registration on the grounds that she had not had the necessary mental capacity at the time of execution and therefore that the power was not valid under s. 6(5)(a). The Master rejected the application for registration and the applicant appealed. In the case of Mrs F, the Master referred to the court under the Court of Protection rules the question whether the power created by the instrument was valid if the donor understood the nature and effect of an enduring power of attorney notwithstanding that she was at the time of its execution incapable by reason of mental disorder of managing her property and affairs. The appeal and the reference were heard together.

Held – it was established at common law that an understanding of the nature and effect of a power was sufficient for its validity, but that a power could not longer be validly exercised if the donor had lost the mental capacity to be a principal. However, the fact that a power could not be validly exercised did not lead to the proposition that it was for all purposes invalid. Having regard to the purpose of the 1985 Act, which was to enable a power to be exercised notwithstanding that the donor did not have the mental capacity required by the common law, and taking into account further that the statutory safeguards for the donor built into the Act made it unnecessary to impose too high a standard of mental capacity for the valid execution of the power, it could be concluded that a power was valid for the purposes of s. 6(5)(a) notwithstanding that the donor did not have the mental capacity which would make it exercisable, provided that she had understood the nature and effect of the juristic act conferring the power. Where there was mental incapacity at the time the power was executed the obligation of the attorney to register the power under s. 4 arose immediately upon execution.

The appeal would be allowed and the reference answered in the affirmative.

Statutory provisions considered

Enduring Powers of Attorney Act 1985, ss. 1, 2, 3, 4, 6 and 8

Cases referred to in judgment

Beaney (Deceased), Re [1978] 1 WLR 770; [1978] 2 All ER 595

Drew v Nunn (1879) 4 QBD 661; 40 LT 671; [1874–80] All ER Rep 1144, CA

Gibbons v Wright (1954) 91 CLR 423 (Aust. HC)

Re K:

Christopher McCall QC for Miss K;

John Morris Collins for the objectors;

Peter Rawson as amicus curiae.

Re F:

Christopher McCall QC for the Mrs F;

Peter Rawson as amicus curiae.

Cur. adv. vult.

HOFFMANN J: There are before the court an appeal and a reference of a question of law from the Court of Protection. The appeal is from an order of the Master dismissing an application for the registration of an enduring power of attorney executed by Miss K under the Enduring Powers of Attorney Act 1985 ('the 1985 Act'). The question of law which is the subject of the reference has arisen in connection with an application for the registration of an enduring power of attorney executed by Mrs F. The appeal and the reference both raise the same point of law, and as it is of some importance for the future administration of the 1985 Act I am, at the request of counsel, giving this judgment in open court.

The 1985 Act was intended to provide an inexpensive method by which a person could confer power to manage his affairs upon a person of his own choice which would remain effective notwithstanding any change in his mental capacity. Before the Act the execution of a power of attorney, however expressed, was useless for this purpose because it would be revoked by the donor's loss of mental capacity.

Section 1(1)(a) of the 1985 Act provides that a power of attorney which is an 'enduring power' within the meaning of the 1985 Act shall not be revoked by any subsequent mental incapacity of the donor. Section 2(1) defines an 'enduring power' as one executed in the manner and form prescribed in regulations made by the Lord Chancellor. The current regulations require the instrument to be endorsed with certain explanatory information which is intended to tell the donor what the effect of executing the power will be.

Section 3 places certain restrictions on what an attorney under an enduring power can do. He may not benefit himself or persons other than the donor except to the extent that the donor might have been expected to provide for his or their needs. He may not make gifts except for presents of reasonable value at Christmas, birthdays, weddings and such like to persons related to or connected with the donor or charitable gifts which the donor might have been expected to make. Section 4 imposes on the attorney a duty to apply to the court for registration of the power as soon as practicable after he has reason to believe that the donor is or is becoming mentally incapable. For this purpose, 'mentally incapable' is defined in the same way as in s. 94(2) of the Mental Health Act 1983:

'. . . in relation to any person, that he is incapable by reason of mental disorder of managing and administering his property and affairs.'

The incentive to register is that once mental incapacity has supervened, the attorney cannot (subject to narrow exceptions) validly exercise the power until it has been registered. Notice of an application for registration must be given to the closest relatives and they are entitled to object to registration on various grounds specified in s. 6(5). These include:

'(a) that the power purported to have been created . . . was not valid . . .

(d) that fraud or undue pressure was used to induce the donor to create the power; and

(e) that, having regard to all the circumstances and in particular the attorney's relationship to or connection with the donor, the attorney is unsuitable to be the donor's attorney.'

Once the power has been registered, it cannot be revoked by the donor without the confirmation of the court. Section 8 confers upon the court wide supervisory powers under which it may, for example, give directions to the attorney with respect to the management of the donor's property and affairs, demand that accounts be kept or documents and information supplied, and finally cancel the registration and revoke the power. In the case of Miss K, relatives objected to registration on the ground specified in s. 6(5)(a), namely:

'. . . that the power purported to have been created by the instrument was not valid as an enduring power of attorney.'

The alleged cause of invalidity was that Miss K did not have the necessary mental capacity at the time of execution. The master received evidence of Miss K's mental capacity and made the following finding of fact:

'I accept the strong evidence that, on the particular date in question Miss K enjoyed a period during which she was able to understand that Mr K was to be her attorney under an enduring power of attorney and that she understood what an enduring power was; but that she was incapable by reason of mental disorder of managing her property and affairs.'

This finding raised the question of law which has been argued in this appeal, namely whether the power created by the instrument was valid if the donor understood the nature and effect of an enduring power of attorney notwithstanding that she was at the time to its execution incapable by reason of mental disorder of managing her property and affairs. The Master answered this question in the negative.

Shortly after she had given judgment in the case of Miss K, the Master heard an application for the registration of an enduring power which had been executed by Mrs F. She was a lady of 75 suffering from presenile dementia. Although she was at times lucid and capable of making decisions with full understanding of what she was doing, at other times she would become confused and suffer loss of memory. The medical evidence was that when she executed the power she fully understood its nature and effect, but that on account of her recurrent mental disability she could not in general terms be said to be capable of managing and administering her property. The case therefore presented the same question of law as the case of Miss K, and without giving a ruling the Master referred the question to this court under r. 39 of the Court of Protection Rules 1984. The appeal in Re K and the reference in Re F were argued together in chambers, and I had not only the benefit of adversarial argument by Mr McCall for the applicants in both cases and Mr Collins for the objectors in *Re K*, but also the assistance as amicus curiae of Mr Rawson, instructed by the Official Solicitor.

The 1985 Act does not specify the mental capacity needed to execute an enduring power and the answer must therefore be found in the common law. It is well established that capacity to perform a juristic act exists when the person who purported to do the act had at the time the mental capacity, with the assistance of such explanation as he may have been given to understand the nature and effect of that particular transaction: see *Re Beaney* [1978] 1 WLR 770. In principle, therefore, an understanding of the nature and effect of the power was sufficient for its validity.

At common law there is, however, the further rule that a power can no longer be validly exercised if the donor has lost the mental capacity to be a principal. The way in which this rule is usually expressed is to say that mental incapacity revokes the power. What is meant by mental incapacity for this purpose has not been fully explored in the authorities. The question is plainly different from the usual question about capacity to perform a juristic act. It is hypothetical rather than factual. The donor did not in fact exercise the power and one cannot therefore ask whether he actually understood the nature and effect of what he was doing. One can only ask whether he would have understood, and this requires one first to decide what he must be supposed to have done and the circumstances in which he must be supposed to have done it. In the Australian case of *Gibbons v Wright* (1954) 91 CLR 423, 445, it was said that a power is revoked if the donor ceases to have the mental capacity to perform the acts authorized by the power. This would seem to mean that, at any rate in the case of a general power, there will be revocation if the donor no longer has the general capacity to manage and administer his property and affairs. It is not necessary for me to discuss the question further because I am content to assume, as did the Master, that the power executed by Miss K would at common law have been revoked, at latest, when she ceased to be able to manage and administer her property and affairs.

The main reason why the Master held that Miss K's power was invalid was because in her view a person suffering from mental incapacity which would have revoked a power could not validly create one. There is at first sight a compelling logic about this reasoning. It is, however, important to bear in mind that in the rule that a power is revoked by the onset of mental incapacity, the term 'revoke' is used as a metaphor. To revoke a power ordinarily means intentionally to perform a juristic act which terminates its legal effect. But the donor who becomes mentally incapable has not performed any act. What happens is that at least for some purposes the power ceased to have effect as if he had revoked it. As in the case of all rules expressed as metaphors or analogies, there are dangers in reasoning from the metaphor as if it expressed a literal truth rather than from the underlying principle which the metaphor encapsulates.

Brett LJ, after reserving judgment for more than 6 months in order to ponder the conceptual problems of revocation by incapacity, expressed the principle as follows in *Drew v Nunn* (1879) 4 QBD 661:

'When the principal, according to law, cannot act for himself, the person who represents him ceases to be able to act for him.'

The rule is therefore concerned with whether the power can be validly exercised rather than with its essential validity. Of course, for most purposes it will make no difference whether the one says that the power has ceased to be exercisable or has become invalid. But the fact that the power cannot be validly exercised does not commit one to the proposition that it is for all purposes invalid. For example, if it was the agent who lost mental capacity, the power would also not be exercisable, but one would not say that the power itself was invalid.

The question is therefore whether, as a matter of construction, a power in 'valid' for the purposes of s. 6(5)(a) only if the donor had the mental capacity which would have made it exercisable. This must be decided by having regard to the purpose of the Act as a whole, which is to enable powers to be exercised notwithstanding that the donor does not have the mental capacity required by the common law. There seems to me no logical reason why the validity of the power for the purposes of s. 6(5)(a) should be affected by considerations of whether it would have been exercisable. The court is not concerned with whether the power has been validly exercised but whether as a juristic act it should registered with a view to its future exercise notwithstanding the donor's loss of mental capacity.

The Master expressed her reasoning in a slightly different way when she said that she did not think that Miss K 'could validly pass to an attorney powers which she herself at the time did not possess'.

This proposition also requires further analysis. In one sense, Miss K did possess the powers to manage her property because she owned it. She could not exercise those powers on a regular basis because she lacked mental capacity. But there is no logical reason why, though unable to exercise her powers, she could not confer them upon someone else by an appropriate juristic act. The validity of that act depends upon whether she understood its nature and effect and not upon whether she would hypothetically have been able to perform all the acts which it authorized.

The Master also referred to s. 4 of the 1985 Act, saying that as the obligation to register the instrument because the donor was or was becoming mentally incapable only arose after execution, if followed that at the time of execution the donor could not yet have been mentally incapable or even becoming mentally incapable. This appears to me fallacious. If the donor is already mentally incapable when he executes the power, there is no inconsistency with s. 4. It only means that the obligation to register arises immediately upon execution.

Mr Collins, for the objectors in the appeal, founded a similar argument upon the long title of the 1985 Act:

'An Act to enable powers of attorney to be created which will survive any subsequent mental incapacity of the donor and to make provision in connection with such powers.'

He said that Act was concerned to protect the power against revocation by any subsequent mental incapacity and therefore contemplated that the donor would have full capacity at the time of execution. I think that this is reading too much into the words. The Act is intended to ensure that the power will continue to be exercisable notwithstanding mental incapacity. But for the reasons I have already given, I see no reason why the test for whether it was validly created should be the same as for whether it would have ceased to be exercisable. In principle they are clearly different.

I think that my conclusions are in accordance with what appears to be the general policy of the Act. In practice it is likely that many enduring powers will be executed when symptoms of mental incapacity have begun to manifest themselves. These symptoms may result in the donor being mentally incapable in the statutory sense that she is unable on a regular basis to manage her property and affairs. But, as in the case of Mrs F, she may execute the power with full understanding and with the intention of taking advantage of the Act to have her affairs managed by the attorney of her choice rather than having them put in the hands of the Court of Protection. I can think of no reason of policy why this intention should be frustrated.

The power does not amount to an outright disposition of assets like a gift, settlement or will. It is fiduciary and further limited as to gifts and payments to the attorney himself by the specific provisions of s. 3. The obligation imposed upon the attorney to register under s. 4 or run the risk that his exercise of the power will be invalidated by s. 1(1)(b), provides the additional protection that the power will be brought to the attention of the court and the relatives to whom notice must be given. The application for registration gives the court an opportunity to consider the circumstances in which the execution of the power was procured and the suitability of the attorney. After registration, the court has its supervisory powers under s. 8. The exercise of the power is thus hedged about on all sides with statutory protection for the donor. In these circumstances, it does not seem to me necessary to impose too high a standard of capacity for its valid execution.

Finally, I should say something about what is meant by understanding the nature and effect of the power. What degree of understanding is involved? Plainly one cannot expect that the donor should have been able to pass an examination on the provisions of the Act. At the other extreme, I do not think that it would be sufficient if he realized only that it gave cousin W power to look after his property. Mr Rawson, as amicus curiae, helpfully summarized the matters which the donor should have understood in order that he can be said to have understood the nature and effect of the power. First (if such be the terms of the power), that the attorney will be able to assume complete authority over the donor's affairs. Secondly (if such be the terms of the power), that the attorney will in general be able to do anything with the donor's property which he himself could have done. Thirdly, that the authority will continue if the donor should be or become mentally incapable. Fourthly, that if he should be or become mentally incapable, the power will be irrevocable without confirmation by the court. I do not wish to prescribe another form of words in competition with the explanatory notes prescribed by the Lord Chancellor, but I accept Mr Rawson's summary as a statement of the matters which should ordinarily be explained to the donor (whatever the precise language which may be used) and which the evidence should show he has understood.

As I read the Master's findings, Miss K understood the nature and effect of the enduring power to the extent which I have described. I therefore allow the appeal and direct that the instrument which she executed be registered. I answer the question of law referred to me in Re F in the affirmative. The costs of all parties in this court and before the Master will be paid on an indemnity basis from the estates of the respective donors.

Solicitors:

Re K:

Anthony Quinn Co. for Miss K;

Michael Dorsey Co., Leeds, for the respondents;

Official Solicitor.

Re F:

Withers for Mrs F;

Official Solicitor

P.H.

[1991] 1 FLR 128

RE R (ENDURING POWER OF ATTORNEY)

Chancery Division

Vinelott J

13 December 1989

Power of attorney – Court of Protection – Application of donor's housekeeper for provision out of donor's estate – Donor incapable of managing her affairs – Court's jurisdiction to supervise donee's conduct – Whether court had power to grant provision – Enduring Powers of Attorney Act 1985, s. 8(2)(b)(i)

The applicant, who was employed by R for over 20 years, initially as a cook and housekeeper but more recently as a companion, alleged that she had provided her services to R at far less than the wages she would ordinarily have expected to earn because of her close relationship with R and because of an expectation, encouraged by R, that she would provide for her for the rest of her life. When R was in her 80s she gave an enduring power of attorney to her nephew, with a general authority to act on her behalf (save for two restrictions) which was registered under the Enduring Powers of Attorney Act 1985. Soon afterwards, R was found by a visitor of the Court of Protection to be incapable of managing her affairs and was placed in a nursing home. R's attorney then gave the applicant notice terminating her employment and sought possession of the flat. The applicant applied to the Master of the Court of Protection seeking provision out of R's estate. The master dismissed the application and the applicant appealed.

Held – dismissing the appeal – the purpose and effect of the Enduring Powers of Attorney Act 1985 was to enable a person to give a power of attorney, which would endure despite a supervening incapacity, to a person of his choice, and to empower that person to deal with his property in the way that he thought fit. The scope of the attorney's authority was enlarged beyond that which it would bear under the general law by s. 3, subject to any express restrictions in the power.

The court's powers under the 1985 Act were primarily directed to the proper supervision of the attorney, and to giving consents and authorisations which were necessary to supplement the powers, but which were not inconsistent with restrictions imposed by the donor of the power. While s. 8 of the Act gave the court jurisdiction to supervise the conduct of an attorney in the exercise of his power, s. 8(2)(b)(i), on its true construction, did not give the court unrestricted power to direct the disposal of the donor's property by way of gift, or in recognition of a moral obligation unaccompanied by any legal obligation; and that, accordingly, the court had no power to direct that provision be made for the applicant.

Statutory provisions considered

Mental Health Act 1983, ss. 95, 96

Enduring Powers of Attorney Act 1985. ss. 3, 8(2)(b)

APPEAL from the Master of the Court of Protection

Timothy Lyons for the applicant

Richard de Lacy for the attorney

VINELOTT J: This is an appeal from the Master of the Court of Protection. It raises a short question concerning the construction and effect of the Enduring Powers of Attorney Act 1985.

I need say very little, and it is undesirable that I should say more than a very little, about the contentious matters which form the background for this appeal. The donor of the power of attorney, Mrs R, is now in her 80s. Not long after she had given the power of attorney she was found by a visitor of the Court of Protection to be incapable of managing her affairs. She is a widow and childless. She has for very many years lived in a flat in Ennismore Gardens and since, I think, 1967 she has had with her in the flat the applicant, who was initially employed as a cook and housekeeper. She says that in more recent years she has been more of a companion, and she says she has served in recent years at far less than the wages she would ordinarily have expected to earn because of her close relationship with Mrs R and, moreover, in the expectation which she was encouraged to form by Mrs R, that Mrs R would look after her and provide accommodation for her for the whole of her life. She says that it was in reliance on that expectation that in 1984 she declined an invitation by relatives to go to live with them in Luxembourg.

On 25 January 1988 Mrs R gave an enduring power of attorney to a nephew. That power was executed in the presence of her doctor and the family solicitor. It is on a printed form. She gave her attorney a general authority to act on her behalf, save that the power was not to extend to the management of her portfolio handled by Mr Raphael Zarn, a stockbroker, and was to be subject to the restriction that the attorney was not to make gifts to friends or relatives. That power was registered under the 1985 Act on 11 May 1988. No question is raised as to the validity of the power and, as I have said, a visitor has found that the donor of the power is now under an incapacity. She was taken first to a hospital following an accident in March, and then in mid-April moved to a nursing home in the country, where she now is.

There has been considerable hostility between the attorney and the applicant, which happily I need not enter into. As a result of the change in Mrs R's circumstances, the attorney gave the applicant notice terminating her employment and later sought possession of the flat, which has a very considerable value (of the order of £400,000) and a very considerable letting value; if improved, it would command a rent of about £800 a week. At the moment it is a drain on Mrs R's resources.

The applicant first applied under the 1985 Act for an order for the cancellation of the power on the ground that Mrs R was, and was likely to remain, mentally capable, or alternatively that fraud or undue pressure had been used to induce her to execute it. Following the report of the visitor, to which I have referred, the application was amended to seek provision out of Mrs R's estate. She asked for an order that such provision be made as the court deemed proper for her maintenance and accommodation, and for reimbursement of sums which she says she has disbursed. On that latter matter, there has been some reimbursement and I cannot, on the evidence before me, decide whether there are other sums in respect of which she has a valid claim. Any further claim will have to be put before the Master of the Court of Protection.

The grounds on which this application is founded are, as I have indicated, statements said to have been made by Mrs R that she would make financial provision for the applicant's future, and that she could trust her to make that provision. On that application being made, the attorney undertook not to restore proceedings he had taken for possession of the flat. The application came before the Master of the Court of Protection on 31 January 1989 when it was dismissed and the applicant appeals from that dismissal. I should perhaps add that the flat has been maintained in the meantime. The proceedings for possession are still pending and have been transferred to the county court. That is all I need say about the background.

The Enduring Powers of Attorney Act 1985 made a very remarkable change in the law. It created a regime for the administration of the affairs of somebody who becomes incapable of managing his affairs which is supplemental to that provided by the Mental Health Act 1983. In effect the Act permits a person, while capable of managing his affairs, to select somebody who will be responsible for managing his affairs if there is a supervening incapacity, so avoiding the expense and – I think, possibly, in the minds of some – the embarrassment of invoking the full jurisdiction of the Court of Protection. A power of attorney has very limited effect until it is registered. When registered, it takes effect according to its terms. The scope of the attorney's authority is enlarged beyond that which it would bear under the general law by s. 3, subject to any express restrictions in the power, and the court is given wide powers of supervision under s. 8. Section 3(4) provides:

'Subject to any conditions or restrictions contained in the instrument, an attorney under an enduring power … may (without obtaining any consent) act under the power so as to benefit himself or other persons than the donor to the following extent but no further, that is to say—

(a) he may so act in relation to any other person if the donor might be expected to provide for his or that person's needs respectively; and

(b) he may do whatever the donor might be expected to do to meet those needs.'

That extension is then further extended by s. 3(5), which gives the attorney power to 'dispose of the property of the donor by way of gift' in making gifts 'of a seasonal nature' or on a specified anniversary to 'persons … related to or connected with the donor' subject to the proviso that 'the value of each such gift is not unreasonable having regard to all the circumstances and in particular the size of the donor's estate'.

The role of the court is set out in s. 8. Under s. 8(2)(a) the court has power to determine questions as to the meaning or effect of the instrument. Under s. 8(2)(b) the court has power to give directions with respect to:

'(i) the management or disposal by the attorney of the property and affairs of the donor;

(ii) the rendering of accounts by the attorney and the production of the records kept by him for the purpose;

(iii) the remuneration or expenses of the attorney, whether or not in default of or in accordance with any provision made by the instrument, including directions for the repayment of excessive or the payment of additional remuneration;…'

Section 8(2)(c) gives the court power to require the attorney to furnish information or produce documents, and s. 8(2)(d) to give any consent or authorisation to act which the attorney would have to obtain from a mentally capable donor. Section 8(2)(e), I must read in full:

'(2) The court may . . .

(e) authorise the attorney to act so as to benefit himself or

other persons than the donor otherwise than in accordance with section 3(4) and (5) (but subject to any conditions or restrictions contained in the instrument); …'

Section 8(2)(f) gives the court power to relieve the attorney wholly or partly from any liability which he has or may have incurred on account of a breach of his duties as attorney.

It is quite plain, and it is not in dispute, that the only authority that the Court of Protection could have to give directions to the attorney, requiring him to make provision for the applicant, would have to be found, if at all, in s. 8(2)(b)(i). The case put by the applicant's counsel is that that subparagraph does give the court unrestricted power to direct an attorney to dispose of any part of the property of the donor of the power, by way of gift or in recognition of some moral obligation unaccompanied by any legal obligation.

I find that an impossible view. Of course, the word 'disposal' is, in some contexts, capable of being given a very wide meaning, and could include a disposition by way of gift. But it seems to me that in the context of s. 8 it cannot have been intended that it should bear that wide meaning. It comes in a paragraph, (b), which is plainly concerned with administrative matters: the management of the donor's property, the rendering of accounts and determination of the remuneration of the attorney. These are all part of the jurisdiction which the court is given to supervise the conduct of the attorney, and to see that he is exercising his powers of management and administration properly. It would be remarkable, in a paragraph directed to matters of that sort, to find an unrestricted power given to the court to dispose of the whole of the donor's property by way of gift.

The court, of course, has a very wide power, in the case of a patient within the jurisdiction of the Court of Protection. It is now conferred by ss. 95 and 96 of the Mental Health Act 1983. However, there the power of the court to direct dispositions of the patient's property is very clearly spelled out, and the rules provide for all persons potentially interested in the patient's estate to be represented, and for full consideration of the effect of any disposition of the patient's property.

Moreover, the construction which it is sought to put on s. 8(2)(b)(i) brings that paragraph into conflict with s. 8(2)(e) which gives the court a power which is supplemental to s. 3(4) and (5); it is a power for the court to authorise gifts or dispositions of property which go beyond s. 3(4) and (5). The power of the court to give that authority is, however, subject to any conditions or restrictions in the power of attorney itself. If the contentions made on behalf of the applicant were right, s. 8(2)(b)(i) would enable the court to give directions for the gift or disposition of the property of the donor which are not subject to conditions or restrictions contained in the instrument. In my view that cannot possibly have been intended.

More generally, I think Mr de Lacy, counsel for the attorney, was right when he said that the purpose and effect of the Enduring Powers of Attorney Act 1985 is to enable somebody to give a power of attorney, which will endure despite a supervening incapacity, to a person of his choice, and to empower that person to deal with his property in the way that he thinks fit. It should be approached on the footing that the court's powers are primarily directed to the proper supervision of the attorney, and to giving consents or authorisations which are necessary to supplement the powers, but which are not inconsistent with restrictions imposed by the donor of the power. I find it unnecessary in these circumstances to consider the further question, whether the restriction in the power of attorney which I read would, in fact, put it outside the power of the court to authorise dispositions of the kind sought in favour of the applicant. In my judgment, therefore, this appeal fails and must be dismissed.

Solicitors:

Lithgow Pepper Eldridge for the applicant

Lovell White Durrant for the attorney

PATRICIA HOLLINGS

Barrister

[1999] 2 FLR 1163

RE W (POWER OF ATTORNEY)

Chancery Division

Mr Jules Sher QC

(sitting as a deputy judge of the High Court)

8 July 1999

Executors, administrators, wills and probate – Power of attorney

W, aged over 90, granted her eldest daughter, X, a power of attorney with general authority to act on her behalf in relation to all her property and affairs. W's other two children, who had an unrelated dispute with X, objected to registration of the enduring power of attorney. Their grounds were (1) that the power was invalid because W lacked capacity to grant it, and (2) that X was unsuitable because of the hostility between the siblings. The master of the court of protection refused to register the power of attorney on both grounds, taking into account in relation to X's unsuitability, an unauthorised gift which she had made to herself and her two siblings. X appealed.

Held – allowing X's appeal and making the order for registration of the power –

(1) The onus was not on X to show that W had possessed the capacity to execute the power of attorney, but on the two objectors to show that W had lacked the capacity to do so. Therefore, even if there was insufficient evidence to satisfy the court that W had possessed the necessary understanding at the relevant time, if the court was not satisfied on the evidence that W had lacked the necessary understanding, it was bound by the Enduring Power of Attorney Act 1985 to register the power unless there was another valid ground of objection. The contemporary evidence from W's GP that W had the necessary mental capacity weighed more heavily with the court than evidence from a psychologist which was based on two interviews with W some months after the power was executed. The court was not satisfied that W lacked capacity.

(2) If an estate was complex, hostility between siblings might well render all of them unsuitable as attorneys for the estate, because it would interfere with the smooth running of the administration of the estate, but where, as here, the estate was simple, such hostility need not impact adversely on the administration of the estate and the court should not interfere on the ground of unsuitability. In relation to the unauthorised gift, although the power of an attorney did not extend to the sort of inheritance tax planning which had been attempted by X, X had been scrupulously fair as between the three siblings, and had not behaved greedily or dishonestly. She was not unsuitable as attorney of W's estate.

Statutory provisions considered

Enduring Power of Attorney Act 1985, s 6(5)(a), (e), (6)

Case referred to in judgment

K, Re; F (Enduring Powers of Attorney), Re [1988] Ch 310, [1988] 2 FLR 15, [1988] 2 WLR 781, [1988] 1 All ER 358, ChD

Adrian Jack for the appellant

David Rees for the respondent

JULES SHER QC: This is an appeal from the decision of the master of the court of protection who refused to register an enduring power of attorney granted by Mrs W to her eldest child, Mrs X, on 4 July 1996 with general authority to act on her behalf in relation to all her property and affairs. As this judgment is being given in open court I shall restrict the recital of facts to the barest minimum necessary to identify the point at issue.

Mrs W is now over 90. Her husband died in 1979. They were hoteliers. The hotel was sold in 1987. In 1993 Mrs W moved to sheltered accommodation. On 29 August 1996 she moved to a residential home and in December 1997 she was transferred to a nursing home where she still resides.

She has three children: the donee of the power, Mrs X, now aged 61, another daughter Mrs Y now 60 and a son Mr Z, now aged 56. Much of the reason for what has turned out to be extremely wasteful litigation in relation to a relatively modest amount of property is due to a wholly unrelated dispute between Mrs X on the one hand and her brother and sister on the other. This dispute concerned two cottages in which the three siblings were, with one other person, in joint ownership as tenants in common. The brother and sister (as well as the other joint owner) wanted to sell at a price which had been offered. Mrs X wanted to hold out for a higher price. Her three joint owners sued her in the county court, causing both sides to run up expensive legal bills. Eventually higher offers came in and the properties were sold above the higher price for which Mrs X was holding out. Apparently even that did not settle the litigation as the plaintiffs continued to dispute the question as to who was to have conduct of the sale.

From the 275 pages in the bundle before me it is obvious that Mrs X, of the three siblings, is the most literary, in the sense at least of being given to committing her communications to writing. She also comes across as efficient in the recording of financial detail so far as her administration of the marketing and sale of the cottages was concerned. She appears from the evidence to be a businesswoman in her own right (unlike her siblings) and to have dominated family financial matters such as the obtaining of planning permission for the site and the campaign to achieve a sale. It is not surprising that she was chosen by her mother, Mrs W, to be her sole attorney.

Unfortunately, perhaps, Mrs X does not mince her words. Her letters are not only prolix but, it has to be said, unnecessarily vulgar. It is from one of these letters that the master quoted in his judgment and it is plain that such offensive letters to her siblings played an important role in persuading the master to reject the power of attorney.

I have had more extensive evidence than was before the master and I have come to a different conclusion. Ordinarily this judgment would be delivered in chambers. However, two points of principle emerge from my different treatment and that has led to this judgment being given in open court.

There survive in this court only two of the grounds put forward by the objectors (Mrs Y and Mr Z) who responded to Mrs X's notices dated 18 April 1998 of her intention to register the power. Those two grounds are the grounds in subparas (a) and (e) of s 6(5) of the Enduring Power of Attorney Act 1985. I quote those two subparagraphs below:

Section 6(5):

'For the purpose of this Act a notice of objection to the registration of an instrument is valid if the objection is made on one or more of the following grounds, namely—

(a) that the power purported to have been created by the instrument was not valid as an enduring power of attorney;

...

(e) that, having regard to all the circumstances and in particular the attorney's relationship to or connection with the donor, the attorney is unsuitable to be the donor's attorney.'

quote as well the next subsection (on which the first issue of principle in this appeal arises).

Section 6(6):

'If, in a case where subsection (4) above applies, any of the grounds of objection in subsection (5) above is established to the satisfaction of the court, the court shall refuse the application but if, in such a case, it is not so satisfied, the court shall register the instrument to which the application relates.'

This is a case, of course, in which 'subsection (4) above applies' because one of the occasions for the operation of subs (4) is that a valid notice of objection to the registration was timeously received: see s 6(4)(a) of the Act. There is no suggestion that this was not the case here.

The important point to notice is that the onus of establishing any of the grounds set out in subs (5) is firmly laid on the shoulders of the objectors. Under subs (6) it is only if the ground concerned is established to the satisfaction of the court that the court can refuse to register the power. Indeed, if the ground is so established the court must refuse. The contrary position is expressly made equally emphatic: if the court is not so satisfied it 'shall register the instrument to which the application relates'.

Very few cases in these days turn on the onus of proof. In ordinary civil litigation the judge is nearly always able to form a view on a balance of probabilities as to whether an event did or did not happen. But the state of a woman's mind some 3 years before the court hearing is inherently an issue in respect of which it is quite likely that the judge may not be satisfied either way.

The first ground: invalidity due to lack of capacity

In this case the essential facts were that at the time of the execution of the power (4 July 1996) Mrs W was 87 and by all accounts was physically well but suffering from a degree of memory impairment. Her GP, Dr H, had written a letter to her solicitor a fortnight before the execution of the power. The letter was dated 22 June 1996 and in it he said:

'I can confirm that I saw her recently with her daughter and found her to be suffering from a degree of memory impairment, however in my opinion she still has the necessary mental capacity to sign a power of attorney. I would add that her mental abilities are at their best in the early part of the day and tend to deteriorate as the day goes by.'

It seemed to me important for the court to see the doctor and ascertain precisely what he meant by the necessary mental capacity to sign a power of attorney and what tests he performed, if any, to reach this conclusion. However, I was told by Mr Jack, counsel for Mrs X, that the doctor had indicated that he could not now remember any detail whatsoever and that he was accordingly unable to help the court.

The hearing below proceeded in the total absence of Mrs X who, unfortunately, was not served appropriate notice of the hearing due to an error in the Public Trustee Office. That would of course have entitled Mrs X to have the proceedings below set aside as of right, but both counsel invited me, in the interest of saving costs, to treat the matter as effectively before me on the original as well as additional evidence put by Mrs X after the hearing before the master.

Against the doctor's evidence was the evidence of a chartered clinical psychologist to whom Mrs Y had taken Mrs W on 22 November and 13 December 1996. Mrs W had been taken from the residential home where she was then living to the psychologist without the knowledge of Mrs X, who first heard about the matter when the psychologist's report was produced in these proceedings.

As the master pointed out the psychologist's report was extensive and detailed. He concluded that:

'... the above detected severity of deterioration across a number of vital areas of cognitive functioning suggests strongly that for the past period running into a number of years, Mrs W has not been in a position to deal properly with the intangible (non-concrete) or hypothetical, or to correctly comprehend, interpret, see implications in, judge, or to direct any business or operation other than that which does not require weighing up the pros and cons, making comparisons, or seeing consequences of action beyond the immediate step.'

As the report did not specifically address the question whether or not Mrs W was capable of executing an enduring power of attorney, the psychologist wrote a supplemental note on 10 July 1998 in which he said:

'I believe that in no way was Mrs W in a condition on 4 July 1996 to execute an enduring power of attorney.'

The doctor's evidence has the inestimable advantage of being that of the patient's GP who saw her regularly, and of being more or less contemporaneous with the execution of the power. It would take a very strong opinion given as a result of an examination some 5 months later to persuade me positively that the patient did not have the necessary capacity. As it was the psychologist recognised in his report that medication could make an assessment of the kind he was making problematic. Yet there is no record in his report of the various forms of medication (including morphine) Mrs W was taking at the time. Mrs X has now given evidence of these: Dothiepin for depression, Inderalla for blood pressure, distalgesic co-proxamol for pain relief and Merellil to keep her calm. Moreover, on 16 January 1997 Mrs W was rushed to hospital and treated for anaemia. The effect of anaemia on her performance of the psychometric tests is unclear.

I have taken into account all the evidence, on both sides, as to various incidents showing a certain degree of confusion over the years. There is no point in recording all the detail here. It is worth noting, however, that Mrs X has for many years handled her mother's financial affairs. Mrs X had been made a signatory on her bank account with Lloyds Bank. Mrs X arranged for the payment of her bills. When it was apparent in April 1996 that Mrs W's mental faculties were getting weaker she wrote, in her own handwriting, to her solicitor, in a perfectly intelligible way in connection with her will, a codicil and the division of what she called her 'household goods'. Mrs W herself, I am told, had been the attorney under an enduring power of attorney for her elder sister so I can assume that she probably knew what an enduring power of attorney was.

I have further evidence before me in the shape of a statement by one of the directors of the nursing home in which Mrs W now lives who says that as late as 12 April 1998 when the notice of intention to register the power was served on her, Mrs W understood the arrangements with Mrs X as the attorney and Mrs W said, 'why would I want to change anything'. I have also been shown a letter written as late as April 1999 in a very shaky hand saying that she wanted the Public Trustee Office to stop interfering with her affairs. I must say that I was a little surprised at the coherence and vehemence of this letter and wondered to what extent it was influenced by others.

All in all, however, I am not satisfied that it has been established that Mrs W did not have the necessary understanding to execute an enduring power of attorney. That was the first ground put forward by the objectors, ie that the power was not valid as an enduring power because Mrs W did not understand the nature and effect of it. The degree of understanding and mental capacity necessary for this purpose has been laid down recently in *Re K; Re F (Enduring Powers of Attorney)* [1988] Ch 310, [1988] 2 FLR 15. The level of understanding required is less than that required to enable an individual to manage her affairs generally. What is required is that she understood:

(a) that the attorney would be able to assume complete authority over her affairs;

(b) that the attorney could do anything with her property that she could have done;

(c) that that authority would continue if she became mentally incapable; and

(d) would in that event become irrevocable without confirmation by the court.

I am not satisfied on the evidence that Mrs W did not have this understanding. This does not mean that I am satisfied that she did have it. The point of this judgment is that this last issue is not the question before me. If, as is the case, I am not satisfied that she lacked the necessary understanding, it seems to me that I am bid by the Act to register the power, and that, subject to consideration of the second ground of objection, is what I propose to do.

In *Re K; Re F* Hoffmann J (as he then was) added, after describing the above four elements, the following sentence:

'I do not wish to prescribe another form of words in competition with the explanatory notes prescribed by the Lord Chancellor, but I accept Mr Rawson's summary as a statement of the matters which should ordinarily be explained to the donor (whatever the precise language which may be used) and which the evidence should show he has understood.'

This sentence forms no part of the reason for the decision. The judge was not concerned with an issue of onus or burden of proof. He inadvertently, in my judgment, turned the onus around so as to make it a requirement that the evidence should positively show the necessary understanding. The master concluded his judgment below thus:

'I must emphasise the final words of the passage I quoted earlier from Hoffmann J's judgment in *Re K; Re F* – "which the evidence should show that he has understood" – because they are often overlooked. The evidence in this case as it was presented to me prior to and at the hearing does not satisfy me that Mrs [W] understood the nature and effect of the enduring power of attorney she signed on 4 July 1996.'

In my judgment the master went wrong in following this part of Hoffmann J's judgment. To sustain the power Mrs X did not have to satisfy him that Mrs W understood the nature of the power; the objectors had to satisfy him that she did not.

The second ground: unsuitability

This brings me to the second and only other surviving ground on which objection is made, and that is that having regard to all the circumstances, and in particular the attorney's relationship to or in connection with the donor, the attorney is unsuitable to be the donor's attorney.

The master decided that Mrs X was unsuitable for two reasons: first, because she had made unauthorised gifts to herself and her siblings of £20,000 each. The master said that he could not condone that. Secondly, and in my judgment more importantly, the master said this:

'In my opinion, the hostility and resentment between Mrs [W's] children renders any one of them unsuitable to be her attorney. The objectors clearly distrust the attorney, and the attorney obviously has no time for her brother and sister. Each party seems determined to thwart the actions and intentions of the other and, if need be, to air their family feud before the courts. Such contentiousness and bickering cannot possibly be in Mrs [W's] best interests, and it would be irresponsible of the court to allow either faction to gain the upper hand in terms of control over their mother. In the circumstances Mrs [W's] affairs should be managed by someone completely independent of the family.'

The gifts

I shall take these two points in turn. First, the gifts. It must be remembered that Mrs X was not at the hearing to defend herself. She did not even know that this criticism would be made. Before me and through her counsel, Mr Jack, she has made it quite clear that now that she understands the law she will undertake to make retrospective application to approve the gifts and not make any further gifts without the court's permission.

The gifts have to be put into proper perspective. There is no suggestion that as between the three siblings Mrs X has not been scrupulously fair. Whatever she gave to herself she gave to each of her siblings. But it is more important to understand why the gifts were made in the first place. Plainly Mrs X is astute enough to have realised that there may be a case for sensible estate planning. She had, I gather from the evidence, sold the flat Mrs W owned and was living in sometime in mid-1996. That realised £100,000. There has been no criticism that this was not a sensible thing to do and the best price that could have been obtained. With Mrs W's other assets this figure put her well above the threshold at which inheritance tax is charged (currently some £231,000 I believe). To reduce the estate Mrs X made on behalf of Mrs W potentially exempt transfers of £20,000 each to the three siblings. Of course, Mrs W would have to survive for the requisite period for this to avoid the tax: but it was a perfectly rational thing to do. Whether it was the right thing to do in Mrs W's interests is another matter entirely and would be dependent upon the extent of her assets and her reasonable needs for the remainder of her lifetime. I say nothing about this aspect. It may have to be considered by the master at some other time.

What the master focused on, quite rightly in my opinion, was that the power of an attorney to make gifts of the donor's property is extremely limited, and certainly, without the authorisation of the court after the power is registered, does not extend to the making of gifts of this kind as part of inheritance tax planning.

But the evidence I have seen does not portray a picture of greed. At worst Mrs X acted misguidedly in the interests of her siblings and herself and not, as she saw it, against the interests of her mother. The worst that can be said of her is that she ought to have known the law if she was to take on the responsibility of such an important fiduciary position, particularly as one of the few things expressly stated in part of the power itself is the following sentence:

'I also understand my limited power to use the donor's property to benefit persons other than the donor.'

There is one further point that ought to be made. Mrs X's evidence is that in making the £20,000 gifts she was not acting under the power at all but on the express authority of her mother. It seems that the proceeds of the sale of the flat were available for distribution and that the gifts were made at about the time of Mrs W's move to the residential home which was in late August 1996, not very long after the power was executed. It may well be that Mrs W was perfectly capable at that time of directing these gifts to be made.

Finally, of course, there is no indication that the two objectors ever complained about the gifts (from which they benefited as much as Mrs X did).

I do not think that the evidence concerning the gifts renders Mrs X unsuitable as an attorney.

Hostility

The second ground of unsuitability is the hostility between the three children. The master considered that that fact alone rendered any one of them unsuitable to be Mrs W's attorney. In my judgment such hostility may well have such consequences but it all depends upon the circumstances. For example, had the estate of Mrs W been complex and had it required strategic decisions in relation to its administration, one would expect the attorney to have had to consult and work with her siblings in relation to the administration. In such circumstances the evident hostility between them would impact adversely on the stewardship of the attorney, no matter who was at fault in creating the hostility in the first place.

But in this case the estate is simple. I asked counsel what the position was and was told that these are the following assets:

(1) a portfolio of investments of a value (as at 23 December 1998) of £211,189;

(2) £20,000 in premium bonds;

(3) a life policy (written in trust) of £30,000.

As to the outgoings there is the cost of the nursing home at some £2000 a month, and then, simply, the need for a modest amount to cover a regular hairdo, telephone bills and the like. And, of course, on the income side there is the old age pension.

In other words there is nothing of any significance left to be done. The assets are under proper control. The income simply needs to be fed through to the nursing home. The evidence is that this has been done by Mrs X very efficiently. She had indicated more than once that she has never intended to charge for her services under the power of attorney and she does not intend to do so. Against this, if the public trustee were to come in, there would be an appointment fee and an annual fee of between £2350 and £3600 pa. If a solicitor were appointed the total cost would be likely to be somewhat less than that.

It seems to me that it is not right to say that (irrespective of the background) hostility of the kind we have seen in this case between the children renders any one of them unsuitable to be Mrs W's attorney. In this case the hostility will not impact adversely on the administration. It would, in my judgment, be quite wrong to frustrate Mrs W's choice of attorney in this way. Whether it is or is not a good idea for a parent in Mrs W's position, when such hostility exists, to appoint one child alone as attorney is another question. But Mrs W did so and, on the evidence, did so knowing of the hostility. That is her prerogative and in my judgment, when the hostility does not interfere with the smooth running of the administration, the court should not interfere on the ground of unsuitability.

That is not to say that this court approves of the strident tones in which Mrs X's correspondence is couched. It is earnestly to be hoped that after all this wasteful litigation she can find it in herself to conduct the family's affairs in a more congenial and co-operative manner.

I shall accordingly allow the appeal from the decision of the master and make the necessary order for the registration of the power. Appeal allowed. Registration of power of attorney ordered.

Solicitors:

Max Barford Co for the appellant

Gaby Hardwicke Yearwood Griffiths for the respondent

PHILIPPA JOHNSON

Barrister

[2001] 1 FLR 832

RE W (ENDURING POWER OF ATTORNEY)

Court of Appeal

Peter Gibson and Arden LJJ and Sir Christopher Staughton

11 December 2000

Power of attorney – Widow granting enduring power of attorney to eldest child – Child's siblings objecting on ground that instrument invalid through want of capacity of donor – Whether burden of proof on objectors or attorney – Enduring Power of Attorney Act 1985 ss 4, 6

In July 1996, a widow in her late eighties granted an enduring power of attorney to her eldest daughter. In April 1998, the daughter applied for it to be registered under the Enduring Power of Attorney Act 1985, having given notice of her intention to her siblings, the objectors. The objections were upheld by the Master in the Court of Protection, but without the daughter being notified of the hearing. The matter was reconsidered on appeal. The Master upheld two grounds put forward by the objectors: (1) that the widow did not have the necessary capacity at the time the order was made, and (2) that having regard to all the circumstances, especially the attorney's relationship with the donor, the attorney was unsuitable. The Master's decision was reversed on those points. As regards the question of capacity he held that the objectors had not discharged the burden of proof which rested on them. He did not make an affirmative finding in respect of the attorney. The objectors appealed on ground (1). They contended also that the decision had been wrong on the facts. With the court's leave the objectors amended their notice of appeal to say that the burden of proof rested on the daughter as the attorney. Since the objection was valid the question to be decided was whether the ground of objection, that the power purported to have been created by the attorney was not valid, was established to the satisfaction of the court. If it was, then the court must refuse registration.

Held – dismissing the appeal – notwithstanding the dicta of Hoffmann J in *Re K (Enduring Powers of Attorney); Re F* and the principle of common law whereby the burden of proof was on the person seeking to uphold a deed or document on which the objectors had relied, s 6(6) of the Enduring Power of Attorney Act 1985 clearly provided that the grounds of objection had to be proved. The judge had been right to treat the burden of proof as resting throughout on the objectors, and, having found that the objectors had not discharged that burden, had been bound to register the instrument. He had not erred in law or on the facts in reaching his decision.

Statutory provisions considered

Law Commissions Act 1965, s 3(1)(e)
Mental Health Act 1983, Part 7
Enduring Power of Attorney Act 1985, ss 4, 6, 7, 8

Cases referred to in judgment

Beaney Dec'd, Re [1978] 1 WLR 770, [1978] 2 All ER 595, ChD
Brown v Pourau [1995] 1 NZLR 352, High Ct of NZ
K (Enduring Powers of Attorney), Re; Re F [1988] Ch 310, Court of Protection
Peters v Morris (CA 99/85) (unreported) 19 May 1987, CA (Wellington)
Waring v Waring [1848] VI Moore 342

David Rees for the appellant
Adrian Jack for the respondent

PETER GIBSON LJ:

(1)   I will ask Sir Christopher Staughton to give the first judgment.

SIR CHRISTOPHER STAUGHTON:

(2)   This appeal concerns the affairs of Mrs W, as I shall call her, a widow who is nearly 91 years of age. On 4 July 1996, she granted an enduring power of attorney to her eldest child, Mrs X. Two years later, on 27 April 1998, Mrs X applied for the enduring power of attorney to be registered under the Enduring Power of Attorney Act 1985. Meanwhile, she had given notice of intention to register on 18 April 1998 to the other two children of Mrs W: I will call them Mrs Y, who is now 61, and Mr Z, who is aged 57. They became the objectors. They had already, on 21 February 1997, obtained a report from a Mr C on Mrs W's mental health, but no action had been taken on that report in the ensuing year.

(3)   On 13 May 1998, the objectors served notice of objection. That led to the present proceedings. The objections were upheld by Master Lush in the Court of Protection. However, his decision was reached in an unsatisfactory way in that Mrs X had not been notified of the hearing date and was not present. It seems to me, there having been real doubt as to whether she had been notified, that the Master would have been wiser not to proceed at that stage. In the event, we should disregard the conclusions of the Master. There might have been an order setting his decision aside and directing a fresh hearing before a new Master; but the parties instead agreed that on an appeal to a judge of the Chancery Division the matter should be reconsidered. That was done in order to save costs.

(4)   The assets of the estate are not large. They are somewhat less now than they were before, no doubt, as the Master ordered the costs to come out of the estate. So did the judge. In the judge's decision it is said that the assets were a portfolio of investments valued in December 1998 at £211,000, £20,000 in premium bonds and a life policy written in trust of £30,000. At the time Mrs W was in a nursing home, which cost £2000 a month. She had some other simple and fairly modest requirements. Of course, she also had on the income side the old age pension.

(5)   The grounds argued before the Master were these. First, that the power purported to have been created by the instrument was not valid as an enduring power of attorney. The reason put forward for that was that Mrs W did not have the necessary capacity and understanding at the time when she made it. Secondly, it was said that undue pressure was used to induce the donor to create the power. Thirdly, that having regard to all the circumstances, and in particular the attorney's relationship to or connection with the donor, the attorney was unsuitable as an attorney of the donor.

(6)   The Master upheld the first and third grounds, that is to say lack of capacity and understanding and unsuitability, but not the second ground, which was undue pressure. The appeal came before Mr Julian Sher QC, sitting as a deputy judge of the Chancery Division. Before him only grounds one and three were argued, the ones upon which the objectors had succeeded before the Master. The deputy judge reversed the Master's decision on both points. He had, of course, additional evidence which was not before the Master.

(7)   There is now an appeal to this court by permission of Walker LJ.

(8)   The third ground, unsuitability, is no longer pursued by the objectors. So the only ground now is that the power of attorney was invalid through want of capacity.

(9) Before the judge the objectors had accepted that the burden of proof as to that rested on them. The judge accepted that, and there was no challenge to it in the notice of appeal. But now the objectors seek to amend their notice of appeal to say that the burden was on Mrs X, the attorney. There has been no objection to leave to amend the notice of appeal being granted; and we do grant it.

(10) The relevant provisions in the Enduring Power of Attorney Act 1985 are as follows. Section 4 provides:

'(1) If the attorney under an enduring power has reason to believe that the donor is or is becoming mentally incapable subsections (2) to (6) below shall apply.

(2) The attorney shall, as soon as practicable, make an application to the court for the registration of the instrument creating the power.'

(11) That, of course, was done in this case.

(12) Then s 6 says:

'(1) In any case where—

(a) an application for registration is made in accordance with section 4(3) and (4), and

(b) neither subsection (2) nor subsection (4) below applies,

the court shall register the instrument to which the application relates.'

(13) The provisions there referred to in subss (2) and (4) deal with two cases. Subsection (2) deals with the case where it appears to the court that there is in force under Part 7 of the Mental Health Act 1983 an order appointing a receiver. But that is not this case. In such a case the court can act of its own motion. Subsection (4) provides:

'If, in the case of an application for registration—

(a) a valid notice of objection to the registration is received … [within a certain period], or

(b) it appears from the application that there is no one to whom notice has been given under paragraph 1 of that Schedule, or

(c) the court has reason to believe that appropriate inquiries might bring to light evidence on which the court could be satisfied that one of the grounds of objection set out in subsection (5) below was established,

the court shall neither register the instrument nor refuse the application until it has made or caused to be made such inquiries (if any) as it thinks appropriate in the circumstances of the case.'

(14) So that deals with two cases: first, whether there is a valid notice of objection; secondly, where the court has reason to believe that appropriate inquiries might bring to light evidence which was relevant.

(15) Then subs (5) sets out for the purposes of the Act what grounds may be included in the notice of objection. Ground (a) is that the power purported to have been created by the attorney was not a valid and enduring power of attorney. That is the case which now remains to be considered in this court.

(16) Then subs (6), which is critical for this case, provides:

'If, in a case where subsection (4) above applies, any of the grounds of objection in subsection (5) above is established to the satisfaction of the court, the court shall refuse the application but if, in such a case, it is not so satisfied, the court shall register the instrument to which the application relates.'

(17) In this case there was a valid objection under subs (4). The question is whether the ground of objection in subs (5)(a), that is to say that there was not a valid enduring power of attorney, is established to the satisfaction of the court. If it is, the court must refuse registration. If not, the court shall register the instrument.

(18) The law relating to this matter has been considered in two judgments to which we have been referred. First, there is the decision in *Re K (Enduring Powers of Attorney); Re F* [1988] Ch 310. In that case Hoffmann J said at 313:

> 'The Act does not specify the mental capacity needed to execute an enduring power and the answer must therefore be found in the common law. It is well established that capacity to perform a juristic act exists when the person who purported to do the act had at the time the mental capacity, with the assistance of such explanation as he may have been given, to understand the nature and effect of that particular transaction: see *In re Beaney, dec'd* [1978] 1 W.L.R. 770. In principle, therefore, an understanding of the nature and effect of the power was sufficient for its validity.'

(19) Later, Hoffmann J referred to what measures should be taken to achieve that. At 316:

> 'Finally, I should say something about what is meant by understanding the nature and effect of the power. What degree of understanding is involved? Plainly one cannot expect that the donor should have been able to pass an examination on the provisions of the Act. At the other extreme, I do not think that it would be sufficient if he realised only that it gave Cousin William power to look after his property. Mr Rawson helpfully summarised the matters which the donor should have understood in order that he can be said to have understood the nature and effect of the power. First, (if such be the terms of the power) that the attorney will be able to assume complete authority over the donor's affairs. Secondly, (if such be the terms of the power) that the attorney will in general be able to do anything with the donor's property which he himself could have done. Thirdly, that the authority will continue if the donor should be or become mentally incapable. Fourthly, that if he should be or become mentally incapable, the power will be irrevocable without confirmation by the court.'

(20) I would, for my part, agree that those four points are a sound indication of what the donor must understand if the power is to be valid.

(21) Hoffmann J went on to say (at 316):

> 'I do not wish to prescribe another form of words in competition with the explanatory notes prescribed by the Lord Chancellor, but I accept Mr. Rawson's summary as a statement of the matters which should ordinarily be explained to the donor (whatever the precise language which may be used) and which the evidence should show he has understood.'

(22) The last nine words have been relied on as showing that the burden of proof lies on the attorney for the purpose of showing that the instrument is valid. I am unable to reconcile that with the burden provided by s 6(6), which, as is accepted by Mr Rees for the objectors, at any rate imposes prime facie a burden on the objectors. With respect to Lord Hoffmann, I suspect that he did not have in mind the question of the burden of proof when he used those words in the form in which he did.

(23) We have also been referred to the case of *Re Beaney Dec'd* [1978] 1 WLR 770. There Mr Martin Nourse QC had something to say about how the requirement of understanding should be put to a donor. He said that the donor in that case was able to give an appearance of understanding that which was not simple, particularly if to the questions he was asked there could be given a yes or no answer, being the answer which was obviously wanted. That is more concerned with the way that understanding can be tested than with the requirement of understanding itself.

(24) The difficulty, as it seems to me, is that old people, as I happen to know, are reluctant to believe that senility is coming upon them and therefore are reluctant to release the powers which they have hitherto enjoyed: hence, I think, the two-stage approach of an enduring power of attorney; stage 1, when the proposed donor is still capable of understanding what she is doing; stage 2, when the attorney has reason to believe that she is no longer capable. An application must then be made for registration.

(25) For my part, I would not be inclined to rely on evidence of one interview, certainly not of the kind described by Mr Nourse. No doubt it is right to ask questions when it is contemplated that a donor shall execute an enduring power; but that is not by any means the final way of determining whether there is the necessary capacity.

(26) The argument for the objectors is that the burden of proof in such a case does not necessarily remain on them. It is put in this way in the outline argument on their behalf:

> '19 The initial burden is upon the attorney. At common law the legal burden of proof lies upon the party seeking to establish the validity of a document. This burden of proof is therefore external to the provisions of section 6.
>
> 20 Section 6(6) supplements, but does not alter, the common law position by setting out the steps that the court must take once it has reached a decision as to whether a valid ground of objection exists. If it exists, the court must refuse registration. Otherwise, the court must register.
>
> 21 Section 6(6) does not reverse the burden of proof in relation to any particular ground of objection. If the objection is based on an allegation of fraud, then it is for the party alleging fraud to prove it. If it is based upon a contention that the document itself is invalid, then it is for the party seeking to rely on the document to prove it.'

(27) That was the way it was put in the outline argument. But before us it seemed to me that Mr Rees was not putting it quite in that way. He was prepared to acknowledge that s 6(6) put a burden in the first instance on the objectors; and if he was not prepared to acknowledge that, for my part I think it is perfectly clear in the section. To take an analogy with computer speak, the way to discover where the burden of proof lies, in my view, is to find the default setting. The default setting is stated quite clearly in s 6(6): if the court is not satisfied on the grounds of objection, then the court shall allow the power of attorney to be registered.

(28) The way that Mr Rees puts it now is that once evidence had been produced which tends to show that there was not the necessary capacity, then the burden shifts, and it lies with the attorney to show that there was capacity.

(29) In support of that he refers to Halsbury's *Commentaries on the Laws of England,* Vol 30, at para 1387:

> 'Every person is presumed to have mental capacity until the contrary is proven, and this presumption applies in civil as well as in criminal cases. However, it is for the executors or other people seeking to set up a will to show that the testator had capacity at the time.'

(30) Mr Rees submits that, just as with wills, so the same is true when somebody proposes an enduring power of attorney for registration. He also referred to a New Zealand case, *Brown v Pourau* [1995] 1 NZLR 352, and particularly to a passage at 363 where there is cited this passage from the earlier case of *Peters v Morris* (unreported) 19 May 1987:

> '"The approach adopted to the matter of proof in all these cases is the same – that before a will can be admitted to probate it must be shown that the testator was a person of sufficient mental capacity; that in the absence of any evidence to the contrary it will be presumed that the document has been made by a person of competent understanding; that once a doubt is raised as to the existence of testamentary capacity an onus rests on the person propounding the will to satisfy the Court that the testator retained his mental

powers to the requisite extent; that in the end the tribunal must be able to declare that it is satisfied of the testator's competence at the relevant time, but that a will not be defeated merely because a residual doubt remains as to the matter.'"

(31) If I may say so, Mr Rees' argument neatly encapsulates what was said in that passage. We were also referred to a case of considerable antiquity, *Waring v Waring* [1848] VI Moore 342.

(32) Where there is only one issue in the case and the burden of proof rests on one party, it seems to me wrong to say that the burden of proof shifts after one witness has been called and given evidence which, if believed, would discharge that burden. Courts do not make up their minds on an issue when they have heard only part of the evidence. Surely one can say, if one wishes, 'Well, the plaintiff is doing quite well. I wonder if there is going to be any evidence from the defendants?' But to say that the burden of proof has shifted seems to me to be wrong. One should make up one's mind on that issue having heard all the evidence on it; and I do not consider that in such a case the burden of proof can be said to shift. At the end of the day, unless the burden as to that issue has been discharged, the person on whom it originally rested does not succeed.

(33) In this case, I think that the judge was right to treat the burden of proof as resting throughout upon the objectors. That is what he did. In the result, he did not feel able to conclude that the objectors had discharged that burden. But equally he did not make an affirmative finding in favour of the attorney, Mrs X. I reject the argument that he erred in law in that respect.

(34) The other ground which has been argued by Mr Rees is that the judge's decision was wrong on the facts. There were two principal witnesses, with other evidence as well. The first of the two principal witnesses was a Mr C, a chartered clinical psychologist. His evidence came in the form of a report of five pages. He had carried out tests on Mrs W's mental capacity on two occasions in November and December 1996. The conclusions that he reached in his report were these:

'As a final comment, the above detected severity of deterioration across a number of vital areas of cognitive functioning suggests strongly that for the past period running into a number of years, Mrs W has not been in a position to deal properly with the intangible (non-concrete) or hypothetical, or to correctly comprehend, interpret, see implications in, judge, or direct any business or operation other than that which does not require weighing up the pro's and con's, making comparisons, or seeing consequences of action beyond the immediate step.'

(35) Later, in a letter dated 10 July 1998, he said:

'I believe that in no way was Mrs W in a condition on the 4 July 1996 to execute an Enduring Power of Attorney.'

(36) There are comments that are made in respect of that evidence: first, that it was what one might call a theoretical discussion of the effect on comprehension, rather than a consideration of the actual things which had to be considered or the actual test for capacity to execute an enduring power of attorney. There was evidence that at the time of the tests by Mr C, Mrs W was taking drugs of several different kinds; and it was acknowledged that drugs might, not necessarily that they would, affect her capacity. There was also the lapse of time between the occasion in July when Mrs W executed the power of attorney and November and December when she was seen by Mr C.

(37) On the other hand, there is evidence from Mrs W's doctor who had treated her for some years. He had seen her quite regularly. He was not called as a witness because by the time the case came on for hearing before the judge he said, with admirable candour, that he could not now remember any detail whatsoever, and he was accordingly unable to help the court. But what was available was a letter that he wrote on 22 June 1996, that is to say about 2 weeks before the power of attorney was executed. It was written not to the proposed attorney or to Mrs W but to the solicitor who eventually witnessed the power of attorney. The letter said:

'Thank you for your letter about Mrs W. I can confirm that I saw her recently with her daughter and found her to be suffering from a degree of memory impairment. However in my opinion she still has the necessary mental capacity to sign a Power of Attorney. I would add that her mental abilities are at their best in the early part of the day and tend to deteriorate as the day goes by.'

(38) There is also evidence that Mrs W had seen her solicitor alone at some time previously; and it is said that she wished to have an enduring power of attorney.

(39) There are three letters which are relied on by the objectors as casting doubt on the capacity of Mrs W. In the first letter from Mrs X to her brother, and I take it her sister, dated 31 October 1994, there is this passage:

'Well, she is very confused and one has to organise her very carefully. She does not wake us up because she is used to coming here.'

(40) This was apparently in answer to the news that when staying with the brother Mrs W had woken them up in the night. That is October 1994. But, in a much later letter which was written to the Public Trust Office, Mrs X wrote this:

'My mother's mental health only started to deteriorate at a stage when she could no longer conduct her affairs when she came out of Eastbourne Hospital having had transfusions for severe anaemia at the end of January 1997.'

(41) Mr Rees points to the contrast of what was said there in a later letter dated July 1998 to what had been said in 1994.

(42) Thirdly there is another letter, dated 29 October 1998, again to the Public Trust Office. It says:

'As I have already stated, my mother was a little confused at times during late 1996. Most of the time she was very logical and she was very much aware of what was happening to her. That is why she previously had got her house in order and told both me and her solicitor what she wanted to happen in the future.'

(43) That is a brief summary of some points in the evidence. The judge, as I have said, was unable to conclude that it was shown that Mrs W had the necessary capacity. He also did not conclude that she was shown not to have the necessary capacity.

(44) I can see no ground for interfering with the judge's conclusions on those two points. It may be a simple view, but it seems to me that the general practitioner who saw Mrs W from time to time, and had done so for some time, was in as good a position as anybody to say whether or not she had the necessary understanding. At all events, if the judge reached that conclusion, I would see no reason to differ from him.

(45) Accordingly, I would dismiss this appeal.

ARDEN LJ:

(46) I agree. The Enduring Power of Attorney Act 1985 established a new mechanism whereby a person could give a power of attorney which would survive his or her incapacity. This was an important innovation because it enabled, among others, elderly people to give powers to attorneys to manage their affairs within the limits permitted by the Act. The Act was passed following a full law reform project by the Law Commission pursuant to the reference under s 3(1)(e) of the Law Commissions Act 1965. The final report is entitled *The Incapacitated Principal* ((1983) Law Com 122). Accordingly, the policy of the Act was very carefully considered; and it may therefore be taken to have been very carefully calibrated. In particular, it is evident that the Act provides a comprehensive set of provisions for registration of the power of attorney and indeed the effective registration is also dealt with in the Act: see in particular ss 7 and 8.

(47) Sir Christopher Staughton has already set out the prescribed procedure for registration. I agree with him that s 6(6) is the pivotal section. In my judgment that subsection clearly proceeds on the basis that the grounds of objection have to be proved. Accordingly, as I see it, the legal burden remains throughout on the objector, the person presenting the notice of objection. If the objector fails to establish his objection, the instrument must be registered. The court has no residual discretion to refuse registration.

(48) Mr Rees has submitted that the position should apply as at common law so that the burden of proof is on the person seeking to uphold a deed or document. He draws an analogy with wills, as Sir Christopher Staughton has explained. But, as I see it, it is open to Parliament to change the common law rules for the purposes of this legislation. In addition Mr Rees accepts that the onus is on the objector when, for instance, there is a question as to the unsuitability of the attorney. As I see it, the Act must be construed as it stands.

(49) The learned Master relied on a passage in the judgment of Hoffmann J in *Re K (Enduring Powers of Attorney); Re F* [1988] Ch 310, namely the words 'and which evidence should show that he was understood' in the passage cited by Sir Christopher Staughton. I agree with what Sir Christopher has said about that passage.

(50) Mr Rees has submitted that the situation could arise in which an objector raises a doubt but fails to show lack of mental capacity. If the respondents to this appeal are correct and if the judge is correct, the court may then be in a position of registering instruments when it is not satisfied as to the donor's capacity. But the scheme of the Act does not require the court to be satisfied as to the donor's capacity. It has a discretion under subs (4) to conduct inquiries if the objection is made on statutory grounds. The Act does not require the court to carry out those inquiries. Indeed, the court may well take the view that where there are two parties contesting an issue, there is no need for it to make further inquiries. Accordingly, in my judgment, Parliament must have envisaged that a situation could arise in which a power of attorney would be registered where an objector had failed to discharge the onus of proof. But it should be taken into account that the Act contains other detailed safeguards for the donor, in particular the restriction on the attorney's capacity to make gifts on behalf of the donor without the court's consent.

(51) As respects the second ground of appeal (that the judge's conclusions on the facts were against the weight of the evidence), I agree that, for the reasons given by Sir Christopher Staughton, the appeal fails.

PETER GIBSON LJ:

(52) I agree with both judgments.

Appeal dismissed. Unsuccessful appellants shall pay costs of successful respondent, but on standard basis. We shall direct that there be interim payment on account of costs of £3000.

Solicitors:

Gaby, Hardwicke, Yearwood & Griffiths for the appellant

Max Barford & Co for the respondent

PATRICIA HARGROVE

Barrister

[2000] 1 FLR 882

RE E (ENDURING POWER OF ATTORNEY)

Chancery Division

Arden J

18 February 2000

Executors, administrators, wills and probate – Enduring power of attorney – Objection to registration – Revocation of power by conduct – Whether execution of second power revoked first – Whether bad relations between family members meant some were unsuitable to act as attorneys

In 1992 Mrs E appointed two of her three daughters, Y and Z, jointly to be her attorneys for the purposes of the Enduring Powers of Attorney Act 1985, subject to a restriction that they did not have authority to sell, charge or lease land or other property in which Mrs E had an interest. In 1997 Mrs E executed a second power, appointing all three daughters, X, Y and Z, jointly as attorneys, with general authority to act without any restriction. This power included a provision that any two of the attorneys might sign documents. In 1998 X applied for the 1997 power to be registered, but registration was refused because an enduring power of attorney could only be created if the attorneys were appointed to act jointly or jointly and severally, and the provision permitting documents to be signed by only two of the three attorneys was inconsistent with that. The 1997 power therefore only took effect as an ordinary power of attorney, revoked by supervening mental incapacity. In 1999 Y and Z applied to register the 1992 power. X objected to registration on the basis that the 1992 power was revoked by the 1997 power, and that Y and Z were unsuitable to be Mrs E's attorneys because of the bad relations between X, Y and Z, who could not agree over management of the mother's affairs. The main area of disagreement was Y and Z's scheme to distribute some of the mother's assets for tax planning purposes, which X resisted. Mrs E, now in her eighties was living in a nursing home, having been diagnosed with a form of Alzheimer's disease. The master registered the 1992 power, ruling that the second power did not revoke the first, and that the attorneys were not unsuitable.

Held – dismissing X's appeal –

(1) The 1997 power was capable of being used prior to the donor's mental incapacity, but did not revoke the 1992 power. Applying the general law of agency, revocation of a power of attorney by conduct required conduct which was unambiguously inconsistent with that power. The burden was on X to show that Mrs E must have intended, by her conduct in executing a second power, to revoke the first power; it was not enough to show that Mrs E must have forgotten about the first power. The two powers were not in fact inconsistent; Mrs E may have wanted to have several simultaneous powers, allowing her to safeguard against possible invalidity of a power, a legitimate and understandable wish.

(2) Y and Z were suitable to be Mrs E's attorneys. Mrs E had appointed them to be attorneys in both of the powers which had been executed, and wherever possible the donor's wishes should be upheld. Hostility between family members did not automatically mean that a family member was unsuitable to act as attorney. The only controversial issue, the tax planning, would have to be decided by the court in any event, and once that matter had been resolved it was unlikely that any great degree of consultation between the daughters would be needed, as the estate was not complex. If a receiver were appointed, a third party would have to become involved, intervening between the donor and her family, and involving the estate in additional costs.

Statutory provisions considered

Enduring Powers of Attorney Act 1985, ss 3, 6, 8, 11

Cases referred to in judgment

Cousins v International Brick Co Ltd [1931] 2 Ch 90, CA

D (J), Re [1982] Ch 237, [1982] 2 WLR 373, [1982] 2 All ER 37, ChD

Goldsworthy v Brickell [1987] Ch 378, [1987] 1 All ER 853, sub nom Goldsworthy v Brickell and Another [1987] 2 WLR 133, CA

Heatons Transport (St Helens) Ltd v Transport and General Workers' Union; Craddock Brothers v Transport and General Workers' Union; Panalpina Services Ltd, Panalpina (Northern) Ltd v Transport and General Workers' Union [1973] AC 15, [1972] 3 WLR 431, [1972] 3 All ER 101, HL

Smith and Jenning's Case (1610) Lane 97, 145 ER 329

W (Power of Attorney), Re [1999] 2 FLR 1163, [2000] 1 All ER 175, ChD

Yaxley v Gotts and Gotts [1999] 2 FLR 941, sub nom Yaxley v Gotts and Another [1999] 3 WLR 1217, CA

Cases cited but not referred to in judgment

Tai Hing Cotton Mill Ltd v Liu Chong Hing Bank (No 1) [1986] AC 80, [1985] 2 All ER 947, sub nom *Tai Hing Cotton Mill Ltd v Liu Chong Hing Bank Ltd and Others* [1985] 3 WLR 317, CA

Ward v Van der Loeff [1924] AC 653, HL

Robert Pearce for the appellant/X

Piers Feltham for the respondents/Y and Z

ARDEN J:

Introduction

This is an appeal against the order of Master Lush, Master of the Court of Protection, dated 9 September 1999 whereby he dismissed objections of the appellant, Mrs X, and ordered that an instrument dated 24 November 1992 ('the 1992 power') be registered as an enduring power of attorney under the Enduring Powers of Attorney Act 1985 ('the 1985 Act'). This appeal is by way of rehearing. The discretion is that of the judge and the judge is not bound by the decision of the master (*Re D (J)* [1982] Ch 237, 245–247). Counsel appearing on this appeal did not appear before Master Lush.

As is well known, the 1985 Act in large measure implemented recommendations in *The Incapacitated Principal* (Law Com No 122 (1983) Cmnd 8977) and provides a means whereby powers of attorney ('EPAs') can be created so as to survive the subsequent mental incapacity of the donor. An EPA must be made in the prescribed form. When the attorney has reason to believe that the donor is, or is becoming, mentally incapable he must make an application to the Court of Protection for registration of the EPA. Before doing so, the attorney must give notice to the donor and the donor's relatives. Until registration, the powers of the attorney are limited. Thereafter, the attorney has the powers conferred by the EPA, which is not revoked by the supervening mental incapacity of the donor. Recourse may be had to the Law Commission's report to ascertain the defect in the law which the 1985 Act was intended to remedy, and in addition to help identify the policy behind the new legislation (*Yaxley v Gotts and Gotts* [1999] 2 FLR 941, 956–957 per Clarke LJ and 963–965 per Beldam LJ).

If a valid notice of objection to the registration of an enduring power of attorney is received by the court within a specified time, the court must neither register the instrument nor refuse the application until it has made or caused to be made such inquiries (if any) as it thinks appropriate in the circumstances of the case (s 6(4)). A notice of objection to the registration of an enduring power of attorney is valid if the objection is made on a number of specified grounds including (s 6(5)):

'(b)   that the power created by the instrument no longer subsists; ...

...

(e)   that, having regard to all the circumstances and in particular the attorney's relationship to or connection with the donor, the attorney is unsuitable to be the donor's attorney.'

If any of these grounds of objection is established to the satisfaction of the court, the court must refuse the application for registration; in any other case the EPA must be registered (s 6(6)). Furthermore, the court must not register an EPA, or refuse the application for registration, until completion of appropriate inquiries if it considers that those inquiries might bring to light evidence that one of the grounds of objection is satisfied (s 6(4)). The 1985 Act makes provision for the revocation or cancellation of an EPA registration of which is refused (s 6(7), (8)). If, however, an EPA is registered it is irrevocable without the leave of the court. The attorney's authority to make gifts is strictly limited (s 3(5)). Accordingly, if an attorney wishes to enter into a scheme to minimise inheritance tax payable on the donor's death, the leave of the court will generally be needed.

The background facts relating to the 1992 power are as follows. Mr and Mrs E had three daughters, Mrs Y, Mrs Z and Mrs X. Mrs Y and Mrs Z are the respondents to this appeal. Mr E died in 1998 and Mrs E is in her eighties. She is living in a nursing home and she has been diagnosed as having a form of Alzheimer's disease.

On 24 November 1992 Mrs E executed the 1992 power. It appointed Mrs Y and Mrs Z jointly to be her attorneys for the purposes of the 1985 Act with general power to act on her behalf in relation to all her property and affairs. However, it was subject to a restriction or condition that 'My attorneys shall not have my authority to sell, charge or lease any land or other property in which I have an interest'.

On 9 April 1997 Mrs E executed a further power ('the 1997 power'). This appointed all three daughters jointly to be her attorneys for the purposes of the 1985 Act with general authority to act on her behalf in relation to all her property and affairs. The words 'save that any two of my attorneys may sign' were inserted in manuscript so as to follow the printed word 'jointly'. This appointment, unlike the 1992 power, was not expressed to be subject to any restriction or condition. The master's judgment states that these words were drafted on the spot by Mrs E's solicitor because it was felt that it could be inconvenient and time-consuming to have to send all documents to Mrs Y, who lived some distance away, for her signature, but I have not taken that factor into account as it is common ground that this finding is not supported by the evidence on this appeal.

On 3 December 1998 Mrs X applied for the 1997 power to be registered. The Public Trust Office rejected her application on the ground that the condition imposed by the power was contrary to the appointment. Mrs X has not appealed against this rejection. Master Lush in his judgment stated that the additional words 'save that any two of my attorneys may sign' were inconsistent with s 11(1) of the 1985 Act, which provides that 'An instrument which appoints more than one person to be an attorney cannot create an enduring power unless the attorneys are appointed to act jointly or jointly and severally' (see also The Law Commission's report, *The Incapacitated Principal*, paras 4.91–4.98). The 1997 power accordingly has effect at most only as an ordinary power of attorney and it is revoked by supervening mental incapacity.

On 5 February 1999 Mrs Y and Mrs Z applied to register the 1992 power. By a letter dated 10 February 1999, the donor's solicitors objected to the registration of the 1992 power on the grounds that it was revoked by the 1997 power and that the attorneys were unsuitable to be the donor's attorneys. From 26 March 1999 Mrs X objected to the registration of the 1992 power. Her grounds were those set out in the letter dated 10 February 1999. On 8 September 1999, following an oral hearing, Master Lush dismissed both grounds of objections and ordered that the 1992 power be registered forthwith. His reasons were as follows:

'The Enduring Powers of Attorney Act 1985 is silent on the question whether a later power revokes an earlier power, and I must admit that this is the first time I have been required formally to adjudicate on this particular issue.

The Law Commission's report, *The Incapacitated Principal,* which was published in 1983 and ultimately led to the 1985 Act, states, at paragraph 4.31:

"We would like to sound a note of caution about the drafting of the attorney's authority under the EPA. Subject to the exceptions mentioned above, the donor would in general be able to insert in the prescribed form of EPA whatever provisions he thought fit whether they related to the subject-matter of the power or to the authority conferred under it. And he could grant as many EPAs in favour of as many attorneys as he liked. This would merely reflect the general principle that people should be able to make such arrangements for the management of their affairs as they please. It will be important, however, for the donor to ensure that the authority bestowed under his EPA (or EPAs if several are granted) effectively covers the whole of his property and affairs. If he leaves a 'gap' so that part of his property and affairs is not covered by an EPA, it may be necessary for the Court to intervene and appoint a receiver. And whilst we would not wish to prevent the donor giving his attorney such limited authority as he thought fit, the fact remains that the less authority that is given to the attorney, the greater is the risk that he would be unable to act for the donor at a later date. If by that time the donor were incapable so that he could not create a new power, the Court might have to take over."

I should emphasise two particular sentences in this paragraph: "And he could grant as many EPAs in favour of as many attorneys as he liked. This would merely reflect the general principle that people should be able to make such arrangements for the management of their affairs as they please".

I imagine that the reason why the law is deliberately silent on the question as to whether or not a later power revokes an earlier power is because it was envisaged that a donor might create more than one power and that such powers might not be created simultaneously.

Paragraph 4.31 of *The Incapacitated Principal* appears mainly to contemplate the situation in which a donor might appoint one attorney to manage one aspect of his or her affairs, and a different attorney to manage another aspect. For example, a donor might in one instrument appoint an attorney to manage his property in England, and in another instrument appoint an attorney to manage his property in Wales.

Elsewhere in their report the Law Commissioners envisaged that a donor might create more than one power in order to achieve the effect of successive appointments. In footnote 214 on page 50 they said:

"We do not recommend that an instrument should be able to provide for successive EPAs; that is, one or more attorneys who would replace the original attorney or attorneys should he or they cease to act. Our main reason for this is that the benefit to be gained by including successive EPAs in our proposals would be out of all proportion to the complexity that such powers would create in relation to some of the more detailed areas of our scheme. In any event, successive EPAs are rendered largely unnecessary because a joint and several EPA would permit the continuation of the EPA in the event of one of the attorneys ceasing to act. It would, however, be possible to create the effect of successiveness by a donor granting EPAs in separate instruments so that the authority of an attorney under one power could commence only upon the termination of the authority of an attorney under another power."

So, for instance, a donor might sign one instrument appointing his wife as his sole attorney and another – perhaps later – instrument appointing his children to be his attorneys if his wife were to predecease him or become otherwise incapable of acting as attorney.

In the absence of any statutory provision to the effect that a later instrument revokes an earlier power, it is necessary to look to the common law for assistance. However, there are no decisions – either reported or unreported – which directly address this point.

There are a number of reported decisions on the revocation of wills, but they are mainly old authorities and are not always entirely consistent. In any event, wills and enduring powers are completely different types of document. To revoke an enduring power the donor must give notice of revocation to the attorneys.

However, some general principles do emerge in relation to the revocation of wills. They are as follows:

- whether a prior will or codicil has been impliedly revoked by a later will or codicil is a question of construction;

- there must be an intention to revoke *(animus revocandi)* on the part of the testator;

- extrinsic evidence of the testator's intention is admissible;

- where there is more than one instrument, the court should, if possible, construe them so that both may stand; and

- if the instruments are so inconsistent that they cannot stand together, neither can be admitted to probate.

If one applies these rules, so far as they are relevant, to enduring powers of attorney, the following principles emerge:

1. A later instrument does not automatically revoke an earlier instrument. This is because it was Parliament's intention that a donor should be able to create more than one enduring power of attorney, if he or she wished. It might be necessary to create more than one power in order to deal with different aspects of the donor's affairs or to take effect at different times or in different circumstances.

2. A later instrument which expressly revokes an earlier instrument will revoke the earlier instrument, but only when notice of the revocation is given to the attorney appointed in the earlier instrument. Where the instrument is registered, the revocation will only take effect when it is confirmed by the courts in accordance with s 8(3) of the Enduring Powers of Attorney Act 1985.

3. In the absence of express revocation, whether an earlier instrument is impliedly revoked by a later instrument is essentially a question of construction.

4. The donor must have intended to revoke the earlier instrument.

5. If there is more than one instrument, the court should attempt to construe them so that, wherever possible, both or all may stand. This reflects the general principle that people should be able to make such arrangements for the management of their affairs as they please.

In my judgment, Mrs E's intentions were as follows.

In 1992 she made a conscious decision to appoint her daughters [Mrs Y] and [Mrs Z], but not her daughter [Mrs X], jointly to be her attorneys.

In 1996 and 1997 there was closer contact and a reconciliation between [Mrs X] and her parents as a result of [Mr E's] illness.

In April 1997 both [Mr E] and Mrs E both decided to appoint [Mrs X] as an additional attorney for the purpose of the Enduring Powers of Attorney Act.

The most convenient way of appointing [Mrs X] as an additional attorney was to sign a new instrument appointing all three of their daughters as attorneys.

On 9 April 1997, when she signed the second power, [Mrs E's] intention was not to revoke the appointment of [Mrs Y] and [Mrs Z], but (a) to confirm their appointment and (b) to appoint [Mrs X] as an additional attorney. In other words, she did not have *animus revocandi* in respect of the earlier appointment.

...

The second ground on which [Mrs X] has objected to the registration of the 1992 power is that, having regard to all the circumstances, her sisters are unsuitable to be the donor's attorneys.

There are no reported decisions on the meaning of "unsuitable to be the donor's attorney" but Parliament's intention when including it as a ground of objection can be found in the Law Commission's report, *The Incapacitated Principal* (Law Com No 122), which was published in July 1983. At paragraph 4.29 the Commissioners said:

> "This needs some explanation. It would amount in effect to a criticism of the donor's choice of attorney. But we would not wish this ground to be sustained merely because the attorney was not the sort of person that a particular relative would have chosen. It is our wish that the donor's choice of attorney should carry considerable weight. Thus, for example, a mother might be content to appoint her son as her EPA attorney despite being aware of a conviction for theft. We would not want her choice of attorney to be upset simply because a particular relative would not want the son to be his attorney.
>
> The question should be whether the particular attorney is suitable to act as attorney for the particular donor. In short, the Court should examine carefully all the circumstances – particularly the relationship between the donor and the attorney."

[Mrs X's] objection in this case was expressed by her solicitors in the following terms:

> "The attorneys are unsuitable to be the donor's Attorneys. Relations between [Mrs E's] three daughters are not good because there is division of opinion as to how [Mrs E's] assets might be applied. It is believed that [Mrs Y] and [Mrs Z] favour some creative tax planning which [Mrs X] believes is inappropriate. We believe [Mrs E's] position would be best served and protected by the appointment by the court of a receiver.'"

The master then referred to *Re W (Power of Attorney)* [1999] 2 FLR 1163, to which I refer below.

Master Lush continued:

> 'In my judgment Mrs E must have been aware of the hostility between her daughters when she created the power in 1992, and she appointed [Mrs Y] and [Mrs Z] as her attorneys notwithstanding that hostility.
>
> I am not convinced that the animosity between her daughters will have an adverse impact on the administration of her estate. The main bone of contention seems to have

been the desirability or otherwise of entering into a scheme to mitigate the impact of inheritance tax on her death.

Attorneys have the very limited powers to make gifts of a donor's property contained in ss 3(4) and (5) of the Enduring Powers of Attorney Act 1985. Larger gifts, such as the kind of contemplated by [Mrs Y] and [Mrs Z], must be authorised by the court in accordance with the provisions of s 8(2)(e) of the Act.

If the attorneys wish to enter into some tax planning scheme, they must make a formal application to the court, and the court will then consider whether, having regard to all the circumstances, the proposed gifts are reasonable and will not impact adversely on [Mrs E's] present and future standard of living.

In the circumstances, I see no reason why the court should frustrate [Mrs E's] choice of attorneys and intervene on the ground of their unsuitability.'

There are two issues on this appeal, both of which were argued before Master Lush:

(1) Is the 1992 power a subsisting power, or was it revoked by the 1997 power?

(2) Are Mrs Y and Mrs Z unsuitable to be Mrs E's attorneys?

I will take these issues in turn.

Issue 1: was the 1992 power revoked by the 1997 power?

There are three differences between the 1992 power and the 1997 power. The *first* difference is that Mrs X is not an attorney under the 1992 power; she is however an attorney under the 1997 power. The *second* difference is that the 1992 power contains the restriction on the disposition of land and other property set out above, which is not present in the 1997 power. The *third* difference is that the 1997 power provides that any two attorneys may sign.

The appellant's submissions

The appellant submits that the 1992 power was revoked by the 1997 power and that Master Lush was wrong to hold otherwise. (The appellant did not argue that the 1992 power was invalid on any other ground as she had done before Master Lush.)

The appellant submits that although the 1997 power has not been registered as an enduring power of attorney, it was nonetheless valid as an ordinary power of attorney as soon as it was executed. As an ordinary power, however, it was revoked by Mrs E's supervening incapacity. The objection to the form of the power based on s 11(1) of the 1985 Act does not affect the validity of the 1997 power as an ordinary power. The power, on the appellant's submission, should be construed as a joint power which is enlarged in the particular respect that any two attorneys can sign. The appellant further submitted that the word 'sign' in the 1997 power should be construed narrowly and as referring only to signing to implement transactions which all three attorneys had decided on.

The appellant submits that as between donor and attorney an ordinary power of attorney is revoked by the doing of any act by the donor which is inconsistent with the continuation of the power and of which the donee has notice. In support of this submission, the appellant relies on *Bowstead and Reynolds on Agency*, arts 119, 122, especially at p 674, note 61, and *Heatons Transport (St Helens) Ltd v Transport and General Workers' Union; Craddock Brothers v Transport and General Workers' Union; Panalpina Services Ltd, Panalpina (Northern) Ltd v Transport and General Workers' Union* [1973] AC 15, 110C per Lord Wilberforce, delivering the joint opinion of their Lordships. The appellant also relied on the American Law Institute's *Restatement of the Law of Agency* (1958, 2nd edn), at pp 302–304. The relevant passage in *Bowstead and Reynolds* reads: '... there may be implied revocation by an act which is inconsistent with the continuation of the agency, coming to the notice of the agent' and the authority cited for this at footnote 61 is *Smith and Jenning's Case* (1610) Lane 97; 145 ER 329. (Another example is *Cousins v International Brick Co Ltd* [1931]

2 Ch 90, where a shareholder who had appointed a proxy to vote for him could nonetheless vote in person.) Likewise the *Restatement* states that a principal can revoke the agency by conduct which is inconsistent with its continuance as where he authorises another agent to act on his behalf. The *Restatement* states that in such a case it is a question of construction whether the agent intends to terminate the authority of the first agent or merely authorise another agent also to act. The appellant relies particularly on a statement in the *Restatement* that the conduct will terminate an agent's authority 'if, reasonably understood', it indicates that the principal no longer consents to the agent acting for him. That the conduct must be such that it can be reasonably understood in this way is the issue for which the passage in the *Heatons* case was cited. In that particular case the withdrawal of authority had been equivocal. What happened in that case was that the principals had merely given advice to the agent and it was held that this did not amount to terminating their authority to act contrary to that advice. The appellant seeks to extend this principle by submitting that there is also a requirement that the conduct of the donor should also be reasonably construed in determining whether it was inconsistent with the continuation of the agency.

The appellant also submits that the execution of the 1997 power is inconsistent with the continuation of the 1992 power thereafter for the following reasons:

(i) It would have been irrational for Mrs E not to have wished to express all the powers her daughters were to have in a single instrument.

(ii) If the 1992 power continued after the execution of the 1997 power, Mrs Y and Mrs Z would thereafter have been simultaneously authorised to act jointly with Mrs X in all matters and to act independently of her in all matters save dealings in land. The effect of this would be that Mrs X's participation would be superfluous in all matters save dealings in land. If in 1997 it had been Mrs E's intention to make Mrs X's participation necessary only in relation to dealings in land, and to achieve this by two instruments rather than one, the obvious course for her to take would have been to grant a further power appointing her three daughters to be her joint attorneys solely in relation to matters falling within the restriction in the 1992 power.

(iii) It is unlikely that Mrs E would have chosen to specify expressly in the 1997 power that any two of her attorneys may sign and to leave unstated that Mrs Y and Mrs Z could continue to act in all matters falling within the scope of the 1992 power independently of Mrs X if they saw fit.

(iv) It is unlikely that Mrs E would have retained the word 'jointly' and deleted the alternative 'jointly and severally' in the 1997 power since if the 1992 power continued after the execution of the 1997 power the combined effect of both was more akin to a joint and several authority subject to restrictions.

There is no evidence as to Mrs E's intentions when she executed the 1997 power. The only evidence is that of Mrs X who states that the 1992 power was never mentioned and that she believes that Mrs E had forgotten about it. There is no suggestion that at the date of the execution of the 1997 power Mrs E was concerned to distinguish between dealings in land and other dealings. Mrs Y and Mrs Z both had express notice of the execution of the 1997 power as they countersigned it. The appellant contends that there is no justification for Master Lush's conclusion that in 1997 Mrs E did not intend to revoke the 1992 power.

The respondents' submissions

The respondents accept that the authority of an agent may be revoked by express notice given by the principal to the agent. They also accept that there can be revocation by conduct of the principal. They submit, however, that there has to be communication of revocation and in addition the conduct must be unequivocal, as in the case of promissory estoppel (see *Goldsworthy v Brickell* [1987] Ch 378, 410–411). Accordingly, it has to be shown that the 1997 power is inconsistent with the 1992 power. They submit that there is no inconsistency between the grant of the 1997 power and the continued subsistence of the 1992 power having regard to the following:

(i) The 1992 power appoints Mrs Y and Mrs Z jointly and does not authorise them to sell, charge or lease any real property of Mrs E.

(ii) The 1997 power is not so restrictive but requires the appellant and respondents to act jointly so that any two may sign.

The 1992 power and the 1997 power therefore overlap but are very far from co-extensive. The respondents also urge the court to take into account that the 1997 power did not take effect as an enduring power of attorney but only as an ordinary power of attorney. This meant that it could not operate after Mrs E became mentally incapable.

Accordingly, on the respondents' submission, no legal impasse was created by the coexistence of the powers side by side.

Conclusions

I accept the appellant's submission that the 1997 power takes effect as an ordinary power even if it cannot take effect as an EPA. The 1997 power is therefore capable of being used prior to the donor becoming mentally incapable. However, in my judgment, the 1992 power has not been revoked by the execution of the 1997 power and the reasons for my conclusion are as follows:

(1) The general law of agency in my judgment shows that to amount to revocation by conduct, the conduct must be inconsistent with the continuation of the agency. Contrary to the appellant's submission, this in my judgment means more than that the conduct should be reasonably understood as amounting to revocation. To be *inconsistent*, it must be unambiguous in its effect. I approach the question of revocation in this way rather than by applying presumptions as a matter of construction, which was the approach of Master Lush.

(2) The onus is on the appellant to show that the 1992 power has been revoked. Accordingly, she has to show that the donor must have intended to revoke the 1992 power. It is not enough to show that the donor must have forgotten about the 1992 power or made no reference to it. Indeed if she had forgotten about it that would suggest that she did not intend to revoke it. As the passages cited by the master from the Law Commission's report show, it is not the policy of the 1985 Act to prohibit successive EPAs.

(3) The 1997 power applies to land whereas the 1992 power does not. Had the 1997 power been limited to land it would have been clear that the two powers were not inconsistent. The present issue has arisen because there are some matters covered by both powers, for example the payment of bills.

(4) There is no contemporaneous evidence as to the donor's intentions, or even any later evidence from her as to what she intended. All that is known is that she did not expressly revoke the 1992 power when she executed the 1997 power. On 4 January 1999 she wrote a letter saying that she agreed that her daughters could apply to register the 1992 power, but this does not inform the court about her intentions in 1997 and I must also bear in mind that the donor had previously objected to the registration of the 1992 power.

(5) I do not consider that it is clear that the 1997 power revokes the 1992 power. There is no reason why the donor should not want to preserve the possibility that the 1992 power might be used if for some reason the 1997 power could not be used. She did not know that the 1997 power was not valid as an EPA when she signed it, but there is no reason why she should not have wanted to cover the situation that it might be invalid. To have several

simultaneous powers would be a legitimate and understandable wish, and not an irrational one as suggested by the appellant.

(6) The appellant contends that the 1997 power requires unanimity, ie that all three sisters had to agree on each transaction to be carried out by the attorneys and that the additional words added by the donor ('save that any two of my attorneys may sign') merely enabled two out of the three attorneys to sign if they had all agreed on a transaction. In my judgment, this interpretation involves adding words that are not expressed, preventing two only from signing unless all three sisters had agreed on the transaction to which the signature related. In my judgment those words cannot be read in. They are not a necessary implication. It is more likely that the donor wished to cover the possibility that one of the sisters was unable to act, for example because she was abroad or ill, or because she was unwilling to agree to something that two sisters approved. This is another situation for which the donor may have wanted to have a contingency plan. There is also some evidence to the effect that the appellant had not been on good terms with her parents prior to the execution of the 1992 power though the appellant contests this evidence. Be that as it may, the effect of the 1997 power as properly interpreted is not in my judgment inconsistent with the 1992 power in any of the respects relied on by the appellant. Rather the 1997 power confirms the tenor of the 1992 power, that the donor was content that two only of the daughters should have power to act as her attorneys. The 1997 power should be seen as at one with the earlier power in this sense, and as an unsuccessful attempt to add the third daughter, Mrs X.

(7) The master based his conclusions on general principles applicable to wills. I do not think that it is necessary to invoke these principles as there is sufficient guidance in the general law of agency. However, I agree with him that a later instrument does not automatically revoke an earlier instrument. The donor must have intended to revoke the earlier power and this must also be the effect of the donor's words or conduct.

(8) I have considered whether it would be appropriate to make inquiries as to the donor's wishes as to who should be her attorney, and I refer to this below. I do not, however, consider that it would be appropriate to make inquiries from the donor as to the position regarding the 1992 power at the time of executing the 1997 power. If her medical condition means that she has a significant and persistent memory loss, she will not be able to assist the court. If her medical condition is satisfactory, she would of course have been able to revoke, or express a wish to revoke, the 1992 power since this dispute has arisen if she had wished to do so. Moreover, if her medical condition is satisfactory, it is likely that one of the parties could have obtained her evidence and have submitted it to the court. Finally, her intentions would not be conclusive by themselves. Revocation must be manifested and in my judgment that has not occurred.

Issue 2: suitability of the attorneys

The appellant's second ground of appeal is that the respondents are not suitable to be the donor's attorneys. The appellant says that the evidence shows that the relations between the three sisters have broken down, principally over the management of the donor's affairs. The appellant points out that there is more significance to be attached to the fact of disagreement where it relates to the affairs of the donor than if it relates to extraneous matters. The appellant says that there is a history of her being excluded by her sisters. She says that the donor wished all three daughters to be her attorneys: this is evident not only from the 1997 power but from a letter which the donor wrote to the court on 13 December 1998. In this letter the donor objected to the appellant applying for the registration of the 1997 power on the ground that 'the decision to make this application should be made by my three daughters, not by one acting alone'. Moreover, the appellant wishes to play an equal part.

The respondents for their part rely on the fact that they are mature and responsible women with no ill-will to the appellant. The only disagreement relates to tax planning. It is hoped to make potentially exempt transfers from the donor's assets among her children equally in order to avoid or mitigate inheritance tax. The appellant has expressed concern as to whether the donor will have sufficient assets left for her needs. It is accepted that the attorneys could not transfer any assets of the donor pursuant to a tax planning scheme without the approval of the court pursuant to s 8 of the 1985 Act.

The court could in theory appoint all three sisters as receivers and in that way seek to put the three sisters in the same position as if the 1997 power had been valid. But neither party seeks that and there is no indication that that would be a viable course. (The appellant says in her evidence that at the present time she has no contact with either of her sisters.) The choice before the court is either to appoint a third party as a receiver or to register the 1992 power. It is against that background that the court is asked to hold, having regard to all the circumstances, the respondents are unsuitable to be the donor's attorneys.

The matters on which the appellant relies revolve around discussions about tax planning for the donor in June to December 1998 in which she was not involved culminating in the execution by the donor of a deed agreeing to an advancement of property out of her late husband's estate in favour of her three daughters in equal shares. I refer to this deed below. The advancement has not taken place because the appellant objected to it. She is one of the executrices of her late father's estate and the proposal cannot proceed without her concurrence.

There is evidence that prior to the death of Mr E both the donor and her late husband wanted to minimise the inheritance tax payable on their deaths by appropriate tax planning. For this purpose they had consulted Mrs Z's husband, Mr Z, who is an accountant. So it was natural that Mr Z should be asked to advise on the donor's estate. The donor's property now consists principally of a life interest in her late husband's estate, a 50% share in their house, other real property, cash on deposit and some investments. Mr Z produced plans to save up to £110,000 tax. The appellant was advised of these plans but she thought that the donor should keep £20,000 more than the scheme provided. This was agreed by the other sisters. In the course of preparing proposals, there was a meeting between Mr Z, the respondents and the donor's solicitor on 11 June 1998. The appellant was not invited to this, and the respondents at first said that they had not been present, contrary to what appears now to be the position. Likewise, it appears that Mrs E's solicitor wrote a letter giving advice so that all the sisters could read it, but it was not shown to the appellant.

In due course Mrs E's solicitors (acting on Mr Z's instructions) produced a draft deed to give effect to the advancement which it was desired that Mrs E should make. They sent it to Mr Z to obtain his instructions on one point. In order to save time, Mr Z arranged for Mrs E and Mrs Z (as executrix of Mr E) to sign it, notwithstanding that it had not been engrossed and notwithstanding that Mrs E had not received any independent legal advice on it. This was also before the appellant had been told about the proposals. The appellant says with some justification that if meetings were being held with Mrs E's solicitor, to which the other sisters were invited, she too should have had the opportunity to attend.

In my judgment Mr Z, Mrs Y and Mrs Z are to be criticised for obtaining the donor's signature to the draft deed, given her medical condition and given the fact that it was only a draft and the fact that she had no independent legal advice. There is medical evidence that Mrs E was not in a position to manage her affairs by December 1998. Mrs E had not received advice about the deed from her solicitor at the stage she was asked to sign.

The court had to consider an objection on the grounds of unsuitability in the recent case of *Re W (Power of Attorney)* [1999] 2 FLR 1163 to which the master referred. In that case, an elderly lady, W, gave one of her children, X, an EPA. Her two other children, who were hostile to X, objected to the registration of this power on the ground (among others) that X was unsuitable to be her attorney. X had made gifts on behalf of W without the consent of the court. The master held that he was not satisfied that W understood the nature and effect of the power and that the hostility between the children rendered them all unsuitable to be W's attorneys. On appeal Mr Jules Sher QC, sitting as a deputy judge of the High Court, held that the making of the gifts had been for sensible tax planning reasons and had been in favour of the three children equally. The other children did not object and there was some evidence that they had been in accordance with W's wishes expressed before she became incapable. Accordingly, he held that matter should be kept in perspective. On the issue of hostility, the court held that it all depended on the circumstances whether hostility made an attorney unsuitable. In that particular case there was little need for consultation and therefore no real likelihood that the hostility would impact adversely on the administration of the estate, as might happen if there was a need for a high degree of consultation between the children. If the Public Trustee were to be brought in, substantial fees would be incurred.

A number of relatives or friends of the donor in this case have written letters to the court giving their views on the suitability of the three sisters to be the donor's attorneys, but I have given these letters limited weight. There are two main reasons for this. First, there has been no challenge to the ability of Mrs Y and Mrs Z to discharge the function of attorneys. Secondly, some of the letters contain views on the personality of the appellant, but it is not necessary for me to decide where the responsibility for any breakdown in relations between the parties may lie.

Having considered the submissions made on this appeal, I do not however consider that the respondents are unsuitable to be the donor's attorneys for the following reasons:

(1) Under both the 1992 power and the 1997 power, the donor appointed members of her family as act as her attorneys and her wishes in that regard should be upheld. It is part of the policy of the 1985 Act that the donor's wishes should if reasonably possible be upheld (see para 4.29 of *The Incapacitated Principal*, set out in the master's judgment). Thus for instance the 1985 Act does not give the court power to refuse to register an EPA except on one of a limited number of grounds. In addition, under s 6(5)(e) of the 1985 Act, the court has to be satisfied not as to the chosen attorney's suitability, but rather to his unsuitability.

(2) To appoint a receiver would mean that a third party would have to be brought into the donor's affairs and between her and her family. This is not in principle a desirable outcome where members of the family have been caring for the donor for a substantial period of time already. Moreover, as I have said, in neither the 1992 power nor in the 1997 power did the donor appoint a third party. The appellant says that she does not think that her mother would be upset if a receiver were appointed. However, the most reliable indications of her wishes that I have are those in the deeds themselves

(3) Mrs Z has had conduct of Mrs E's affairs for some time. Mrs Y and Mrs Z are more likely to know what the donor would want than a receiver, who may well be a stranger.

(4) On the question of the hostility between the three sisters, I agree with Mr Sher QC that this does not automatically mean that the attorney should be some other person. It must depend on the facts. The tax planning issue has been the only matter of controversy in this case and it will have to be decided by the court in any event. It has not been suggested that once that matter is resolved there will have to be any great degree of consultation between the respondents and the appellant as to how the donor's affairs should be managed. Her estate, though presently not insubstantial, is not complex. It will consist mainly of a limited number of investments after the anticipated tax planning scheme has been implemented.

(5) On 15 December 1998 the respondents made a sensible suggestion to submit the outstanding issues on the tax planning scheme to mediation by a solicitor. This offer has been refused by the appellant. They have also offered to consult the appellant on all decisions if she would abandon the present appeal. These suggestions demonstrate their willingness to try to resolve any difficulties with the appellant by negotiation and compromise. I have criticised them for obtaining Mrs E's signature to the draft deed of

advancement, but there was no intention to act otherwise than in Mrs E's best interests and in accordance with her wishes. I also consider that it is regrettable that the appellant was not kept properly informed of the steps being taken. However, I do not consider that what has happened in those respects should be seen in isolation. Mrs Z in particular has given a considerable amount of time to managing her mother's affairs and there has been no complaint about that. I do not consider that, given all the circumstances of this case, either she or Mrs Y could be held to be unfit or unsuitable to act as attorneys for the donor in the future management of her affairs. Moreover, they clearly have access to legal and accountancy advice if that is needed.

(6) Another issue is whether the appointment of two out of the three sisters is likely to be against the donor's interests because it will lead to disharmony among the family which will have an adverse effect on her. No one, however, has suggested that this will happen. The three sisters are all responsible and mature individuals: one is a finance manager for a large UK subsidiary of a French company, one is a schools inspector and one (the appellant) has recently been in the employment of a firm of solicitors as a legal accounts assistant. I would not expect any of them to cause any distress or anxiety to the donor because of any disharmony between themselves.

(7) There would be significant costs involved in appointing a receiver which would not be incurred if Mrs Y and Mrs Z are attorneys.

(8) I have considered whether the court should make inquiries from the donor as to whether she would be concerned if two of her daughters were to be her attorneys, but not the third. Counsel helpfully made suggestions as to the type of inquiries that could be made, such as whether the donor wanted the same people to continue to manage her affairs as at present. I do not however think that such inquiries would elicit significantly more information than I have at present and accordingly I do not consider that such inquiries would be appropriate. Moreover, the question is not what the donor would now prefer but whether Mrs Y and Mrs Z would be unsuitable to be her attorneys. I note that the Law Commission's report envisaged only a limited role for inquiries by the court and stated that the court would make independent inquiries of its own where there were suspicious circumstances or in cases where there were no relatives to be informed (see *The Incapacitated Principal*, paras 4.46 and 4.48). That is not to say that inquiries will only be appropriate in such circumstances: the court must form a view about the usefulness of inquiries based on all the circumstances of the particular case.

(9) I do not consider that the attorneys under the 1992 deed should be treated as unsuitable simply because they do not include the appellant. Naturally if circumstances permitted it, it would have been desirable that she should have the same role as her sisters in relation to her mother's affairs but as I see it this is not open to the court because the donor chose to appoint her two sisters under the 1992 power. I hope that she will now accept that this was a decision which her mother (for whatever reason) was free to make, and abide by it, as best she can.

For the reasons given above, I dismiss the appeal and direct that the 1992 power be registered forthwith.

Order that the power be registered.

Solicitors:

Ferguson Bricknell for the appellant/X

Darbys Mallam Lewis for the respondents/Y and Z

PHILIPPA JOHNSON

Barrister

[2000] 2 FLR 1

RE C (POWER OF ATTORNEY)

Court of Appeal

Waller and Chadwick LJJ and Sir Christopher Slade

21 December 1999

Enduring power of attorney – Registration – Objections – Inquiries – Terms – Report prepared by chartered accountant – Disclosure

The father, who was showing signs of memory loss, was advised by his doctor to execute a power of attorney in April 1998. In June 1998 he executed a power of attorney in favour of J, the woman he had been living with for many years, and M, a business associate who was also an old friend. The son opposed registration of the power on the basis that the father had not had capacity to grant the power in June 1998, that undue pressure had been used to induce the father to grant the power and that M was unsuitable to be the father's attorney. The son was particularly concerned about the transfer of substantial parts of the father's assets to J and to M. The judge took the view that the objections were without substance, and ordered registration of the power of attorney subject to certain conditions, including preparation by a chartered accountant of a report investigating all transactions over £25,000. The report was solely for the use and consideration of the Court of Protection and the attorneys, but the court had the power to disclose the report or any part of it to the family after 7 days' notice to the attorneys. The son sought disclosure of the report. The attorneys applied to the court for an order that the report should not be disclosed. The judge took the view that, although there was nothing on the face of the report to suggest that there was anything wrong with the relevant transactions, the report should not be disclosed, as disclosure would simply lead to further litigation. The son appealed against the registration of the power, and sought permission to appeal the judge's refusal to disclose the report.

Held – dismissing the appeal and refusing the application for permission to appeal – the first issue before the judge on an application to register the power of attorney was whether it was appropriate in the circumstances of the case to make inquiries into the question whether any of the grounds of objection were established. While there had been good reasons for registering the power, and the appeal therefore failed, there had been little or no express consideration of the issue of inquiries, and the judge's reasons for dismissing the objections should have been expressed in a way which left the objectors in no doubt that their concerns had been taken fully into account. The judge was entitled to reach the conclusion that there was no useful purpose to be served by disclosure of the report to the children, and much risk of distress to the father. There was also some risk of damage to the father's financial interests if the transactions were subject to hostile examination in litigation.

However, some further investigation into the suitability of M as an attorney was appropriate, in the light of a transaction in which, on the face of it, M took substantial benefit at the expense of the father. The matter should be remitted to the Court of Protection for consideration of its power to cancel registration on the ground of an attorney's unsuitability.

Statutory provisions considered

Enduring Powers of Attorney Act 1985, ss 4, 6, 8

Alastair Norris QC *for the appellant*
Hazel Williamson QC *and* Mark Cunningham *for the respondents*

CHADWICK LJ: This is the judgment of the court. It is given in respect of two matters: first, an application for permission to appeal from an order made on 13 May 1999 by Jacob J, when sitting as a nominated judge of the Court of Protection in proceedings under the Enduring Powers of Attorney Act 1985; and, secondly, an appeal from an order made on 1 December 1999 by the same judge on a subsequent application in the same proceedings. The proceedings relate to a power of attorney executed by an elderly donor, to whom we shall refer as 'C', on 2 June 1998 in favour of the lady with whom he had long been living as his wife and a business associate who had been his friend for many years. We shall refer to the attorneys as 'Miss J' and 'M' respectively. Registration of the power, under s 6 of the Act, is opposed by the donor's son, to whom we shall refer as 'D', and other children of the donor.

The background to the proceedings

The circumstances in which the application for registration was made are unusual. They may be summarised as follows:

(1)   The suggestion that C should execute a power of attorney under the 1985 Act appears to have first come from his medical adviser, Dr Ian Perry, in the course of a telephone conversation with the donor's solicitor on 24 April 1998. That telephone conversation took place shortly after the donor, together with Miss J and the solicitor, had attended at Dr Perry's consulting rooms for the purpose of executing a will. A contemporary attendance note, confirmed by affidavit evidence from both Dr Perry and the solicitor, makes it clear that they were satisfied that he had testamentary capacity at that time.

(2)   The solicitor did not take the matter of an enduring power of attorney forward until 2 June 1998. On that day, at a meeting at the solicitor's offices which had been arranged for some other purpose and at which the donor, Miss J and M were present, the solicitor raised the suggestion with the donor. C expressed a wish to proceed immediately. The solicitor asked a colleague, also a solicitor, to come to his office. The power of attorney was executed by the donor, Miss J and M in the presence of the two solicitors on that day. There was no doctor present. That was not surprising, given that the meeting had not been convened for that purpose and the donor's wish to proceed immediately. Both solicitors present had the question of capacity in mind. They have each sworn affidavits to the effect that they were satisfied that C knew and understood what he was doing.

(3)   No steps were taken to register the power of attorney at that stage: or thereafter until 25 February 1999. But, in the meantime on 7 January 1999, D, the donor's son, had made application to the Court of Protection, under s 98 of the Mental Health Act 1983, for the appointment of a receiver in respect of his father's affairs. The application was supported by a medical certificate signed by Dr John Meadows on 6 November 1998. Although the certificate contains the statement that Dr Meadows was the medical attendant of the donor and had acted as such since 14 October 1996, it is not in dispute that Dr Meadows had seen the donor only on one occasion, that is to say on 14 October 1996 on referral from Dr Perry. Dr Meadows did not think it necessary to consult Dr Perry before signing the certificate on 6 November 1998; nor to inform him of what he had done.

(4)   As a result of the application to which we have just referred, which was made without notice to C, Miss J, C's solicitor or Dr Perry, a receiver ad interim was appointed on 13 January 1999. The order was served personally on the donor on 21 January 1999. As may be imagined, it came as an unwelcome surprise to him.

(5)   On 1 February 1999 the donor instructed his solicitor to apply to the Court of Protection to discharge the order of 13 January 1999. In making that application the solicitor disclosed the existence of the power of attorney which had been executed on 2 June 1998. The Court of Protection directed that one of the Lord Chancellor's Medical Visitors should make a report. Dr Ann Bailey visited C for that purpose on 12 February 1999. In the light of that report the

Master of the Court of Protection directed that the interim receivership should continue: but he directed, further, that the attorneys should apply for registration of the power of attorney.

The attorneys applied for registration of the power by notice dated 25 February 1999. Notice of that application was given to the donor's five children. Objections were lodged by solicitors on behalf of D; and by the other children in person.

On 15 April 1999 the donor, through his solicitor, made application to the Court of Protection that the objections to the registration of the power should be summarily dismissed and that the power should be registered forthwith. That application was supported by the two attorneys, Miss J and M. On 22 April 1999 D applied for directions for the hearing of the objections; including, in particular, directions for the disclosure of documents relating to (i) instructions given by C to his solicitor since January 1998, (ii) all powers of attorney or contracts entered into between M and C (without limitation as to time), and (iii) details of all financial transactions between either of the attorneys and C since January 1996. The attorneys' application to register the power, C's application to dismiss the objections and D's application for directions came before Jacob J on 13 May 1999.

The proceedings so far

Jacob J took the view that the objections were without substance. He saw no need for directions preparatory to a hearing. He dismissed the objections summarily. He ordered registration of the power of attorney under the Act. But he did so upon terms set out in the schedule to his order, which required (amongst other things) that the attorneys should instruct a named chartered accountant to prepare a report for the Court of Protection. The report was to set out the nature and value of all transactions which had taken place since 1 June 1996 concerning the assets of the donor; being transactions in respect of which the value exceeded £25,000. Further, and for the future, the attorneys were to report to the Court of Protection, twice yearly, all transactions exceeding £5000 which had taken place in the preceding 6 months; and were to give notice to the Court of Protection, in advance, of their intention to effect any transaction which exceeded £25,000. That was to be accompanied by a certificate from the named chartered accountant that, having regard to the financial position and interests of the donor, the transactions appeared to him unobjectionable.

The order of 13 May 1999 contained, at paras 4 and 5 of the schedule, provisions as to use and disclosure of the report. The report was to be addressed and delivered to the Court of Protection. Three weeks after delivery to the court, it was to be copied to the two attorneys, Miss J and M. It was directed that the report was to be solely for the use and consideration of the court (to take such steps, if any, as it saw fit) and the attorneys. The Court of Protection might disclose the report, or any part of it, to members of the donor's family, but only after 7 days' notice to the attorneys so as to give them the opportunity to make such application to the judge as they might think fit.

The report was sent to the Master of the Court of Protection in the form of a letter dated 12 August 1999. The master raised a query, to which the named accountant responded on 24 August 1999. On the same day, solicitors instructed by D, who must have become aware that the report had been sent to the court, wrote 'to request the Court of Protection to exercise its discretion to release a copy of the report to [D] now, so that he can satisfy himself and his brothers and sisters that nothing untoward has occurred with his father's financial affairs and assets'. The master informed the attorneys' solicitors of that request. The attorneys applied to the judge – as, clearly, Jacob J had intended that they should have the opportunity to do – for an order that the report should not be disclosed to the children. That application was fixed for hearing before Jacob J on 1 December 1999. The judge acceded to the application. He directed that the report should not be disclosed. He gave leave to appeal against that order.

In the meantime, D has applied to this court for permission to appeal against the order of 13 May 1999. That application came before Evans LJ, with whom I was sitting, on 4 November

1999. That court took the view, first, that the then anticipated hearing before Jacob J might, in the light of the report that would be available to him at that hearing, provide an opportunity to resolve the issues that remained between the attorneys and the children, and, secondly, that, if there remained unresolved issues, then the Court of Appeal would be in a better position to decide whether this unfortunate litigation should proceed to an appeal if it knew what view Jacob J had taken of the report, and (if appropriate) were able to have sight of the report itself. Accordingly, the application for permission to appeal against the order of 13 May 1999 was adjourned so that it could come back before this court in the third week of December 1999. In the event, that application has been heard with the appeal against the order of 1 December 1999.

The statutory framework

The functions of the court on application for registration of an enduring power of attorney made under the 1985 Act are set out in s 6 of that Act. The court, in that context, is the Court of Protection – see s 13(1) of the Enduring Powers of Attorney Act 1985 and s 93(1) in Part VII of the Mental Health Act 1983. Section 6(1) of the 1985 Act requires that the court shall register the instrument provided that neither subss (2) or (4) of s 6 applies. Section 6(2) requires that, where it appears to the court that there is in force an order under Part VII of the Mental Health Act 1983 appointing a receiver for the donor, then, unless it directs otherwise, the court shall refuse the application for registration. In the present case, the court had directed that the application for registration be made, notwithstanding the receivership ad interim. Before making that application the attorneys were required, by s 4(3) of the Act, to give notice to the persons described in Part I of Sch 1 to the Act. Those persons include the donor's children. Section 6(4) is in these terms, so far as material:

'If, in the case of an application for registration—

'(a) a valid notice of objection to the registration is received by the court before the expiry of the period of five weeks beginning with the date or, as the case may be, the latest date on which the attorney gave notice to any person under Schedule 1, …'

the court shall neither register the instrument nor refuse the application until it has made such inquiries (if any) as it thinks appropriate in the circumstances of the case.'

Section 6(5) sets out the circumstances in which a notice of objection to the registration of an instrument is valid. They include, so far as material:

'(a) that the power purported to have been created by the instrument is not valid as an enduring power of attorney;

…

(d) that fraud or undue pressure was used to induce the donor to create the power;

(e) that, having regard to all the circumstances and in particular the attorney's relationship to or connection with the donor, the attorney is unsuitable to be the donor's attorney.'

Section 6(6) requires that, where s 6(4) applies and any of the grounds of objection in s 6(5) are established to the satisfaction of the court, the court shall refuse the application to register the instrument; but if the court is not so satisfied, it shall register the instrument to which the application relates.

Where an instrument has been registered under s 6 of the 1985 Act, the court has the functions prescribed by s 8 with respect to the power, the donor, and the attorney. Those functions include giving directions to the attorney with respect to the management or disposal by the attorney of the property and affairs of the donor (s 8(2)(b)(i)); requiring the attorney to furnish information or produce documents or things in his possession as attorney (s 8(2)(c)); and cancelling registration of the instrument registered under s 6 on being satisfied that fraud or undue pressure was used to induce the donor to create the power (s 8(4)(f)) or that, having regard to all the circumstances, the attorney is unsuitable to be the donor's attorney (s 8(4)(g)). In the case of an instrument creating joint attorneys – which this was – references in ss 6(5)(e) and 8(2) and (4) include references to any attorney.

The position, therefore, is that the court had power to register the instrument – notwithstanding the appointment of the receiver ad interim – and was required to do so unless it was satisfied that one or more of the grounds of objection set out in s 6(5) was or were established in respect of one or both attorneys. For that purpose the court was required to make or cause to be made 'such inquiries (if any) as it thinks appropriate in the circumstances of the case'. Once the instrument had been registered the court had the extensive powers of control over the attorneys conferred by s 8(2) of the Act. It was, as it seems to us, in the exercise of those powers that the judge gave the directions which are contained in the schedule to his order. This can be properly described as a registration subject to conditions as to an investigation of past transactions, and to restrictions as to the regulation of future transactions.

The objections

The 1985 Act required notice to be given to the donor's children – see s 4(2) and Sch 1, para 2(1)(b). The purpose of the requirement that notice be given is to enable the persons to whom notice is given to object to the registration of the instrument creating the power. In the present case the objections lodged by D were contained in a letter from his solicitors to the Public Trust Office dated 19 March 1999. They were: (i) that the donor did not have capacity to grant the power on 2 June 1998; (ii) that undue pressure was used to induce the donor to grant the power; and (iii) 'that M is unsuitable to be the [donor's] attorney, and that accordingly [Miss J] and [M] are unsuitable donees of a joint power'. Similar objections were lodged by the donor's daughters (by letters dated 10 March 1999 and 19 March 1999) and by his other two sons (by letters dated 16 March 1999 and 23 March 1999). In the form lodged, the objections could fairly be described as lacking in particulars; but, no doubt, it was the intention of the objectors to remedy this by the filing of evidence, for which purpose directions were sought in the application made on behalf of D dated 22 April 1999. In any event there was before Jacob J a substantial skeleton argument, settled by counsel and dated 10 May 1999. Subsequently, in connection with the application in December 1999, D swore an affidavit; but this, understandably, is primarily directed towards the question whether the accountant's report should be disclosed rather than to the objections to registration.

The medical evidence

The judge treated the children's assertion that the donor lacked capacity on 2 June 1998 (the date on which he signed the instrument) as the principal objection. In our view he was right to do so. All the evidence before him suggested that C had been shrewd, successful and strong-willed in the course of a long life which had brought him substantial material rewards. If he knew and understood what he was doing in June 1998, it was inherently unlikely that he would have allowed his will to be overborne by undue pressure. Further, if he knew and understood what he was doing, he was likely to be a sound judge of the suitability of his chosen attorneys to look after his interests. He had known each of them for many years. He was likely to know whether they were of such integrity that they could be trusted with the powers which he was to confer upon them; and he was likely to know whether they would be competent to deal with the complexity of his business and financial affairs.

The medical evidence before the judge may be summarised as follows:

First, there is the medical certificate of Dr Meadows, given on 6 November 1998 on the basis of a single consultation which (although Dr Meadows describes it as having occurred 3 years earlier) had, in fact, taken place on 14 October 1996. Dr Meadows had written to Dr Perry on 15 October 1996:

'Thank you for referring this very pleasant gentleman who is seventy eight and failing intellectually, though he preserves all the social graces and has some insight. His memory is poor, calculation difficult, he is prone to confusion and he has some difficulty in finding words at times in running speech. There is nothing obviously wrong on the more physical front and the pattern is very much as one sees in idiopathic decline in intellectual function of the elderly.'

In his certificate, given some 2 years later, Dr Meadows diagnosed:

'Alzheimers disease/presenile dementia. Deteriorating memory, proneness to confusion, considerable word finding difficulty, inability to concentrate, impaired comprehension.'

He added the comment:

'My opinion is based upon consultation 3 years ago. It is inconceivable that there has been an improvement. I am told that his mental condition has deteriorated which is as expected.'

In a letter addressed to the Public Trustee Office and dated 11 May 1999, Dr Meadows confirmed that he stood by that certificate.

Secondly, there is the evidence of Dr Perry, a consultation physician who had known C for about 15 years and who had been his medical adviser since 1993. His opinion might be thought to be of particular relevance because, in April 1998, he had been asked to direct his mind to the question whether C had capacity to make a will; and it was he who had suggested to C's solicitor that consideration be given to C giving an enduring power of attorney. He had experience in the relevant field; he was consultant to the Wessex Alzheimer Society. He had referred C to Dr Meadows in October 1996 'because I wanted a neurological opinion to make sure that [he] did not have a brain tumour or other similar condition and that his presenting symptoms were only of an age onset (possibly early Alzheimer's disease)'. In his affidavit sworn on 27 January 1999 Dr Perry observed that he had never been convinced that C was suffering from Alzheimer's disease. His view was based on a perceived improvement in C's condition from 1997. He deposed:

'8   I see from my notes that on reviewing [him] on 21 October 1997 there had been a definite improvement in his memory and I was satisfied with that improvement when I saw him again on 28 January 1998 and 2 April 1998.'

Thirdly, there is the report of Dr Alice Parshall, a consultant psychiatrist approved under s 12 of the Mental Health Act 1983. She was asked to prepare a psychiatric report on C in connection with the application to discharge the receiver ad interim. She interviewed C for a period of over an hour on 2 February 1999. In her report, dated 3 February 1999, she expressed the view that:

'... the clinical picture which has emerged in [C] is not typical of progressive Alzheimer dementia ... the picture now is more consistent with normal ageing complicated by a significant cerebral injury [suffered in 1995] from the latter of which some rehabilitation may have taken place ... In summary however, while [C] does show "mental disorder" in the broad terms of the Act I have been presented with no evidence of recent decline and there would be no grounds to make a recommendation under the Act.'

Dr Parshall observed, in the final paragraph of her report, that C appeared to be aware of the responsibility of owning assets and showed no mental disorder likely to make him dispose of assets recklessly. She stated that it was not her view that he would readily be exploited financially.

Finally, and perhaps of the greatest significance, there is the report of the Lord Chancellor's Visitor, Dr Ann Bailey. She had seen Dr Meadows' certificate, Dr Perry's affidavit and Dr Parshall's report. She interviewed C on 12 February 1999, both in the presence of Miss J and alone. It is significant, in the present context, that she found no indication that either of Miss J or C dominated the other. As she put it, 'they were true partners'. Her diagnosis was of

FOO.2 Atypical Alzheimer's disease; possibly precipitated by the accident in 1995. She went on, in the final paragraphs of her report:

> 'I consider that the mental disorder, particularly the impaired concentration, significant memory loss, a disinterest in current affairs and the fact that C has multiple business interests render him incompetent of fully managing his affairs. I feel h̄ has insight into this problem.
>
> Over the last year it would appear that [C] has taken steps to put his affairs in order. He has always been aware of his cognitive problems. It is my opinion that in June 1998 he would have had the capacity to create an enduring power of attorney.'

It is significant, also, that Dr Bailey formed the view that, on 12 February 1999, C understood the nature of a power of attorney (although perhaps not the special characteristics of an enduring power); that he knew that he had given powers of attorney to Miss J and M; and that he knew that those powers could be revoked.

The hearing on 13 May 1999

The first issue before Jacob J on 13 May 1999 was whether it was appropriate in the circumstances of the case, as they appeared from the material then available, to make or cause to be made inquiries into the question whether any of the three grounds of objection advanced by the donor's children were established. That was the issue raised by the donor's own application of 15 April 1999, seeking summary dismissal of the objections. It was also the issue raised by the legislation itself – see s 6(4) of the 1985 Act. If, but only if, he were satisfied that it was not appropriate to inquire beyond the material then available could the judge proceed to decide, there and then, whether to register the instrument of 2 June 1998 or to refuse registration. If he was not so satisfied, then he was bound to consider what inquiries should be made. That was what he was invited to do by the application for directions, dated 22 April 1999, which had been issued on behalf of D. If the judge thought that some inquiries should be made, it was for him to decide what those inquiries should be. He was not bound to make the directions sought if he did not consider them appropriate; but he was required to consider whether any, and if so what, directions were required in the circumstances.

It is clear that the judge formed a view, after hearing the submissions made by counsel instructed on behalf of the donor and before hearing counsel for D (or the other objectors in person), that a possible way forward was to register the instrument but to impose terms on the attorneys. He first expressed that view at pp 33–34 in the transcript of the proceedings on 13 May 1999. At p 36 (line 26) he gave a clear indication that the parties should work towards that solution, if they could: '... I would much rather this did not end up in any kind of judgment if it is at all possible. It is always better if you can do without judgment, and as everybody is here now this is the time to try and sort something out briefly'. There was then a short adjournment to enable Mr Norris QC, instructed on behalf of D, to take instructions. He then sought to explain to the judge the concerns of his client and the other children. He said this, at p 37 of the transcript (lines 8–30):

> 'If I was asked to summarise what the real concerns on this side are, it is that over the last three years substantial parts of father's assets have been transferred to [Miss J] and to [M]. Over that period, father has, on all sides it is agreed, been vulnerable. The family would like some investigation into the transactions which have happened in the past three years. They involve giving away the patient's house of two flats which are worth about £1 million and a half share in a property development which is worth between £3–4 million. Those we know about. There are other transactions involving Liechtenstein anstalts, offshore bank accounts and so forth about which we simply know nothing at the moment. We would like somebody to look at those. Not in the sense that we want them set aside; we simply want them examined at the moment to see what actually happened ... It is also the case that father has made a Bahamian Will. We do not know what that

says, we do not particularly care what it says. Our concern is not what will happen to father's property another day but what is available for father now. That is the principal concern.'

These were the concerns which the judge sought to address by the order which he was to make. He observed (transcript, p 39, lines 29–31) that he was getting the very clear message that C did not want an outsider involved in his affairs; to which Mr Norris' response was that it was not a question of whether he wanted it or not, the question was whether it was for his benefit that that should be done.

The hearing continued in the form of a debate as to the details of the solution which the judge had in mind. There was little or no express consideration of the issue which the judge was required by the statute to address – namely, whether inquiries were appropriate before making a decision whether or not to register the instrument of 2 June 1998. But the following exchange (transcript, p 55, line 17 to p 56, line 9) is of significance:

'MR NORRIS: I hate this horse trading, my Lord, but it does seem that the family's concerns are simply not being addressed in this scheme.

MR JUSTICE JACOB: This is not a case about the family's concerns. At the moment there is an appointment of a power of attorney in these two people … I looked at the medical side of that and I came to the conclusion that the medical evidence was overwhelming in favour of the fact that the gentleman was compos mentis at the time he did it.

MR NORRIS: Your Lordship has not looked at the question of pressure. Your Lordship has not looked at the question of suitability.

MR JUSTICE JACOB: No, I have not. I thought the medical one was the strongest. Sometimes one takes the view that there are several points being run just because one of them is not a very strong one. If you want me to go through the whole lot, I will but I could just end up by confirming the whole thing. I am just trying to find a way to do it. I am not going to have the family having a look into all this when that was not what the donor wanted.

MR NORRIS: My Lord, this jurisdiction is all about the Court supervising the administration of the donor's assets. It is the very reason why the family is informed about the registration of the power and why the Law Commission called that notification of the family a keystone of the protective machinery.

MR JUSTICE JACOB: Of course it is, and the family does know about it and now the Court is going to be looking at it and the Court has taken control. It does not mean that the family can come barging in.

MR NORRIS: But, my Lord, the family is not seeking to come barging in, as I have endeavored to make plain.'

It is clear that the judge took the view that there was nothing to be gained by further inquiries, either into the question of capacity or into the related questions of undue pressure and unsuitability. It would, we think, have been helpful if he had explained why he reached that conclusion; but we are satisfied that his reasoning does emerge from the transcript of the proceedings before him. He was satisfied, from the medical evidence that was before him, that the donor had the necessary capacity at the time when he signed the instrument on 2 June 1998. He must have taken the view that there was little chance that oral evidence from the doctors – and the opportunity for cross-examination – would alter the conclusion which he had reached on that point; or, at the least, that such benefit as might be obtained from oral evidence did not justify the expense and delay that oral evidence would entail. There was really no evidence of pressure on the donor, other than the pressure inherent in his own perception of his failing intellect. There was a case for inquiry into the suitability of (at least) M; in the circumstances that there was, plainly, potential for a conflict of interest which M might have exploited in the past. But, clearly, the judge thought that the appropriate way to resolve that question was through the reporting procedure which he proposed to include in his order.

While recognising the reasons which led the judge to take the course which he did on 13 May 1999, we think there is much force in the criticism of his approach to the application which has been made to him. The 1985 Act gives objectors the right to have their objections considered by the court before an instrument creating an enduring power of attorney is registered. It is of particular importance, in a field as sensitive as this, that they are not left with the impression that those objections have been brushed aside. There is, we fear, a danger that that is the impression which was given by what occurred on 13 May 1999. We are satisfied that the judge had good reasons for taking the course which he did; but we are firmly of the view that those reasons could and should have been spelt out in a way which left the objectors in no doubt that their concerns had been taken fully into account.

The order of 1 December 1999

At the hearing on 1 December 1999 Jacob J had the benefit of the report from the named accountant. That would have satisfied him of two matters: (i) that the donor had more than enough assets to provide for his comfort and maintenance in his remaining years – a matter about which Mr Norris had expressed concern on behalf of the children at the hearing of 13 May 1999; and (ii) that there had been no transactions between the donor and either of the two attorneys other than those identified by Mr Norris at that earlier hearing. The judge had, also, the benefit of explanations – set out in confidential exhibits to affidavits sworn by Miss J and M – of their dealings with the donor.

The judge took the view that no useful purpose would be served by disclosure of the report to the children. He said this, at p 4F–H of the judgment which he gave on 1 December 1999:

> 'When I ordered this report I hoped, as I say, it would produce peace. I have no doubt whatever that if it is disclosed it will produce war. Almost every single one of the transactions will be the subject of further investigation. There is nothing on the face of the report to suggest there is anything wrong with these transactions, but from what I have seen of the material so far I can see nothing but continued litigation – speculative litigation at that.'

He went on, at p 6F–G:

> 'I am sorry that the procedure which I devised did not lead to peace. The Court has seen the report. Whilst, of course, one cannot say from the report that there is not behind the report something untoward, it is a pure matter of speculation whether there is or not. I can see no reason why the family should be allowed to indulge in that speculation to the distress of the patient.'

We have read the report and the other confidential material which was before the judge. Because it is confidential material we can say little about it. The appellant must be content that, having read that material, we can express our view that the judge was entitled to reach the conclusion that there was no useful purpose to be served by disclosure of the report to the children; and much risk of distress to their father. We would observe, also, that we are satisfied that there is some risk of damage to his financial interests if the other parties to transactions in which he is engaged came to the view that those transactions were to be the subject of hostile examination in the context of litigation.

The way forward

We are not persuaded that there is any purpose in an appeal against the order made on 13 May 1999. That order has been made and events have now moved on. We do not think that there is any real prospect that the Court of Appeal would think it sensible to set that order aside. There is ample power, if necessary, to deal with the situation which now exists under the provisions in s 8 of the 1985 Act.

Nor are we persuaded that the decision on 1 December 1999 to refuse disclosure of the report was flawed. It was, of course, a decision made by a judge of the Court of Protection in the exercise of his discretion. This court should not interfere with such a decision unless satisfied that the judge erred in principle. We can find no such error. Indeed, so far as our view is material, we think he reached the correct decision on 1 December 1999.

In those circumstances, and for the reasons which we have sought to give, we would dismiss the appeal against the order of 1 December 1999; and refuse the application for permission to appeal against the order of 13 May 1999.

We do not think it sufficient to leave the matter there. We think some further investigation into the suitability of M as an attorney is required. We think it appropriate to remit the matter to the Court of Protection, with a direction that express consideration be given to the question whether there is a case for the exercise by that court of its power under s 8(4)(g) of the 1985 Act on the ground that M's relationship to or connection with the donor make it suitable for him to remain the donor's attorney. The particular matter of concern to this court is the transaction evidenced by the letters of 28 and 29 October 1997 to which reference was made by Mr Norris in the court below. On the face of those letters the transaction is one from which M appears to have taken a substantial benefit at the expense of the donor. It is obvious that M is not, himself, a person who can inquire into the propriety of that transaction. We should make it plain that we have formed no view on that question. We think that should be left to the Court of Protection. But we are satisfied that the question needs to be addressed with more care than it appears to have received so far.

Order accordingly.

Solicitors:

Charles Russell for the appellant

Nicholson Graham & Jones for the respondents

PHILIPPA JOHNSON

Barrister

INDEX